MONEY FLOWS IN THE UK REGIONS

Money Flows in the UK Regions

JOHN SHORT
with
DAVID J. NICHOLAS

Gower

Published by
Gower Publishing Company Limited,
Westmead, Farnborough, Hants., England.

British Library Cataloguing in Publication Data

Short, John
Money flows in the UK regions
1 Flow of funds—Great Britain—Mathematical models
I Title
339.2'6'072 HC260.F55

ISBN 0-566-00421-6

Printed and bound in Great Britain by
Biddles Ltd, Guildford and King's Lynn

Contents

List of tables vii

List of figures xi

Preface xii

Acknowledgements xiii

Introduction xiv

1 **Insights from the literature**

Introduction 1
Regional accounting systems 2
Regional accounting in the UK 6
The regional strategies 9
Recent developments 11
Conclusion 12

2 **A money flows model of a national economy**

A description of national income 14
The components of final output 19
A system of accounts 22

3 **A money flows model for regions** 31

Regional money flows model 37

4 **The generation of data for a regional money flows model: general observations and conclusions**
Introduction 43
The personal and company sectors 43
The general government sector and public corporations (other than nationalised industries) 45
Flows from the European Economic Community 48
The financial accounts 49
The findings 56
Conclusions 57

APPENDICES

1 **The personal and company sectors** 59
The personal sector 59
The company sector 75

2 **The general government sector and public corporations (other than nationalised industries)**
Public expenditure 84
Agriculture, fisheries, food and forestry 85
Trade, industry and employment 87
Roads and transport 94
Housing 96
Other environmental services 97
Law, order and protective services 98
Education and libraries, science and arts 99
Health and personal social services 100
Social security 101
Public expenditure by economic category 101
Public corporations 110
Tax revenues 132

3 **The financial sector**
The sectors 161
Financial flows in the context of the regional money flows model 162
The regional distribution of certain financial flows 178

Bibliography 216

Tables

Table 1	Data availability matrix	56
Table 2	Personal income 1974	68
Table 3	Personal income 1975	68
Table 4	Personal income 1976	69
Table 5	Personal income 1977	69
Table 6	Personal expenditure 1974	70
Table 7	Personal expenditure 1975	70
Table 8	Personal expenditure 1976	70
Table 9	Personal expenditure 1977	71
Table 10	Personal capital account 1974	71
Table 11	Personal capital account 1975	72
Table 12	Personal capital account 1976	73
Table 13	Personal capital account 1977	74
Table 14	Company sector: appropriation account 1974	80
Table 15	Company sector: appropriation account 1975	80
Table 16	Company sector: appropriation account 1976	81
Table 17	Company sector: appropriation account 1977	81
Table 18	Company sector: capital account 1974	82
Table 19	Company sector: capital account 1975	82
Table 20	Company sector: capital account 1976	83
Table 21	Company sector: capital account 1977	83
Table 22	Central government: regionally relevant current expenditure 1974/75	112
Table 23	Central government: regionally relevant capital expenditure 1974/75	113
Table 24	Local authority regionally relevant current expenditure 1974/75	114
Table 25	Local authority regionally relevant capital expenditure 1974/75	115

Table 26 Public corporations regionally relevant capital expenditure 1974/75 116
Table 27 Total public expenditure 'in' the regions of 116
the UK 1974/75 116
Table 28 Central government: regionally relevant current expenditure 1975/76 117
Table 29 Central government: regionally relevant capital expenditure 1975/76 118
Table 30 Local authority regionally relevant current expenditure 1975/76 119
Table 31 Local authority regionally relevant capital expenditure 1975/76 120
Table 32 Public corporations regionally relevant capital expenditure 1975/76 121
Table 33 Total public expenditure 'in' the regions of the UK 1975/76 122
Table 34 Central government: regionally relevant current expenditure 1976/77 122
Table 35 Central government: regionally relevant capital expenditure 1976/77 123
Table 36 Local authority regionally relevant current expenditure 1976/77 124
Table 37 Local authority regionally relevant capital expenditure 1976/77 125
Table 38 Public corporations regionally relevant capital expenditure 1976/77 126
Table 39 Total public expenditure 'in' the regions of the UK 1976/77 126
Table 40 Central government: regionally relevant current expenditure 1977/78 127
Table 41 Central government: regionally relevant capital expenditure 1977/78 128
Table 42 Local authority regionally relevant current expenditure 1977/78 129
Table 43 Local authority regionally relevant capital expenditure 1977/78 130
Table 44 Public corporations regionally relevant capital expenditure 1977/78 131
Table 45 Total public expenditure 'in' the regions of the UK 1977/78 131
Table 46 Inland revenue receipts 1974/75 140
Table 47 Customs and excise duties 1974/75 140
Table 48 Inland revenue receipts 1975/76 141
Table 49 Customs and excise duties 1975/76 141

Table 50 Inland revenue receipts 1976/77 142
Table 51 Customs and excise duties 1976/77 142
Table 52 Inland revenue receipts 1977/78 143
Table 53 Customs and excise duties 1977/78 144
Table 54 National insurance, etc, contributions 1974/75–1977/78 147
Table 55 Local authority: funding of current expenditure 1974/75–1977/78 148
Table 56 Local authority: funding of capital expenditure 1974/75–1977/78 149
Table 57 European Regional Development Fund 1975–1977 159
Table 58 European Coal and Steel Community 1974–1977 160
Table 59 European Agriculture Fund–guidance section 1974–1977 160
Table 60 European Investment Bank 1974–77 160
Table 61 Public sector: transactions in financial assets 172
Table 62 Banking sector: transactions in financial assets 173
Table 63 Other financial institutions: transactions in financial assets 174
Table 64 Industrial and commercial companies: transactions in financial assets 175
Table 65 Personal sector: transactions in financial assets 176
Table 66 Overseas sector: transactions in financial assets 177
Table 67 National Savings by region 179
Table 68 Trustee Savings Bank: estimated net increase in funds by region 181
Table 69 Trustee Savings Bank: net increase in funds by region 181
Table 70 National Savings Committee: regional coverage of total gross savings by channel of investment 183
Table 71 Estimate of funds of Life Assurance and Superannuation schemes by regions 189
Table 72 Local authority superannuation 1975/76 189
Table 73 Local authority superannuation 1976/77 190
Table 74 Local authority superannuation 1977/78 190
Table 75 Superannuation funds: use of funds 1974/75–1977/78 191
Table 76 Insurance companies use of funds 1974/75–1977/78 191
Table 77 Finance houses: source of funds 1974/75–1977/78 192
Table 78 Finance houses: loans and advance 1974/75–1977/78 192
Table 79 Finance house: estimated advances by Region 1976/77 and 1977/78 194
Table 80 Building societies: survey results (net receipts) 1974–1977 199

Table 81 Building societies: survey results (net advances) 1974–1977 200
Table 82 Building societies: liabilities and assets 1974/75–1977/78 201
Table 83 Estimated net receipts received by building societies by Region 1974/75–1977/78 202
Table 84 Estimated net advanced by building societies by Region 1974/75–1977/78 202
Table 85 Estimated loans for house purchase: the banking sector 1974/75–1977/78 203
Table 86 Loans for house purchase: new loans: 1974/75–1977/78 203
Table 87 Loans for house purchase: local authorities 1974/75–1977/78 204
Table 88 Special financial agencies: shares and lending by Region 1974/75–1977/78 207
Table 89 Banking sector: Current and Deposit accounts 1974/75–1977/78 209
Table 90 Banking sector: market loans and commercial bills 1974/75–1977/78 209
Table 91 Banking sector: Estimated Current and Deposit accounts of personal sector by Region 211
Table 92 Banking sector: estimated advances to personal sector by Region (excluding for home purchase) 211
Table 93 Unit trusts 1974/75–1977/78 212
Table 94 Investment trusts 1974/75–1977/78 213
Table 95 Property unit trusts 1974/75–1977/78 213
Table 96 Unit trusts: estimated sales to persons by region 1974/75–1977/78 214
Table 97 Notes and coin: estimated holding by region (persons and companies) 1974/75–1977/78 214
Table 98 Tax instruments by sector and region 1974/75–1977/78 214
Table 99 British government securities: sectional holdings and estimated regional personal holdings 1974/75–1977/78 215
Table 100 Credit extended by retailers and identified trade credit by sector and estimated regional credit by persons and companies 1974/75–1977/78 215

Figures

Figure 2.1 Circular flow model of national product 18
Figure 2.2 Flows between sector accounts 28
Figure 3.1 The basic matrix 39
Figure 3.2 Money flows to and from each region of the sectors of region A 40
Figure 3.3 Money flows involving multi-regional finance institutions 41

Preface

This study on sector-regional financial flows was developed from previous research on the regional distribution of public expenditure undertaken by John Short while working with the Northern Region Strategy Team. This particular study was financed initially by a grant from the Department of the Environment, and subsequently by the Social Science Research Council.

This book is based on the research report which was presented to the sponsoring departments, however neither the original report nor this version do not necessarily represent the views of the Department of the Environment, and the methods of analysis employed are not necessarily endorsed by them.

Acknowledgements

The research was carried out in the Department of Economics at the University of Durham under the direction of John Short with research assistance from D. J. Nicholas.

The research team is grateful for the help of numerous organisations who when asked to produce data which required time and effort were willing to do so, collating data at the regional level which preserved the confidentiality of their clients. The CSO is thanked for the use of their detailed statistics on the company and private sector in Appendix 1. For the material in Appendix 2, acknowledgement is due to the many government departments, local authorities and public corporations who provided statistics. The material in Appendix 3 has relied on the help of many parts of the financial sector such as the building societies, assurance companies, the Finance Houses Association, Special Finance Agencies, the Trustee Savings Bank, as well as many individuals working in that sector. Without their help, the new ground which the research has dug into and turned over, however slightly, would have remained fallow. Thanks go also to our colleagues in the Department of Economics for providing the atmosphere conducive to research, particularly to Richard Morley for also being a patient sounding-board, and Mrs Audrey Greathead, Liz Dunne, and Mrs Audrey Richardson who have efficiently and cheerfully met the various deadlines over the years in the typing and production of the research.

Data forming the tables in this book have been reproduced by permission of the Controller of Her Majesty's Stationery Office.

Introduction

The purpose of this study is two-fold. The first is concerned with the production of a model which classifies the various types of money flows between the sectors of a national economy in the regional context in a consistent manner. The second purpose is to produce data relating to these flows for the regions of the United Kingdom identifying the sources of these data and discussing the methodology used in their production. As such this research report is organised in a neutral vein, neither attempting to analyse the data which have been produced nor relating them to wider issues. Such an analysis for the public sector flows has been undertaken in Short (1981), *Public Expenditure and Taxation in the UK Regions.*

The overall report is split into four parts. The main report discusses the model which has been adopted to classify regional money flows, and outlines the availability and production of data for the model for the main sectors which have been adopted. These sectors form the statistical appendices. In Appendix 1 the personal and company sectors are examined, Appendix 2 covers the public sector covering central government, the local authorities, and the public corporations (other than nationalised industries), and finally Appendix 3 deals with the financial sector.

The main report is organised as follows. After this introduction, the literature relating to the subject of regional accounting is examined as to the evolution of regional models on the one hand, and the generation of data for the UK on the other. To enable a model of regional financial flows to be constructed, the national income and expenditure accounting model which has been adopted throughout the world to study a country's income generation is examined and related to money flows in Chapter 2. The regional dimension to this model is incorporated into this national money flows model in Chapter 3, and Chapter 4. Chapter 4 presents the general findings relating to the availability of data on regional money flows which have been discussed in greater detail in the statistical appendices. In the final chapter some general observations and conclusions relating to availability of data are outlined.

1 Insights from the literature

Introduction

The purpose of this chapter is to present the findings of a general but not comprehensive examination of literature on regional data systems both from a conceptual and practical viewpoint in relation to the overall research.

What is a region? What are the ideal boundaries of a region? What are the social, economic and political as well as the physical dimensions of a region? What is regional science and analysis? (Perloff, 1954; Izard, 1960). Questions such as these are not tackled directly in this work. However, the identification and understanding of the relationships involved in money flows within a region and between regions will certainly provide some insights into such problems.

The research project itself is characterised by the identification of these flows below the aggregate level in the regional context. A classification system relating to regions and the available data and their measurement, are the overall objectives. Related to these, certain characteristics of of the relationship between regions and the nation as a whole, and some overall guidelines can be identified from the previous work. In addition, certain attempts have been made to look beyond the aggregate level, and these will be examined.

Material on the methodology and problems of regional accounting are examined later in the chapter. Following on from this, independent work carried out in the UK is examined. Recent developments in providing regional data for the UK are then considered and this leads on to a consideration of the regional strategies which have been conducted in the 1970s in the UK with respect to their use of data relating to money flows (primarily public sector). Finally, there is a short conclusion.

Regional accounting systems

In the late 1950s and early 1960s, there was much discussion on the validity of designing accounts at the sub-national level.

Three volumes (among others) have been provided which contain a variety of papers on topics related to the general subject.

Regional Income (N.B.E.R., 1954) is a collection of papers broadly related to regional issues, containing ten papers. The first four relate to some of the conceptual issues generally applicable to any study of inter-regional differences; the next group of three papers inspect some empirical investigations of inter-regional differentials; and the final group examine problems encountered in estimating income below the regional level.

Design of Regional Accounts (Hochwald, 1961) presents a wide range of papers. Hirch in his paper explores the possibilities of expanding personal income into a comprehensive index of regional health and well being. The Ruggleses suggest how the various types of national economic systems can be broken down into regional accounting systems. Lever, for his part, constructs a set of regional income and produce accounts to record local trade relations with the 'rest of the world'. Other papers relate the use of regional accounts to certain policy issues; examine the impact of external forces on regional employment as a result of projecting regional activities in the context of national demand projections; and some show the impact of government policies on capital formation and output.

Regional Economic Planning (Izard and Cumberland, 1961) is a collection of papers from a study conference built around the subject of techniques for analysis for regional and national economic development. The conference was designed to act as a bridge between economic theorists, planners and administrators, in order to make available to the administrators the most recent and comprehensive techniques of regional economic analysis, and also to provide the theorists and planners with deeper insights into the practical problems which administrators have to face. The volume provides a history and a review of regional economic planning; an examination of certain structural problems common to all regions, with general recommendations for appropriate policy; and an analysis of the various techniques of regional and national economic analysis. In this last section there is a paper by Stone, to which further reference will be made.

In general, the papers which are of most interest to this work are those dealing with the conceptual issues involved in regional accounts. These will be dealt with collectively with reference to individual papers as the general conclusions are similar. The general consensus from all the papers is that regardless of data limitations, regional accounts offer a flexible framework for economic analysis. The Ruggleses ask whether national economic accounts can provide the kind of information needed for regional economic analysis and whether it would be fruitful to provide regional data in the national data for these purposes. Generally the contributions start from the assumption that data cannot be obtained in most cases and examine the resultant problems of measurement as they affect the designing of the accounts. Some look at what can be done with existing data such as income statistics. However, as data questions are a separate part of this work, such discussions of data bottlenecks relating to other countries and time periods is not of interest.

A more fruitful line of examination leads to the conceptual issues which have to be faced in the regional context. However, first of all it is appropriate to consider what are the basic elements of accounts. Accounts are defined by their transactors and the transactions they record. In business accounting, transactors are always legal entities whose transactions, in a double entry system, are related to change in their balance sheets. In economic accounting, transactors may be sector aggregates or legal entities as in all money flows and many income accounts, or they may be physical constructs such as 'industry' in input-output accounts. Any regional accounting system, to form an internally consistent framework, must carefully define its components and their aggregation into exogenous and endogenous sectors (Hirch in Hochwald, 1961).

It is in the defining of components into exogenous and endogenous sectors where many conceptual problems have been identified. As a result, the general principles as to the treatment of corporations financial intermediaries, and non-resident activities, have to be decided upon if the accounts are to be comparable over regions. More important, these principles have to allow meaningful and accurate descriptions of regions. Hochwald divides the conceptual issues as he sees them into three parts. The first problem relates to data, but that does not concern us here. The second group of problems are institutional and the final group relate to policy problems.

To the extent that the income creating activities of national institutions are not confined to a particular region, serious problems of regional allocation arise about the transactors to be included, about the grouping of these transactors into regional sectors and about the range of transactions to be covered by the regional accounts. Taking each in turn, Hochwald examines the problems involved.

1 *Transactors.* As both individuals and corporate institutions often represent different forms of economic activity and

different stages of economic development, the range of activities subsumed under a single total of national income may not be comparable among regions. Many national transactors are involved in multi-regional activity and correct allocation to a region of income generated, especially from head offices, poses difficulties. Even when local residence of an income recipient is identified, the same transactor may operate in different regions as a consumer and producer. The distinction between income received and income produced is of significance in clearly defining the regional aggregates to be measured and the regional transactors to be included in regional income estimation.

2 *Sectors.* National income estimates derive their usefulness for economic analysis and public policy from the detail they show for the major categories that appear of strategic importance in explaining variations in the total. However, the division for the national economy may not be altogether suitable for the regional dimension. Nevertheless, in comparing across regions, it is important that all industries and regions are defined consistently.

3 *Transactions.* The range of activities, whether real or imputed, must be the same for all regions. Where inter-regional price differences are important, these must be accounted for in the system. Care must also be taken to ensure that inter-regional transactions are allocated to the regions concerned especially where institutions cross regional boundaries in their own organisational make-up.

Hochwald's policy problems relate to the openedness of the regional economy *vis-a-vis* the national economy. Because of the many transactions which a region undertakes with the rest of the world, especially with the nation of which it is a part, it is unlikely that the sector structure, and transactions coverage, of regional income accounts will be complete. As a result it is likely that a region will be analysed as an integral part of a larger market and for policy purposes, analyses such as the industrial origin of income received by the region's residents, or a record of regional production of key industries as they adapt to changes in national demand may be more helpful than regional expenditure estimates required for the technical completion of a regional accounting system. What Hochwald is suggesting is that the usefulness of certain pieces of information at the regional level is minimal, as there would appear to be little or no scope for action in relation to these data as far as meaningful policy is concerned.

This last point is one which is common to all of the three volumes so far cited. The accounting system should be designed to serve policy issues and effort should be geared to reconciling the available data with the concepts best suited to the policy issues. This assertion argues against the aims of the present research—the production of a neutral model. However the present work is a departure from the 'data availability' models in so far as it tries to develop a model and then relates the data to this model. However, the passage of time should have improved the availability of data.

Stone in his paper *Social Accounts at the Regional Level: A Survey,* sets out 'in an orderly manner methods of regional description and analysis which centre around the national accounts'. The interesting points for this research lie in his identification of the 'outgoings and incomes' of a region's production, consumption and accumulation accounts in relationship to itself, other regions, the rest of the world, and the central government. He takes out the consuming and accumulating of central government from the regions and treats them as a separate region, while including government's producing activities along with all other forms of production in the region concerned. However, the armed forces are entirely removed from the regions and are entered on a separate government account. The relationships between all regions and the rest of the world are shown by a set of accounts which are made to balance by the introduction of appropriate transfers.

For example, the incoming in the aggregate production account of a region equals the consumption of the residents in the region, the investment made by the residents, the sales by the region to central government, and net exports to other regions and the rest of the world while the corresponding outgoings matching these are gross domestic product at factor cost (less stock appreciation) and indirect taxes less subsidies paid in by region. Stone traces through each of the corresponding outgoings and incomings in a 9 x 9 matrix which in its 27 entries describes 46 flows (an entry can be both incoming and outgoing—for example gross domestic product of the region is an incoming relating to the income and outlay account [consumption]).

Stone provides estimates of regional accounts for the UK at the aggregate level for consumption, production and accumulation in each region in 1948, as well as the region's account with the central government and the rest of the world, covering gross domestic product at factor cost, consumption by residents, gross investment, savings by residents, sales by region to the central government for consumption purposes, current transfers received by the region from central government, direct taxes paid by region to central government, net capital transfer from central government to the region, indirect taxes less subsidies paid by the region, net borrowing by the government from the region, net borrowing by all other regions and the rest of the world from the region, net exports by the region to all other regions and the rest of the world, net receipts of factor income by region from other regions and the rest of the world, and current transfers received by region from other regions and the rest of the world.

More recently Catsambas (1978) has produced estimates of federal taxes and expenditure flows for the states in the USA for 1972. This study has concentrated on the methodological aspects of incidence and examines the individual taxes and expenditures in relation to the separate states.

The papers discussed in this section have dealt with the question of regional accounts at the aggregate level and apart from Stone have concentrated on American experiences which have been constrained through examining the best way of using existing data, rather than considering general systems as a whole. The next section looks at the work carried out in the UK in the field.

Regional accounting in the UK

Woodward's Regional Social Accounts for the UK (1970) can be considered as a major pioneering work in the regional data field. Although some estimates of various parts of regional GDP had been previously produced (Stone), Woodward's work provided the first major breakthrough in so far as he attempted to disaggregate the various components of regional GDP.

The purpose of Woodward's paper was twofold: firstly, the estimation of regional accounts for the regions of the UK for 1961 and for 1964 (depending on data availability) and secondly, suggestions for the improvements in the statistical sources. His basic aim was to disaggregate the components of GDP and domestic expenditure shown in the national accounts for the UK (following the CSO National Income and Blue Book definitions). He distributed these components among the various regions by making use of all the available data avoiding the hypothesis that the components are distributed in accordance with each region's population. As a result the final figures have resulted from a mixture of direct data and data generated by various proxy methods.

In general, the income approach to measuring GDP was adopted, lack of information on the service industries proved too great to attempt estimation through production, and estimation by expenditure was not carried out as data on both imports and exports were unreliable. Nevertheless, domestic expenditures for each of the regions was estimated.

Basically, Woodward divided GDP by taking factor incomes: wages and salaries, incomes from self employment, gross trading profits of companies, gross trading surplus of public enterprises and rent, and allocated them to each region in turn. The national sources of data were followed as far as possible, but difficulties arose which often meant that they could not be used. For example, in estimating the gross trading profits of companies, the Inland Revenue Annual Report shows company profits for each of the four countries comprising the UK which are compiled by adding the statistics from individual tax districts. Added together they provide figures for the UK. However, tax assessments on company profits are made in the tax district where the registered office is located. Thus, for example, many assessments on Scottish companies are made by the Inspector of Tax District in London in which the registered office happens to be located. The Quinquennial Census of Production also provides information on gross profits incomes of companies, but only for manufacturing industries. Furthermore, many companies have several productive units in different regions and a centralised administrative unit. The Census of Production excludes employees not on the productive site and allocated net output to the regions where the manufacturing units are located. As a result, the true picture is not revealed either.

GDP by industry and region was also estimated. However, one of the purposes of attempting an industrial breakdown of GDP was to point out the weaknesses in the statistical sources. This section was compiled by adding together the estimates of factor income from a wide variety of sources, the reliability of the estimates varying widely from one industry to another. Formidable problems arose. To quote Woodward:

> We do not even know accurately the amount of GDP arising from individual manufacturing industries for the country as a whole, since the estimates of gross trading profits can only be derived from Inland Revenue sources, which classify firms by industry according to the financial unit rather than establishment. In addition, the Census of Production, the only source of regional data about individual manufacturing industries, does not show net output defined in the same way as the Blue Book. Moreover, if we get round these problems ....., we are still faced with the major problem that at the industrial order level, a particular industry may represent quite different things in different regions.

Woodward also shows domestic expenditure for each of the regions by estimated consumers' expenditure, public authorities' current expenditure and gross domestic fixed capital formation. His classification of items to particular headings in this section may be faulted. For example, he includes both military expenditure and national administration expenditure in regional domestic expenditure. While both of these generate factor incomes in a region, they cannot be treated as domestic expenditure in any particular region, as the benefits from these expenditures are not solely for the region where this factor income is generated. Stone, in contrast, treats all government expenditures as separate from domestic expenditure and only considers the factor incomes as part of the region, although he does have a government/region matrix separated from the rest of the region. However, there are government expenditures which form part of domestic expenditure in a region (hospitals .....). One solution to this problem lies in between Stone and Woodward's and is described elsewhere (Short, 1981). Also, Woodward, in estimating gross domestic fixed capital formation, excluded amounts spent on land and buildings.

Another major area of social accounts which he estimated was 'net beneficial expenditure by the public sector'. This corresponded to the Public Sector Combined Current and Capital Account in the Blue Book. However, Woodward adapted this table quite considerably for regional estimation. He excluded overseas military services, and net loans and grants abroad, most central government current expenditure and all military expenditure on goods and services. Since estimation was 'concerned with the benefit of public expenditure, that is gifts of money, goods and services' all payments for a consideration such as lending were also excluded. Also capital expenditure on trading services and housing were excluded. The only capital expenditure items which were included were those related to social and environmental services, such as schools, hospitals, sewerage and roads as well as capital grants to universities, and improvement grants. On the receipts side, borrowing, rent, interest and dividends were excluded. (Part of debt interest accruing to financial intermediaries was also omitted, but on practical rather than theoretical grounds.)

Thus the Woodward definition of public expenditure in the regional context is a rather narrow one excluding all elements of the public sector which could be said to operate in the market, and including only those elements where no market provision was present. Rightly excluded were those items which are national in character and cannot be attributed to any one region. However, the exclusion of items such as capital expenditure on housing (even though housing subsidies were excluded), would seem to bias the figures as some regions are traditionally dependent on the provision of housing by the public sector. Also, where a region obtained a loan from the government which could not be obtained elsewhere, or at a preferential rate of interest, this should be considered in this category.

It is important, however, to view Woodward's paper as a major contribution to the data gathering exercise in the regional context. It was pioneering in British regional statistics. As he indicated, one of his purposes was to point out data deficiencies as well as attempting to provide estimates, however variable, of the components of GDP. Although this review has been negative in so far as it has concentrated on the major problems of estimation, it could have also examined those areas where the estimates given were accurate. Despite the difficulties, Woodward's work provided the only available estimates on regional data for some time, and as a result, they were used extensively. As well as Woodward, estimates of expenditure flows have been provided for Scotland alone by McCrone (1965) for the 1950s and Begg et al (1975) for the decade 1961–71.

The regional strategies

That Woodward's work was the main source of regional data in the early 1970s shows that no great progress had been made in the field. The Strategic Plan for the North West, (1973), Technical Paper No. 2, *Needs and Resources,* uses his Social Accounts 'extensively' (sic). However, the emergence of these regional strategies provided a new impetus for regional data. These regional strategies concentrated on the public sector in the main in the quest for data. Their reasoning behind this is as given by SPNW:

> It is perhaps worth reminding ourselves why we have drawn attention to public expenditure, its level and pattern, as an issue for strategic planning. It is because public expenditure is probably the most important single means of securing a better overall quality of life for the population in the North West–it is not an end in itself, but it is the indispensable means of securing the most important single objective the SPNW set for itself. (Technical Paper No. 2 SPNW 79)

However, while strategies desired information on public expenditure, their success was varied. The two strategies West Central Scotland and the North West, reached similar conclusions on the availability of data:

> The task of compiling this report has confirmed that the regional statistics of central government departments are not maintained in a form readily adaptable to forthcoming Regional Boundaries. (West Central Scotland Plan: (1974) Supplementary Report 3, Public Expenditure)

An important recommendation made by both these strategy teams was that special measures should be taken for comprehensive statistics of past public expenditure by region to be prepared on a systematic and routine basis.

Nevertheless, the WCS plan and SPNW did attempt to collect whatever data they could on public expenditures relating to their regions. However, their approach was *ad hoc* in so far as no distinction was made between using public expenditure as a contributor to gross regional product in the region on the one hand, and supplying services on the other. Defence and national administration were treated in the same manner as hospitals and housing.

Both the WCS plan and the SPNW geared their overall approach to the annual review of public expenditure made by the government (Public Expenditure Survey Committee [PESC]), using the national projections embodied in the annual survey and the functional classification breakdown of expenditure. This system was adopted by the most recent strategy (Northern Region Strategy Team (NRST, 1976), in its attempt to obtain better statistics:

> ..... PESC provides the only systematic and comprehensive method available for classifying public expenditure on a consistent programme-by-programme basis, both over time and across all spending authorities. For this reason, we have taken the PESC system as the framework for our study. We have thus used the PESC definition of public expenditure and have also classified our statistics in accordance with the PESC classification. A further reason for adopting the PESC definition and classification was that it greatly facilitated consultation with government departments, since this is the basis of their routine statistical work. (NRST Technical Report No.12 p.8)

A major departure of NRST classification was in distinguishing between public expenditure made in a region supplying services which were of benefit to the residents of the region rather than the nation as a whole (expenditure made 'in and for' a region or regionally relevant expenditure), and expenditures which were made 'in' a region and contributed to gross regional expenditure. In short, expenditure 'in' a region, is an analysis of total public expenditure, while the expenditure 'in and for' analysed that part of public expenditure which is relevant only to the region which directly benefits in social welfare terms. Following this approach, NRST produced public expenditure statistics for the regions of the UK for the period 1969–70 to 1973–74 (regionally relevant) and for the North for 1972–73 (contribution to gross regional expenditure).

The 1976 Review of the Strategy for the South East followed NRST's methodology in the work of the Resources Group. However, the overall objective of the South East Team differed from NRST in so far as the SE Team was concerned with physical development in the main, while NRST was concerned with the overall regeneration of the region's economy.

As well as work carried out by the Regional Strategy Teams, there have been two Royal Commissions which have touched on the regional element of public expenditure and revenue. The Royal Commission on the Constitution (Kilbrandon Committee) commissioned a paper entitled

Financial and Economic Aspects of Regionalism and Separatism by D. N. King, (1973) and took written evidence from the Revenue Departments (1973) on the question of revenue returns from the regions. The information on public expenditure contained in the paper by D. N. King is not as detailed as the NRST's work. However, both King and the Revenue Department provide more information and detail on revenue than previously published. The second Royal Commission was on Local Government Finance (the Layfield Committee, 1976), and examined the relationship between local and central government finance.

Recent developments

It is only in the recent past that official figures estimating GDP for, in the first place, the four countries comprising the UK, and secondly, the standard planning regions, have been produced. (Estimates of gross domestic product for England, Scotland, Wales and Northern Ireland, (Economic Trends, June 1976), and UK Regional Accounts (Economic Trends, November 1976 initially) and in the Studies in Official Statistics series, No.31, Regional Accounts.) The figures for the four countries have resulted from a move by the CSO to reconcile the GDP figures for each of the four countries. Previously independent estimates from the countries themselves had been made. The estimates are based on the 'factor incomes' approach. (CSO 1976a, 1976b, 1978)

The UK Regional Accounts (published annually) present a much more detailed account of GDP estimates for the regions of the UK. As well as aggregate factor incomes, industrial details are presented as well as details of consumers' expenditure, taxes on expenditure and subsidies, total personal income and personal disposable income and gross domestic capital formation by industry and by purpose of government. More recently local authority data have been included. Detailed methodology is discussed in the Studies in Official Statistics No.31, Regional Accounts.

The statistics relating to the regions presented by the CSO are not all-embracing. Data on the public sector (apart from those mentioned above) are not included and the financial sector is not considered at all. However, to a certain extent the latter are outside the scope of the CSO's intentions of providing regional social accounts.

As well as the impetus for more information on regional accounts which has come from the regional strategies, the European Economic Community require regional information for its own regional policy. Work on regional accounting is currently being carried out by the statistical services of member countries on the initiative of the Statistical Office of the European Communities.

In 1976, the Statistical Office of the European Communities (Eurostat, 1976) published *Regional Accounts: Economic Aggregates 1970.* The coverage for the British regions was not great as the CSO, as already mentioned, has only recently started detailed work in the field. Nevertheless, some global data for 1970 were produced.

As well as providing some data which will be updated and expanded as the national statistical offices manage to incorporate a regional arm to their normal statistical services, this publication includes a description of the methodology used in the exercise of examining the main conceptual problems in relating to the definition of the units and operations which had to be taken into account at the regional level. Nevertheless, the choice of what should be included at the regional level was essentially pragmatic, reflecting on the one hand, the statistical information needed for describing the structure and evolution of the regional economies, and on the other, taking into account the current state of regional accounting activities in the member states and the general development of regional statistics.

This would seem to suggest the scope and description of a regional economy would expand the more the information became available. Once trade flows for regions were established, the methodology would then reflect this. While it certainly is practical to organise things on this basis, it may be better to establish a methodology which gives a full description of the regional economy, and measure as much of the region as possible given existing data. As data become more sophisticated then the quantification can become fuller.

Conclusion

What the literature review has shown can be divided into two parts. The first part deals with the conceptual problems involved in the treatment of a region as a part of a nation. The material shown in this section is that of two decades ago and is related to the debate on the value of accounts at the regional level. The discussion is taken at the aggregate level and centres around a system of accounts reflecting the national accounting system.

The second part deals with the attempts to provide data relating to expenditure and income at the regional level in the UK. This ranges from the early attempt by Woodward to provide regional social accounts through to the official estimates of the CSO and Eurostat. Woodward's work, although now dated, is useful in so far as it is a good guide to indirect estimation. The Northern Region Strategy Team's work on public expenditure is of interest because it takes an existing system, PESC, and adapts it to the regional level with a high degree of disaggregation. The official work provides up-to-date estimates on regional social accounts.

The overall importance of these to the research project is that they suggest that the possibility of attaching figures to the classification system devised in the project may be high. The greater degree of disaggregation contained in these official or unofficial estimates or their sources means that they can be adapted to suit the model adapted in the present work.

2 A money flows model of a national economy

A description of national income[1]

In this chapter, the national income accounting framework is used as a basis for the analysis of money flows. What is national income? The national income is a measure of the money value of goods and services becoming available to the nation from economic activity. It can be regarded in three ways:

1. As a sum of incomes derived from economic activity, which can be broadly divided, for example, between incomes from employment and income from profits.
2. As a sum of expenditure, the main distinction being that between expenditure on consumption and expenditure on adding to wealth (or investment).
3. As a sum of the product of the various industries of the nation.

This is why national income, national expenditure and national product are interchangeable phrases, measuring the same concept.

As the national product is a measure of the goods and services becoming available from economic activity, it is important to be sure of which activities contribute to it. In doing so, it is necessary to distinguish clearly between those transactions which relate to productive activities and other transactions which simply re-distribute income between the different members of the community. The former contribute to the creation of goods and services while the latter merely transfer the ability to purchase goods and services and are not the counterpart of any addition to the current output of goods and services. Nevertheless, when considering money flows, this transference of purchasing power is important.

It is this classification of all transactions, into those that represent productive activities and those that do not, that is important in deciding what is to be included in national product. However, this has to be modified, for purposes of estimation, because all the values of transactions in productive activities are not added together to arrive at total product. Consequently, a second distinction is necessary. This is the distinction between transactions in intermediate products and final products. The former are those productive activities, the results of which are used in the production of other productive goods or services. Final products are, on the other hand, consumed for their own sake. If sales of intermediate products are added to the sales of the final product, this would constitute double counting. By measuring national product as the sum of final products, it is not necessary to estimate the inputs into the final demand. Alternatively, by adding the sum of the goods and services which enter into final product—the value added at each stage of production—one can obtain the value of the final product also.

The three methods of measuring national product will now be examined in greater detail.

The expenditure method

Consider the following economy in which the only transactions are:

1 Industry A sells wood pulp to industry B for £10.

2 Industry B sells paper to industry C for £50.

3 Industry C sells books to final consumers for £200.

In this economy it is assumed that there are no other transactions, no foreign trade and no stocks. The total of all these transactions is £260, but this is not really the true value of the product which the economy produces. This is £200. The £260 that would be obtained by adding all the transactions at every stage is much in excess of the true value of what the economy is really obtaining for its activity, simply because certain elements of output are counted more than once as the value of wood pulp sold to industry B is embodied in the books sold by C.

One way, therefore, of quickly finding the national product from such a list of transactions is to look at the figure of final product or final demand, ignoring all intermediate transactions. This will provide an estimate of national product and is known as the value of expenditure on national product.

The output method

The output, or production method, or industry of origin method, amounts to calculating what each separate industry adds to the value of final output. This is the value added by each industry to the raw materials or other goods and services that are bought from other industries before passing on the products to the next link in the whole chain of production.

In the example given above, industry A bought no intermediate inputs and sold its output for £10. This constitutes its value added. Industry B purchases its inputs (£10 from A) and sold its product for £50. Value added in industry B was £40. Industry C purchased its inputs (£50) from B and sold books for £200, adding in the production process another £150 to the value of the inputs bought.

The sum of the three industries' value added is £10, plus £40, plus £150, which equals £200–the same figure obtained by looking at the value of final sales to consumers. Using this method, the intermediate inputs are not ignored (as in the expenditure method), but since only the value added included in each activity is included in the final total, no double counting takes place.

The income method

The third way of calculating national product is in terms of the incomes accruing to the basic factors of production used in producing the national product. If all basic factors of production are classified into land, labour and capital, all payments of incomes originating in the production process can be classified into payments to these three factors of production: labour receiving wages and salaries, land receiving rental payments and capital the remainder–which can be defined as profits. Other payments are made by firms in the course of production, such as payments for raw material inputs, but the firms supplying these inputs in turn pass on their net value added to the factors of production used in producing them.

Thus out of the value added by each industry, payments have to be made to the three factors of production. The sum total of all factor payments must equal the sum total of value added by industry, which in turn equals the value of sales to final product. The table below illustrates the situation in terms of the three-industry economy

Value added	Industry	Distribution of value added		
		Wages	Profit	Rent
10	A	8	2	0
40	B	30	8	2
150	C	60	80	10
200		98	90	12

Another way of looking at the three ways of measuring national income is as a system of flows. For this purpose it is useful to introduce the terminology of the productive sector, which produces goods and services and pays out the incomes generated, and the household sector which represents the receipts of incomes by private individuals and their expenditures of these incomes on private consumption. The circulating flow will then consist of the flows of payments from the household sector to the productive sector for its final product, and then the payment of the resultant value added to the household sector in return for the contribution to production which it has made. This represents a circular flow. The three different ways of measuring national product then appear as merely three different points at which the flow of money round the circuit is measured. If measured at the point where the money is flowing into the productive sector, then it is the expenditure method that is being used. If measured where it leaves the productive sector, then it is the value added that is being measured. If measured at the point where the income recipients receive the income, then it is the income method that is being used.

Figure 2.1 shows two sectors: the household and the productive sector, and the flows from these sectors. On the one hand there are the money flows of wages and salaries from the productive sector to the household sector and on the other hand, corresponding to these money flows, are the flows from the household sector of their services in the form of labour. In like manner, there are money flows from the household sector to the productive sector in return for flows of final goods and services in the other direction.

The national product is also concerned with transactions which do not have any money flows involved. To understand this it is necessary to delve deeper into what national income accounts are attempting to measure. National income is a measure of the money value of goods and services becoming available to the nation from economic activity. This is different from saying that the actual money flows reflect the flow of real goods and services in the economy. What the national income is measuring is the value of real goods and services in money terms, not the actual money flows which take place. In most cases money flows are in the reverse direction to the flows of real goods and services. However, there are some exceptions to this rule.

In certain cases income is often received in kind, namely in the form of goods for which no payment as such is made. Nevertheless, these are still considered income. To include them in the measurement of national income, one imputes the values that they would have had if they had entered into a market transaction in the normal way. A similar situation exists with respect to the owner-occupation of dwellings. Dwellings are conventionally classified as investment by the household sector and

Fig.2.1: Circular flow model of national product

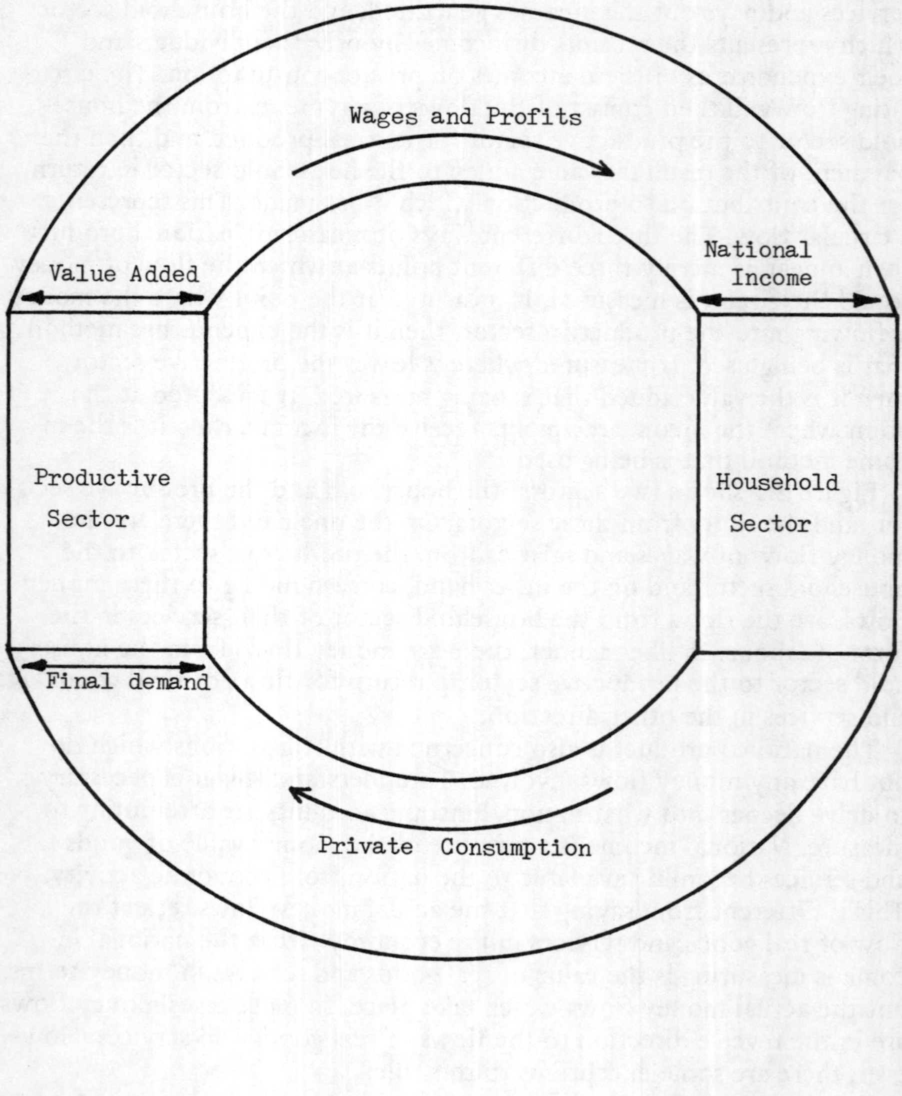

therefore as productive assets, but as such an output has to be attributed to them just like all other parts of the productive sector. By definition, owner-occupied dwellings are not rented out, therefore a rent has to be arrived at by imputation. This represents a payment by the owner-occupier to himself as payment for the services of the dwelling. In reality no money flows take place. A similar situation exists with investment. The national product measures the creation of the product over a given period, and both the process of production and the passage of time involve a gradual using up of the nation's productive assets. In order to measure the net additions to the nation's wealth or the national product, this capital consumption or depreciation should be taken into account and deducted from income, product and expenditure. In reality, this replacing of the capital stock used up in production in any year may not be carried out, and, therefore, no real expenditure on this occurs and hence no money flows take place.

Another major difference between the way national accounts conventions differ from a money flows description of the economy is regarding the point of time at which transactions ought to be measured. The sale of an article involves the placing of an order by the buyer, the delivery of the article, the rendering of an account by the seller, and the actual payment by the buyer; these operations usually take place on different dates. There are two main bases of accounting which are applicable to the problem faced here. These are the cash (payments and receipts) basis, on which transactions are recorded when money passes; and the accruals (or payable-receivable) basis, on which transactions are recorded when the expenditure is incurred. The principle adopted for the national accounts is to record transactions as taking place at the time when the expenditure is incurred as this represents the time when the addition to outputs has taken place.

The components of final output

The system of measuring the national product—the unduplicated value of the flow of goods and services produced by the nation in the year—has been outlined in terms of a two sector economy comprising households and production with consumption and labour as the link between the them. The relationship of actual money flows to national product flows was also highlighted. In this section, the description of the economy is widened to incorporate the different sectors of the economy and the role they play in the system. In the next part, this will be further expanded to incorporate the inter-relationship of the sectors.

The various sectors of the economy will be introduced by examining the uses to which final product is put. It was seen earlier that the output of the productive sector was either used up in the production of other goods and services or was not. Any output that was not used up in the production of goods and services must be either used up for its own sake–consumption, or not used up at all but set aside for the purposes of adding to the nation's wealth, its stock of capital investment. Parts of output can also be exported and used up as consumption or investment in other countries.

Consumption expenditure can be sub-divided into private consumption and public consumption.

Private consumption

This is mainly comprised of the consumption of households, but also of non-profit making bodies such as charities and certain educational establishments, like universities. These are not regarded as productive bodies but as types of mutual benefit societies entered into by private individuals. The expenditure of these bodies on goods and services, such as the salaries of their employees or equipment they use, are treated as part of consumers' expenditure in final product. If these organisations had been considered as part of the productive sector, their salary payments would have been part of value added and the goods they purchased treated as intermediate goods. To counterbalance the inclusion of the expenditures of non-profit making bodies under private consumption, all payments by individuals to such bodies have to be excluded from consumers' expenditure on final product. This exclusion is because such payments are not regarded as expenditures by the household sector on the output of the productive sector, and therefore, do not generate factor incomes. They are merely transfer payments from some members of the household sector to others and they do not cross the production boundary.

It is only when these non-profit making organisations use their receipts from fees, etc., to purchase goods, that the payments are regarded as crossing the production boundary and therefore as consumers' expenditure. Similarly, only the income that such bodies may receive from outside the household sector, such as dividends on investments, will be included as additions to personal income. The incomes they receive from the personal sector are merely transfers of purchasing power within the sector. This point is an important one in considering the question of money flows and it is one that will be examined in greater detail later.

Public consumption

The second sector involved in consumption is the public sector. The public sector comprises the government and local authorities. Only expenditure on current goods and services is treated as consumption. All capital formation carried out by the government is considered under investment, and all transfer payments made by the government are considered under the sector which generates the final demand in the production process.

An important consideration with respect to these public sector expenditures is that the public sector acts as the producer as well. Expenditure on final output corresponds to some production and value added in the productive sector. In the case of public sector expenditure, one of the most important 'industries' producing the final output that the public sector buys is the public sector itself. For it is the public sector which produces the defence, foreign policy, health and education services which it then proceeds to buy on behalf of the public. In producing these services the government is acting as part of the productive sector of the economy, and the value added that it creates in the course of the production is part of value added by industry of origin. The value added in the public sector comprises the wages and salaries plus the intermediate goods and services, like books, which the public sector buys for educational services.

The second category of final demand is investment. Investment is that part of the current output of goods and services which is devoted to adding to the stock of capital and hence to raising the future potential income flow. There are three main categories of investment which are important: domestic fixed capital formation; changes in stocks and investment abroad.

Domestic fixed capital formation comprises the flow of capital goods such as machinery and factories and that part of work in progress for which progress payments are usually made. Depreciation is the difference between gross and net domestic fixed capital formation. Changes in stocks ('unfixed' capital formation) include any raw materials or semi-finished goods or finished goods which have not yet entered into final demand, that is, they have neither been sold to final users nor had a progress payment paid on part completion. Investment abroad is merely the investment carried out by residents on one country in another. This can be offset by investment by foreigners in the former country. The difference is referred to as net investment abroad and can be positive or negative.

Three sectors are involved in making fixed investment—the personal sector by purchasing dwellings, the company or productive sector by purchasing plant and machinery which are used for producing intermediate and final goods, and the public sector by purchasing buildings for hospitals and schools.

A description of economic activity has gradually been built up showing how the various ways of measuring the nation's product relate to each other and how the various sectors contribute to the total. These relationships will be expanded in greater detail below.

A system of accounts

Double-entry accounting

This section will show how the various money-flows are linked together in an interlocking system of accounts. To do this, it is first useful to consider the nature of accounts, particularly the double-entry system of accounts. Any transaction requires two transactors, the one who pays and the one who receives. Each transactor can be allocated an account in which his receipts are recorded on the credit side and his payments on the debit side. Since a receipt by one transactor is a payment by another, a credit item for one must be a debit item for another. Thus any transaction must appear in the accounts of both transactors, on the debit side of one account, and on the credit side of the others. A double entry accounting system is simply one in which both aspects of each transaction appear; once as a receipt and again as a payment in another account.

A further feature of the system is that all accounts are made to balance. If, for example, an account has an excess of receipts over payments, then it has saved. By adding the savings of this account to the payments side, the two sides will balance. Similarly, if an account has an excess of payments over receipts, an item representing borrowing could be added to the receipts side of the account in order to preserve the equality of both sides; alternatively, savings, at a negative value, could be kept on the payments side.

There are three main classes of account which are of interest:

1 The production account which shows only the payments and receipts associated with that transactor's productive activities.

2 The appropriation account which shows all current receipts and payments including those—such as transfer payments—which may not arise out of productive activities.

3 The capital account which shows transactions of a capital nature that affect the transactor's balance sheets of assets and liabilities.

Accounts may be consolidated in various ways. Any sector of the economy will embrace a vast number of transactors and the accounts of them all may be combined into one account for the whole sector. Transactions between members of the same sector would thus appear on both sides of such an account. If all such items are deleted the resulting consolidated account shows only that sector's transactions with other sectors.

In the following section, these accounts are used to describe the sectors of the economy and show the inter-relationships which exist between them.

The production account

This is the account which shows the value of what the productive sector finally produces and what are the claims on this product.

Payments	*Receipts*
National income	Private consumption
Wages	Public consumption
Distributed profits	Gross domestic capital formation
Undistributed profits	Subsidies
Direct taxes paid by firms	Exports and property income from abroad
Indirect taxes	
Imports and property income paid abroad	

In this account what is being said is that, on the one hand, the productive sector produces a series of positive final outputs: private consumption, etc., and, on the other hand, it has to make payments such as wages, profit, etc. However, in this case payments do not equal gross national income nor total receipts equal gross national expenditure. To get these, imports and indirect taxes have to be treated as negative receipts. This arrangement then shows gross national product (expenditure) at factor cost equal to the sum of the incomes of the factors of production. If however, no allowance was made for indirect taxes and subsidies, then gross national expenditure would be measured at market prices.

This production account can be shown as a flow diagram, see below, where the flows refer to money. Receipts are shown by the arrows entering the box and payments by arrows leaving it.

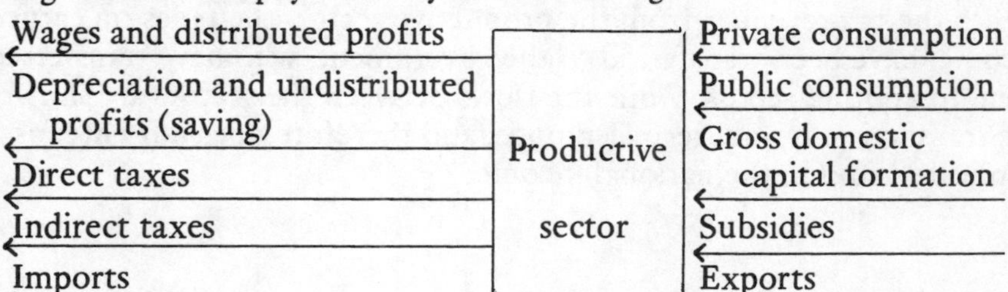

Each of the arrows entering the production account originate in an account of its own, which can be analysed also.

Credit items in production account	*Account to which item shown is debited*
Private consumption	Personal account
Public consumption	Public sector account
Gross domestic capital formation	Capital account
Subsidies	Public sector account
Exports	Rest of world account

This relationship between the categories of credit items distinguished in the production account may be represented diagrammatically in the incomplete flow diagram on p.25. The arrows show the direction of payment and the entry of an arrow into a box indicates that the account to which the box refers is to be credited with the transaction concerned, whereas the transaction is a debit item in the account from which the arrow has originated. The double entry accounting principle also requires the existence of counterpart credit items for the various items shown on the debit side of the production account. By building up the credits and debits flows, it will be possible to get a complete description of the flows.

The personal account

This account covers households and the non-profit making organisations such as charities. Wages and salaries paid to this sector from the productive sector will enter as a credit item on this account. The sector's purchases of consumer goods and services from the productive sector, together with its payment of tax, appear as a debit item in the account of the household sector (and as a credit to the productive and public sectors respectively). Other important credits are the incomes received by households in the form of transfer payments form of transfer payments from the government such as old age pensions and grants to students. Transfer payments do not form part of national income because they are not payments resulting from productive services. What is happening is that the tax revenues from the productive sector, the taxes on earned income, have been transferred to the government, who have transferred them to another sector. While the flows between the sectors are shown, the transaction is only recorded once, and therefore does not enter as a duplicated sum in the national income.

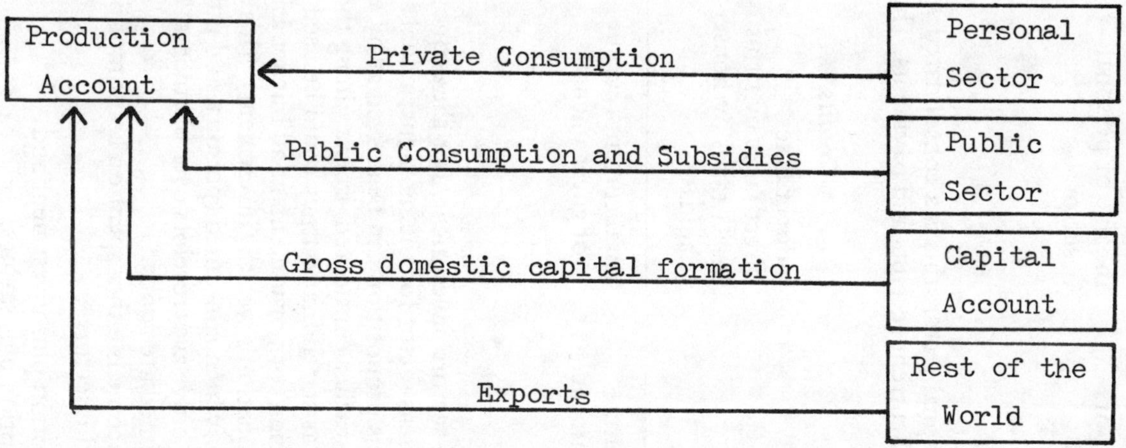
Production Account
Private Consumption
Personal Sector
Public Consumption and Subsidies
Public Sector
Gross domestic capital formation
Capital Account
Exports
Rest of the World

Debits	Credits
Private consumption Direct taxes on households Savings by households	Wages and distributed profits Transfer payments
Expenditure and savings of personal sector	Income of personal sector

The public sector account

Like the account for the personal sector, this is a consolidated appropriation account, showing all current receipts and payments. This is as follows:

Debits	Credits
Public consumption Transfer payments Subsidies Savings	Indirect taxes Direct taxes by firms Direct taxes by households
Total current expenditure and savings of government	Total current revenue of government

The capital account

This account covers all three sectors' investment. For the economy as a whole, but ignoring the overseas sector for the moment, actual savings equals actual investment. This proposition can be arrived at by examining the definitions that were earlier considered. In examining the components of final output, it was stated that output could be used up for its own sake (final consumption) or not used up at all but set aside for the purpose of adding to the nation's wealth (investment). This applied to all sectors of the economy which consumed (personal and public). The productive sector could only save (receipts over payments) as its consumption is only of intermediate goods.

For each sector current income is either spent on consumption or saved. Therefore, taking all the sectors:

Output = consumption plus investment and
Income = consumption plus savings.

As output and income have been shown to be equal, savings and investment must be equal.

The capital account for the economy as a whole (ignoring the overseas sector) can be shown as follows:

Debits	*Credits*
Gross domestic capital formation by the personal, public and productive sectors	Savings by the personal, public and productive sectors.

However, there is one important factor regarding this equality between savings and investment. This savings equal investment proposition relates to the economy as a whole, not to individual sectors. For example, the personal capital account may be such that not all savings are invested in dwellings and it could be classified as follows:

Personal sector's capital account

Debits	*Credits*
Gross domestic capital formation	Savings
Residual (positive)	

On the other hand, the public and productive sectors may invest more than they actually save themselves, and their account would be as follows:

Public and productive sectors' capital account

Debits	*Credits*
Gross domestic capital formation	Savings
Residual (negative)	

What the proposition that actual savings equals actual investment is saying is that if there is a surplus of funds in the personal sector, this will be matched as a negative residual by the public and productive sectors. The sum of these residuals on the capital account is zero. All this is really stating is that between the sectors there are money flows in the form of borrowing and lending which correspond to debits and credits in the normal sense. These debits and credits are financial assets which correspond to the real assets which are being created.

The final account to be considered is the one relating to the overseas sector. This is important in two ways. The first relates to the current account. Items for domestic consumption may be imported from abroad, while items of domestic production may be exported. The second relates to the capital account. As it is possible for domestic sectors to borrow form abroad to finance capital expenditure, this source of finance needs to be included alongside the capital account.

Similarly, overseas sectors can borrow from domestic sectors. Also, overseas sectors may invest in fixed capital formation in the UK, and likewise, UK sectors can invest in fixed capital formation overseas. An account for the overseas sector would look like this:

Fig.2.2: Flows between sectoral accounts

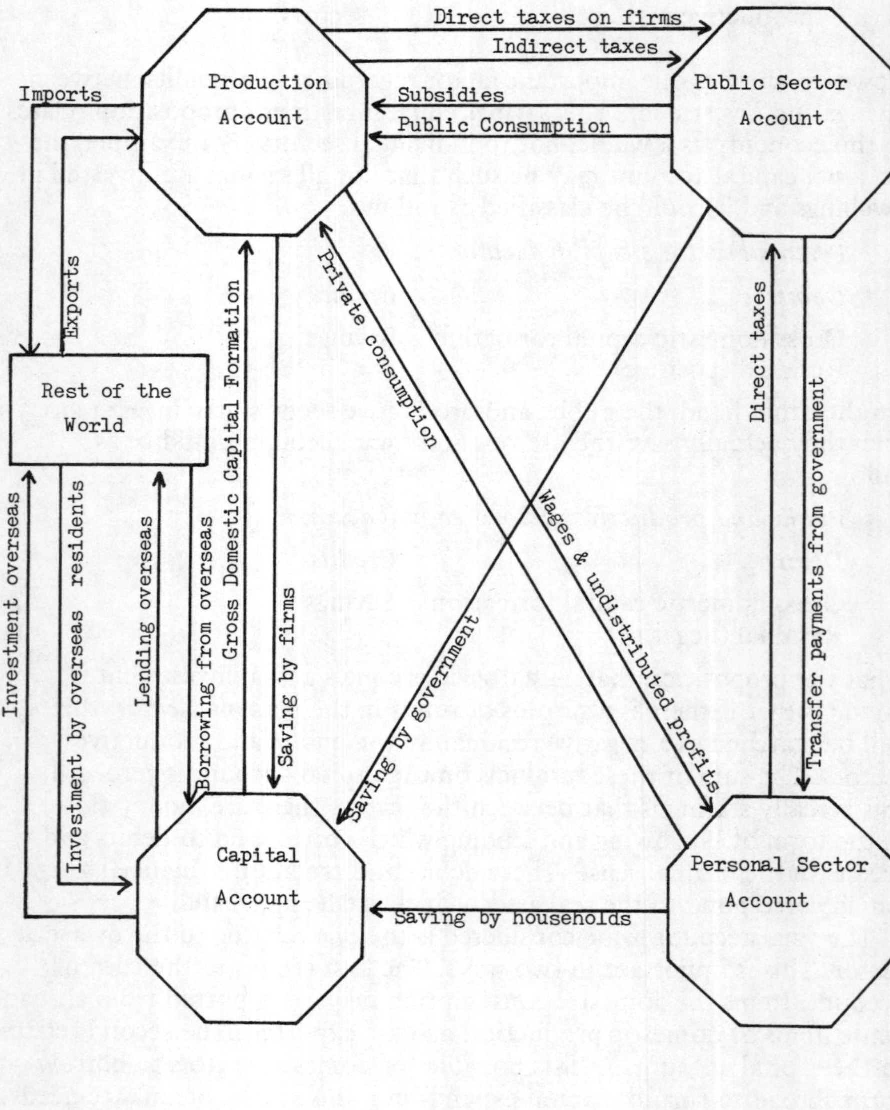

Current account

Debits	*Credits*
Imports	Exports
Other payments (interest, gifts and other transfers)	Other payments (interest, gifts and other transfers)

Capital account

Debits	*Credits*
Investment by overseas residents	Investment overseas
Borrowing from overseas	Lending overseas

However, in a national accounting framework these would be all on the receipts side with all the debits classed as negative receipts; this is to maintain the equality of national income and national expenditure. Otherwise total income would differ from total expenditure.

All these accounts then taken together in one flow diagram shown in Figure 2.2

The money flows described in Figure 2.2 show the interaction between the various sectors in the economy. However, these are not the only flows which take place in the economy. Mention has already been made of intermediate products which go to make up the final products—the subject of the production account. There are flows which take place between the intermediate producers and the final producers: goods and services in one direction, money in the other. In like manner, there are flows within the household sector. One person sells a second-hand car to another and there is a transference of money between the two. National income does not increase because the value of the car has been included when first produced. It could be possible to measure all these internal transactions by using the double entry method of accounting by crediting the seller and debiting the buyer of the car. Similarly, there are flows between different government departments. The Inland Revenue collects taxes, but transfers them to where they are spent. One government department may carry out work for another. (Although in the final model used, central government and local authorities will be treated as separate entities so that the flows between them will be recorded.)

Of all the intersectoral flows, one set—the relationship between intermediate and final producers—is analysed nationally and is of interest to policy makers. These are described by input-output accounts. However, other inter-sector flows are not usually of great interest. There may be some value in attempting to separate unincorporated business from the household sector, but on the whole it is the inter-relationships of different sectors that is important and of interest.

The model which has been outlined in this chapter, examining intersector flows, will form the basis of the regional money flows model. It is to the adaptation of this basic model that the next chapter turns.

Notes

1 This section follows W. Beckerman, 1976.

3 A money flows model for regions

The previous chapter built up a picture of an economy for a single nation, showing the money flows between three domestic sectors: the productive sector, the personal sector and the public sector, and between these three and the foreign sector. This chapter introduces regions into the analysis and examines the problems which arise.

Before introducing regions into the analysis, it is useful to consider the nation itself and of what it consists, as no precise definition has been given so far. The national income, product and expenditure of a country are the income, product and expenditure of those persons, enterprises and institutions which are regarded as that country's residents. They are not the same as the income and product originating within the geographical boundary of the country or the expenditure occurring there. International transactions, those between residents of the country in question and non-residents, need to be included to complete the picture.

Residents comprise individuals living in the country, the central government and local authorities, and all business enterprises and non-profit making organisations located in the country, including branches and subsidiaries of overseas companies but excluding overseas branches and subsidiaries of domestic companies. Agencies of the government operating abroad, such as embassies or military units, are regarded as residents, and conversely, the agencies of foreign governments are regarded as overseas residents.

The definition of residence for an individual centres around whether the individual is liable to income tax. Broadly speaking, in the UK, persons are resident if they maintain a place of abode there for six months or more during the year or if they visit the UK regularly for substantial periods. Persons who fulfil any of these conditions are subject to UK tax in respect of the whole of their income wherever originating, with only certain minor exceptions. UK government officials and forces stationed abroad are regarded as UK residents. Similarly, officials and forces of other governments stationed in the UK are excluded.

Such a definition applies to the generation of national income; national income is that which accrues to residents wherever located. For money flows this has to be modified in so far as wages and salaries, and income from self employment generated abroad by residents has to be seen as an inflow if it is remitted back to the country. If it is not remitted back, it does not enter into the money flows. Similarly, wages and salaries, and income from self employment generated by non-residents of the UK in the UK, enters into the money flow, and if it is remitted out of the country then it is an outflow. However, in the majority of cases, residents reside in the country and wages and salaries, and incomes from self-employment, generated enter the money flow directly. As far as property income from abroad, earned by persons, the normal convention applies; this is an inflow both in the money flow as well as the national accounting sense.

The definition of residence for a business in the UK is as follows. For income tax purposes a company, wherever registered, is treated as resident if the central management and control of the business is exercised in the UK; its profits, wherever originating, are then liable to UK tax. Residency for Inland Revenue purposes also includes branches and subsidiaries of overseas companies operating in the UK. For the national income accounts, an enterprise which is a UK resident but whose trading operations take place wholly or partly abroad is in principle divided into two parts: firstly, overseas branches or subsidiaries earning trading profits on overseas operations and secondly, a head office and branches earning trading profits on operations in the UK, if any. Branches are treated as residents of the country in which they are located and subsidiaries contribute to national income not as part of domestic income, but as income from abroad. Correspondingly, the UK branches and subsidiaries of overseas companies contribute to domestic income but not to national income, their profits being part of income paid abroad.

For money flows, the important considerations are the flow of profits into and out of the UK, and the amount generated within the UK and retained there. Profits earned abroad and remitted to the UK are an inflow of money; profits remitted abroad are an outflow.

Total government spending irrespective of where it is spent enters into the national accounts. However, with respect to money flows, flows abroad such as on defence forces or embassy staff, etc., which are considered resident in terms of the national income accounts, have to be treated as outflows. Similarly, inflows from other nations, although not resident in a national accounts sense, are included, and should be classified as inflows from the rest of the world. For local authorities, as they are centred around a particular locality in the UK, their residency is in the UK as in the national accounts; they, of course, may buy equipment from abroad which would be covered in imports, or borrow from abroad which would be covered in the capital account of the balance of payments.

In the international situation, the origin and destination of money flows appear fairly straightforward conceptually. Can a parallel analogy be applied to the relationship between regions within a single nation? Is it possible to treat each region as a separate nation and apply the set of rules regarding money flows outlined for a nation to each of them? The short answer to this is 'No'. The consideration of regions poses some fairly awkward conceptual problems. The first problem is concerned with government and multi-regional organisations and the problems of defining the origin and destination of flows of a common currency. The second major problem is concerned with the role of the central government as the central government operates on behalf of the country as a whole and in some cases cannot be assigned to any region in particular. However, it is possible to devise a model which will describe inter-regional money flows; this will be done by examining the situation regarding persons, companies and the public sector.

The personal sector in the regional context can be treated in the same way as it has been in the international context. Residents of a region earn wages and salaries, or income from self-employment; if these are earned outside the region and are remitted back, then they are inflows. Property income from abroad is that earned outside the region. In the international situation, it is unlikely that people will work in one country and live in another country, so the flows of wages and salaries, and income from self-employment are likely to be minimal. However, in a country like the UK, the scope for persons living in one region and working in another is obviously much greater. Residency has to be either based on workplace or restplace. The arguments for basing residency on restplace appear stronger as the majority of expenditure decisions are likely to be centred around home and family. Inflows then would be related to earned income from self employment from region of work to region of domestic residency. (However, as the numbers involved are likely to be small, a useful assumption to make would be that there is no difference between place of residency and work.)

As far as the other aspects of personal sector income are concerned, inter-regional flows are straightforward, conceptually. Property income from abroad covers all flows on profits, dividends and interest from outside the region, whereas under the heading profits, dividends and interest are centred around the region itself. These two groups can be classed together rather than as two separate headings. Rent can be received in the region itself and the rest of the world.

On the expenditure side, expenditure by the personal sector may be distributed according to the region where the value added was generated. This is akin to an import account for each region which will in turn generate an export account for each other region. By treating expenditure as the sum of value added in each region, final flows will be measured. For example, a car purchased in the North comprises the value added generated by the selling garage and the value of the car as it came into that garage. If the car was built in another region, there would be a flow of money out of the North corresponding to the wholesale value of the car. However, this is only the first round flow. It is unlikely that all the materials for the car were made in the same region where it was assembled. Indeed, there may be a considerable import content to the assembling region (from other regions and abroad) in the car. The final flows—value added at each stage—would describe the situation where all the imports were allowed for. Indeed, some of the imported parts may have an import content themselves, and possibly even from the regions where the assembly has taken place. Therefore, there would be considerable complexity involved in tracking down all of these. Nationally, this measurement is fairly straightforward, as all exports and all imports are recorded. If there are re-exports of imports, these will cancel out when the net figure is obtained, and, as this is the important consideration regarding the recording of trade, the problem is resolved. At the regional level, there is a serious practical problem of measurement. However, such a method goes beyond the money flows model outlined earlier. The money flows system entails the initial flows rather than the final situation once all subsequent flows have been incorporated. On the expenditure side, then, only the initial flow is of interest.

In the international situation, the origin and destination of company profits appears fairly straightforward. Profits earned abroad by subsidiaries of UK companies are remitted back to headquarters. Profits earned by British subsidiaries of non-UK companies are flows out of the country. In both cases these allow for the fulfilment of tax responsibilities. Once profits have been earned, they are either retained or distributed to shareholders. Retained profits are treated as company savings and form part of the capital account, either financing capital expenditure in the company itself, or forming part of financial assets, eventually financing capital expenditure by another company or another sector. Distributed profits form part of the income of the personal sector.

In the case of a country, retained profits and distributed profits are either a flow within sectors (therefore, measured in their creation) or a flow between sectors (including the overseas sector). However, the introduction of regions can complicate this. There are two types of companies that can be identified. The first is the company which operates solely within a single region and does not have overseas subsidiaries. The second is the multi-regional company with a headquarters based in one region. As far as the first is concerned, the origin of profits is within the region itself; retained profits finance capital expenditure in the region or go into financial assets, the destination of which in theory can be analysed. Distributed profits can also be similarly analysed. The origin and destination of profits can be matched.

Consider the multi-regional organisation. Assuming that accounting procedures allow a breakdown of where profits are earned, the region of origin will be available irrespective of where the headquarters are located. Once all of the profits are remitted to the headquarters and are pooled as company profits, then in so far as their ultimate destination is concerned, profits earned in one region are indistinguishable from profits earned in another. It could not be said that the profits earned in region X flowed to region Z, via headquarters. The picture is further complicated by the two uses of profits. The destination of distributed profits is fairly straightforward even though the origin and destination of a particular batch of profits cannot be precisely matched, but the problem of tracing the destination of undistributed profits is much more complex. Capital expenditure is financed out of savings or out of borrowing, or a combination of both. If all company capital expenditure were financed out of savings, then both the origin and destination of retained profits would be known, but not matched. This is a measurement problem rather than a conceptual one.

The problem which headquarters present to the tracing of the origin and destination of money flows has arisen because, once money of the same currency is pooled together, it is impossible to tell from where money has originated once it reaches its ultimate destination. The same problem arises in the case of financial intermediaries such as banks, building societies and assurance companies. Deposits paid into building societies form the basis for lending. A building society which operates in one region, attracting its deposits solely from residents of that region, and lending to other residents of the region, can easily be analysed with reference to asset and liability sheets. However, when more than one region is considered, deposits once pooled together cannot be distinguished from each other in relation to the destination of these deposits in the form of loans. All that could be known is the total amount put into deposits by residents of a region, and the total amount lent to regions.

A third area where this situation arises is with the government. The government raises money through taxation, borrowing, and money creation. From the funds raised in this way, it pays wages and salaries, transfer payments, and buys the goods used in carrying out its responsibilities. Again, the origin of flows to the government and the destination of flows from the government may be measured with respect to the regions concerned, but not matched together.

One method of treating the government and company headquarters in in an inter-regional context would be to consider them as supra-regional, as if regions in their own right. By showing them in this way, origin and destination of flows would be identified, but not matched. If the financial institutions only lent their deposits to persons or companies, then it would not be necessary to have recourse to creating an extra region to account for pooled regional resources because the total flows of deposits and borrowing by each region could be analysed. This would give region of origin and region of destination similar to the supra-regional method. However, the financial institutions do not lend all their deposits to persons and companies in regions, they lend to the government and multi-regional companies also. As a result, it is necessary to create a supra-regional identity for them also.

Treating government as a supra-regional organisation provides an interesting method of analysis for government expenditure in the inter-regional context. Using the supra-regional method, it is possible to show the money flows which emanate from the government to a region in response to the purchase of goods and services. However, nothing is known of the ultimate destination of these goods and services; they may be for the region in which they were produced, or otherwise. The destination of these goods and services is also of interest. The position of the government with regard to regions is further complicated. Part of the role of the government is to provide services for the nation as a whole. Some of these services, like the provision of health services, can be attributed to the region where the expenditure takes place. A hospital in a region can be assigned to that region in so far as it contributes to the health of the residents of that region, rather than the residents of another. A doctor in general practice can be assigned to the region where he practices. Both of these are treated as government expenditures. Nevertheless, there are two considerations when analysing government expenditures in the regional context. The first relates to the region where the services are provided, the second to where the actual money flows take place. In most situations these will be the same as in the case of payments in the form of wages and salaries, but some equipment may be 'imported' into the region, in this case the money flows will be to a different region. However, some services provided by the government cannot be attributed to any one region in particular. Services such as defence are national in character and are indivisible with respect to benefits as regards regions. While the service of defence cannot be attributable uniquely to any one region, the money flows in the form of wages and salaries, and payment for equipment such as warships can be assigned to the region in which the service personnel are located or the warship built.

This distinction between national and regional spending can be treated together by using the government as a supra-regional organisation in an analysis of government spending. National expenditures which take place in a region can be treated as an export of goods and services to the government, and therefore, an inflow of money. 'Regional' expenditures would be assigned to the region where the money flows take place, and they could also be matched with the region for which the goods and services are destined. Thus there would be a flow of goods and services between regions, paid for by the government. This analysis is akin to saying that each region has its own central government sector for non-national services, and national services would be represented by the supra-region sector representing government. In this manner, national expenditures in a region are classed as part of gross regional expenditure analogous to gross national expenditure. The regional expenditures such as those on health would form part of gross domestic regional expenditure, analogous to gross domestic expenditure, because the region alone benefits from the expenditures. What is being described here is an analysis of the aggregate money flows to regions resulting from expenditure on goods and services by the government on behalf of the nation as a whole, and its individual regions.

The money flows will describe the first round flow, rather than the value-added generated in each region as a result of government expenditure.

The other major sector is the local authorities. As these are centred around geographical areas and can be summed to regions, there are no conceptual problems involved in their analysis.

Regional money flows model

The model to be used can be summaried as follows. The inter-regional money flows model classifies the many transactors in an economy into various sectors. These sectors, the personal sector, the company sector and the government sector follow the National Accounts conventions.[1] In many cases, it may be useful to sub-divide these sectors further (depending on the nature of the analysis). The personal sector comprises households, unincorporated businesses and private non-profit making bodies. The company sector can be sub-divided into the commercial and business sector; and the financial sector. These can be further sub-divided, the former into private and public ownership, and the latter into the banking, insurance and other financial institutions. The government sector can be divided into the central government and local authorities. These follow the National Accounts conventions.

The transactions which are analysed are those made by the final transactors for all of the sectors except in the case of the financial sector. For each sector, the revenue flows, and the expenditure flows which are subsequently generated, are examined for both capital and current transactions where appropriate. For financial institutions, the analysis is extended and they are analysed in their role as financial intermediaries, channelling money to final spenders from savers. No intra-sectoral transactions within a region are considered. These are all consolidated. Each transaction carried out by a transactor appears twice in the accounting system, as a credit to one transactor and a debit to another. The capital and current accounts of each sector are linked through savings, and the capital accounts of all sectors are linked through the financial assets and liabilities which they possess.

Each transactor is assigned to a region according to the concept of residency. The personal sector is classified by the region of domestic residency. The company sector is classified by the region where the unit of production is located and the government sector is classified by the region where it governs. This classification system does not, however, provide a comprehensive coverage of all transactors.

There are two major problems. The first is that some institutions, as transactors (notably central government), cannot be assigned to any particular region even though the transactions they carry out can: the central government governs the whole nation. The second lies in the purpose of the model—the matching of the origin and destination of money flows by regions. Many institutions—banks, building societies, companies, and the government—receive money from regions as deposits, profits or taxes which are then all pooled in a central fund at 'headquarters'. These funds are then distributed in the form of loans, capital expenditure, transfer payments, etc. However, origin and destination by region cannot be matched. These institutions, like the government, have a residency outside of any particular region with respect to decision-making.

For organisations like these, one solution is to classify residency as to these flows as supra-regional, that is outside any particular region, covering the nation as a whole. Flows to and from the government or those financial institutions which operate on a countrywide basis can then be analysed in the form of transactions which take place in regions, by a transactor out with the regions, by examining the flows from the supra-region to regions, and vice versa.

To these regions and supra-regions are added, as a separate group, the transactors who reside outside of the UK and are classified as the rest of the world. The institution of the EEC is also considered separately as it is an important channel for money into regions.

Figure 3.1 illustrates these flows in matrix form. The matrix shown here describes the eleven regions of the UK, the rest of the world, the EEC, the central government, multi-regional companies and countrywide financial institutions. Including the totals, this gives a seventeen by seven-

Fig.3.1: The basic matrix

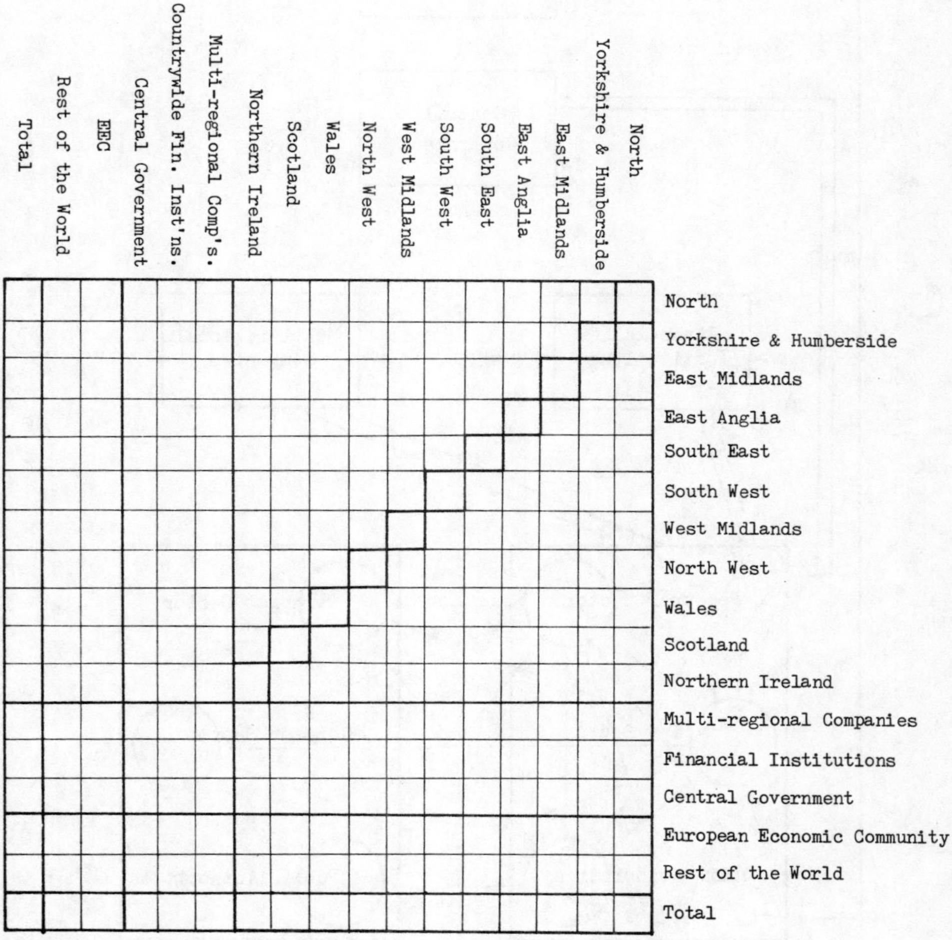

Fig.3.2: Money flows to and from each of the sectors of region 'A'

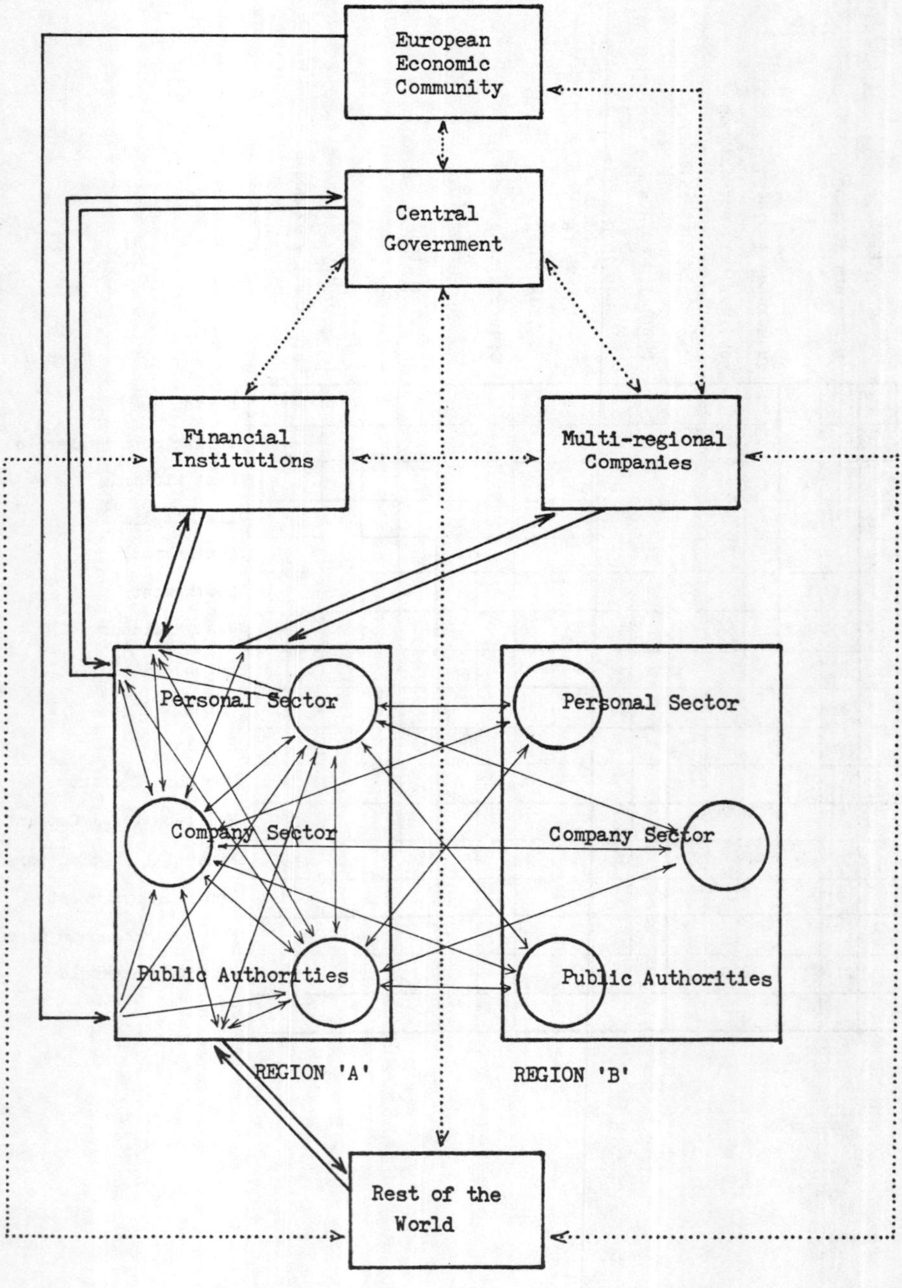

Fig.3.3: Money flows involving multi-regional financial institutions

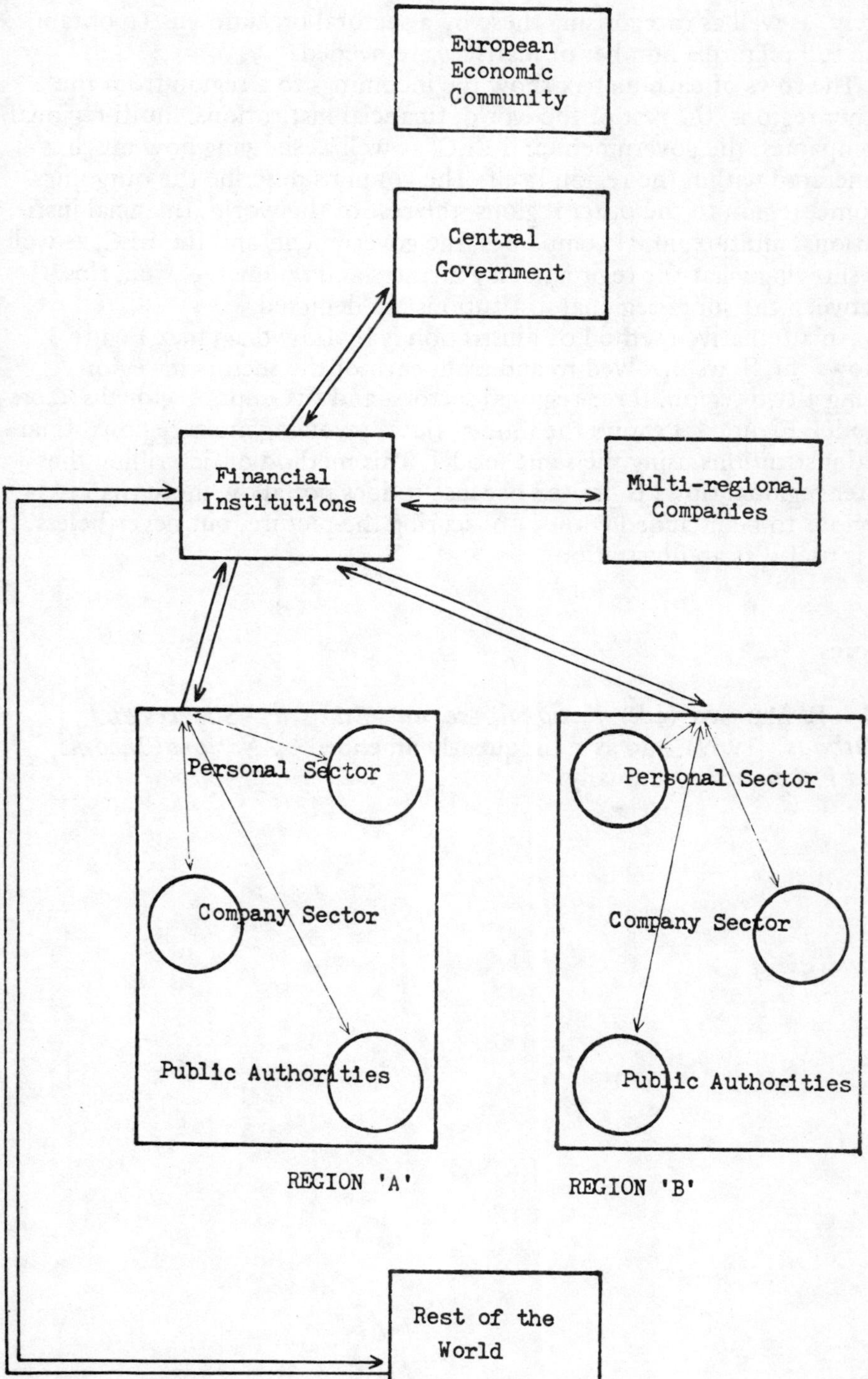

teen matrix. However, to analyse and understand all the flows which take place, it is necessary to treat income and expenditure flows separately, as well as categorising these by a sectoral breakdown. To obtain the full picture a number of matrices are needed.

The rows of each matrix show the incomings to a region from the other regions, the rest of the world, financial institutions, multi-regional companies, the government and EEC, as well as showing how much is generated within the region itself. The columns describe the outgoings from a region to the other regions, the rest of the world, financial institutions, multi-regional companies, the government, and the EEC, as well as showing what the region itself generates and retains. As well, flows between the supra-regional institutions are depicted.

An alternative method of illustration is by flow diagrams. Figure 3.2 shows the flows involved to and from each of the sectors in region A, using a two-region, three-regional sectors, and five-supra-regional sectors model. Figure 3.3 shows the money flows involving multi-regional financial institutions using the same model. This method of describing the inter-regional flows is limited because it does not allow more than two regions to be included without obscuring the picture, but nevertheless, it is useful as an illustration.

Notes

1 R. Maurice, (ed.), *National Accounts Statistics–Sources and Methods,* (1969), and as subsequently amended by *National Income and Expenditure,* annually.

4 The generation of data for a regional money flows model: general observations and conclusions

Introduction

The data and the sources and methods employed to obtain them are discussed in detail later (see pp.59–215). In Appendix 1 the personal and company sectors are covered. The general government sector and public corporations (other than nationalised industries) are included in Appendices 2 and 3 in the financial sector covering the assets and liabilities of the private, public and financial sectors is treated in detail. This chapter provides a summary of the problems involved in obtaining data and the sources and methods employed in their collection.

The personal and company sectors

The personal sector

Considerable effort is made by the Central Statistics Office to estimate the regional dimension of the economic role of the personal sector in constructing regional accounts which they now produce annually. Consequently, given the resources available to the research team, it was felt that full use should be made of the CSO's efforts in this field, and it would not be worthwhile attempting to duplicate their work. Indeed, given the time available for the research, and the range of economic activity not as yet covered by the CSO in the regional field, it was appropriate that the research should concentrate on filling the gaps.

The CSO exercise is closely related to the national income and expenditure accounts as presented in the annual 'blue book', and a conscious attempt is made to ensure the direct comparability of the regional to the national accounts. As a result, the CSO estimates are on a calender year basis compared to the financial years used elsewhere in this report. Furthermore, the CSO adopt the accruals accounting system rather than the money flow system outlined in the present work; these differences have been discussed in Chapter 2.

It was felt that as much use as possible should be made of the CSO exercise, while adapting their results, where possible to our needs. The CSO were most helpful and made unpublished estimates available to the project. As a result, the coverage of the personal sector owes much to the work already undertaken by the CSO. Given this, current income and expenditure are more fully represented than the capital account.

The particular source used in compiling these data was *Economic Trends* of November 1978 which is compatible with the estimates presented in National Income and Expenditure, 1967–77. For 1977 only preliminary estimates are available from the CSO as presented in *Economic Trends*, June 1979; and the final figures for 1977 would be expected to be produced in November. These, however, are subject to some delay due to the preparation of the Annual Census of Employment for 1977 being delayed. These preliminary estimates are not directly compatible with the published national accounts and are not as comprehensive as previous years' final statistics.

Given the above observations, there are certain inconsistencies between the data presented for the personal sector in Appendix 1 and the 'ideal' data required for the model. Nevertheless, the use of these CSO estimates are justified on the grounds that it released resources for obtaining data on other sectors, and secondly it is highly unlikely that any data produced otherwise would actually be an improvement on that of the CSO.

The company sector

In the previous chapter the company sector has been divided into two: the public sector covering public corporations and the private sector. The public corporations refer here to the nationalised industries such as British Steel, and new towns, water authorities, etc., are considered in the general government sector.

The company sector poses several difficulties and the coverage of the activities of the company sector at the regional scale are particularly limited. The identification of the flows involved in the company sector shows that for the nationalised industries much of the inflows are related to flows between supra-regional sectors (the industries themselves and mainly the central government and the financial sector). Indeed, the main non-supra-regional item is the undistributed income flow which is derived from the appropriation account of the sector. No information exists on the regional distribution and it is allocated using the CSO's estimates of regional gross trading profits and surpluses. A similar situation exists for the private sector and the undistributed income is allocated likewise. The other major items for both public and private companies are capital transfers (mainly from central government). These cover regional development grants, investment grants and the like. Figures for total capital transfers from the general government are presented in Appendix 2. These, however, include loans which form part of the financial accounts. Furthermore, some of these go to persons (grants for house improvements, loans for house purchase). However, for the company and personal sector as a whole, these can be obtained from Appendix 2.

On the expenditure account, gross domestic fixed capital formation is the main item. Here, recourse can be made to the work of the CSO. Regional estimates of gross domestic fixed capital formation by industry and by purpose of government are included in the regional statistics which they produce. From this information it is possible to estimate the capital expenditure by the company and personal sector by region. As the personal sector's capital expenditure is for the most part on dwellings and these are given separately, an estimate for the company sector can be obtained.

The coverage of the company sector is one which could undoubtedly be improved; however such an exercise would have to be carried out in conjunction with the CSO's work in this field in order to avoid duplication and to obtain access to primary sources.

The general government sector and public corporations (other than nationalised industries)

The flows associated with the general government sector comprising the central government, local authorities, and public corporations (other than the nationalised industries) are considered in detail in Appendix 2 where the expenditures and revenues of these sectors are examined separately.

The expenditures of the general government and the public corporations included in this section form most of public expenditure. Loans to the nationalised industries have not been analysed. The methodology adopted for the analysis of public expenditure is that outlined in the section describing the regional money flows model and used in Short (1978). These analyse public expenditure in two distinct but related ways: the first relates expenditure to the region where the services provided are consumed; the second relates to the region where the actual money flows take place. In most situations, these will be the same as in the case of payments in the form of wages and salaries, but some equipment may be imported into the region and, in this case, the money flows will be to a different region. However, some services provided by the government such as defence are indivisible with respect to the benefits for different regions, and cannot be attributed to any one region. Nevertheless, the money flows in the form of wages and salaries, on payment for equipment can be assigned to the regions. Thus the services which are regionally relevant are classified by region in terms of the services provided on the one hand, and all services (regionally relevant and national) are assigned to each region in terms of the money flows generated.

The sources and methods used in assigning public expenditures to the regions are detailed in Appendix 2. The overall quality of the data with respect to regional coverage is good. Local authority spending in each region of England is produced by the Department of the Environment and apart from some problems with some authorities after local government reorganisation the data has generally been available. Certainly for the future, these data can be expected to be produced. For Wales, the Welsh Office publish local authority statistics. For Scotland, there is a similar publication, and although there was considerable delay in their publication, due to reorganisations in the period covered by this study, the statistics will be available in the future.

For central government spending, the quality of data varies between spending programmes and departments and indeed, within spending programmes. A considerable part of the data are published as a matter of course: social security expenditure, expenditure on roads, and on regional development, grants to universities, etc. Other data have been provided by the departments on request without their having recourse to particular special exercises.

Data on health expenditure, DHSS administration and Ministry of Defence contracts were obtained in this way. In other cases, some Departments have produced details of their expenditures in the regional context where their records have allowed this. In some cases, these have been provided with caveats as to the precision of the estimates. Such statistics related to the operations of the Ministry of Agriculture, Fisheries and Food, and the Departments of Industry and Energy. In other cases, the departments felt that the data provided by the initiation of a special exercise were sound. Examples of these were the data provided by the Department of Employment as to expenditure on employment support schemes.

Data on the public corporation's spending were obtained from published sources, (Covent Garden, Scottish Special Housing Association and Scottish and Welsh New Towns), or from the government departments under which the public corporations operate, (English New Towns, and Ports from the Department of the Environment), or from the corporations themselves (Regional Water Authorities). In this last example, although the water authorities are organised on a regional basis, their boundaries are different from the standard planning regions, the water authorities provided data on their operations within their boundaries so that their expenditure across country could be categorised on a standard region basis.

The final method of obtaining regional data was by assigning the national control totals to each region using a suitable proxy where direct data do not exist. For the most part these proxies relate to a physical variable such as manpower, consumption patterns or output.

With respect to the revenues received by the central government, local authorities and public corporations the generalisations relating to expenditure apply. However, there are considerable flows from the central government sector to the other two, and these are considered separately.

The source of data for the local authorities is the local authority returns to the Department of the Environment which are aggregated across regions. These provide details of rate income, specific government grants and rate support grant on the current account, and central government capital grants, and loans on the capital account. The relevant publications for Scotland and Wales contain the same data. However the general upheaval caused by reorganisation has meant that data for 1974–75 for the English regions is not complete, and that certain data for 1975–76 to 1977–78 for Scotland are only available from the *Rates and Rateable Value in Scotland* publication. However, in the future these data should be produced for all the regions.

For the central government compilation of data on the flows required a variety of sources to be employed in the main, the methodology which was used was tax-based proxies and this accounted for about three-quarters of the data. Sources such as the Inland Revenue's *Survey of Personal Incomes* allowed figures for direct taxes to be obtained. For indirect taxes such as Value Added Tax, data on the regional distribution of the relevant tax base, such as regional spending patterns weighted by the appropriate VAT rate, were used. National Insurance and other contributions were allocated on the basis of wages and salaries in each region. Car tax was apportioned according to the distribution of new car registrations. In some cases regional data on certain tax bases are not available (e.g. betting and gaming taxes) and in such cases, a crude proxy such as adult population was employed.

On the capital account, the government raises the majority of its funds through the financial markets and this is discussed in detail in the separate chapter on the financial sector (see p.161).

For the public corporations, the relevant flow is the loans they obtain from the Public Works Loan Board to finance their capital expenditure. Details of the loans to the new towns, water authorities, etc., are given in the PWLB annual report.

In total, it has been possible to produce data on the regional incidence of both public expenditures and revenues. The data have been generated by employing a mixture of direct data on the regional distributions, and in some cases, the use of proxies where no direct data exist. What the exercise has demonstrated is the high coverage of public expenditure from direct data sources and on the revenue side using direct data or tax-base proxies which produce reliable data.

For such an exercise to be continued in the future, the goodwill of certain departments which have generated data by initiating special data gathering exercises is important. Their continuance, plus the encouragement of similar efforts by departments where data on the regions are weak would certainly be necessary. However, there are areas where the quality of data are high, particularly in the production of local authority statistics, and health expenditures to mention but two.

Flows from the European Economic Community

Included in Appendix 2 are the flows from the various funds of the European Economic Community. These flows can be divided into two: the first are those which are to the government and the government uses them as income to support its own spending programmes in the areas concerned. For example, grants from the European Regional Development Fund to industry are not made to the originators of the projects, but they go to the Department of Industry. The projects themselves receive only national regional development grants (for which they qualify automatically) and the European grants are used to boost the government's income. The second are those which go directly to the region without being channelled through the government. The infrastructure grants of the Regional Development Fund are included here. Consequently, the data are shown in the form of flows to the supra-regional sector and to the individual regions where appropriate.

The sources of data on the flows from the EEC are the European Commissions press releases and background reports which between them itemise each allocation made to the UK. These are often supplemented by Parliamentary answers in *Hansard.* However, there are difficulties involved in handling the EEC sources on two grounds. As the data series are not continuously established, it is difficult to assemble consistent data over a time period. As well, most internal EEC documents use the Unit of Account denominations for monetary quantities and as the 'exchange' rate of which with the £ sterling fluctuates through the year, the collection of annual flows in £ sterling of payments from funds that may be spread over the year becomes difficult.

Given that the EEC produce background papers and press releases on the various flows to member countries, and their regions where appropriate, it would seem that it could be possible to produce the detail which is required for the accounting system and framework outlined in this project without much more effort.

The financial accounts

Financial accounts are sometimes called the 'flow of funds' accounts, or the sector financing accounts. Financial accounts are designed to set out the financial transactions of the different sectors of the economy systematically and in a convenient form. They provide a statistical framework for considering financial transactions and enable the operations of one sector to be directly related to those of other sectors.

The financial transactions can be presented in two ways. The sector financing account presents a time series for a particular sector's acquisition of financial assets and liabilities. The other method, the financial assets transactions, gives details of the sales and purchases of a particular asset or group of assets by each of the different sectors. The two types of account can be combined to form a matrix with these two way classifications of assets in sectors, giving details of the transactions in each of the various types of financial assets by the various sectors in a single period. As the financial assets are classified in a uniform way, the acquisition of a particular kind of financial asset by one section can be associated with changes in the other assets and liabilities of that sector and those of the other sectors.

The financial accounts are classified by six sectors: personal, public, industrial and commercial companies and overseas which in the main are the creators of financial surplus and the demanders of funds; and the banking, and other financial institutions sectors which operate as intermediaries to channel these surplus funds to the final spenders. However, not all of the financial surpluses are transmitted via financial intermediaries: for example, the government borrows directly from the personal sector (National Savings) and from the overseas sector (intergovernment loans). Furthermore, there is often transactions between financial institutions which channel savings from one sector and ultimately to the final spender.

Thus the system may be viewed as a continuum where at one end the savers and borrowers comprise a fairly homogeneous unit and the surpluses are transmitted via a financial intermediary such as a building society. At the other end there is no such link between the savers and the borrowers. Savers pass on their surpluses to financial institutions who in turn pass some of these funds to other financial institutions which may be more specialised in a particular type of financing operations, these in their turn lend to final spenders. The special finance agencies operate in such a manner. In between these extremes fall banks, who deal with heterogeneous groups in both the savings and lending operations; and National Savings, unit trusts, life assurance, etc., who transmit funds between wholly heterogeneous groups.

Therefore the operations of the financial accounts can be fairly complex at a national level. Introducing an extra dimension such as the regional one complicates matters further, both on the levels of presentation and collection of data. As discussed in the presentation of the overall financial flows model, (see p.37), because of the impossibility of classifying institutions which transcend regional boundaries, a supra-regional category has been created. Flows from regions to these supra-regional sectors and vice-versa can then be measured. In terms of a matrix, incorporating all of the regions and supra-regions, flows for each financial assets can, in theory, be identified. In practise, it is better to present the relationship between regions and the supra-regional entities without recourse to the full matrix, identifying only those elements which are represented.

At the national level, data are not collected for each of the sectors separately. For particular assets and liabilities, the figures are taken from the statutory returns of the institutions involved and assigned to the particular sectors which have been identified. In most cases there is often a discrepancy between, for example, purchases of an asset and the recorded sales by a sector. The residual is then allocated to the non-reporting sectors, often on a fairly arbitrary basis. If such problems exist in the national context where a sophisticated data collection system operates, these are multiplied when the extra regional dimension is introduced.

In this section the lessons and generalisations from Appendix 3 are drawn upon with specific examples given where appropriate from each sector.

The personal sector

Surpluses. Data are not collected directly from the personal sector nationally; they are provided from the returns of other sector's (building societies, banks, etc.), or they are estimated as a residual when all other sectors have been accounted for. The collection of data at the regional level is no exception. Given the national intra-sectoral flows, the regional ones will not be different. If all National Savings are flows between the personal sector and the public sector nationally, all National Savings in a region will be flows from the personal sector to the government sector.

Where it has been possible to survey the various financial institutions as to their regional operations, and where the personal sector are involved, data have been generated. The main form of savings by the personal sector are deposits with building societies, banks (including savings banks), national savings, unit trusts and life assurance and superannuation funds. Nationally these are estimated for the personal sector from the returns of the institutions involved.

For the regional model, data were obtained from the building societies and from the Trustee Savings Bank. Regional figures for the Department of National Savings were estimated using data from the voluntary regional committees for National Savings; and figures for the life assurance and superannuation funds were obtained by using estimates from the Family Expenditure Survey (although some elements such as local authority superannuation funds for each region can be obtained). The major gap in this section is the banking sector where no direct data could be obtained, or any suitable proxy generated; as such it represents a major gap where further work is necessary. However, any such work would have to be carried out with the consent and co-operation of the banking sector itself.

Other financial assets held by the personal sector have been estimated nationally as a residual: notes and coin, British government securities, local authority debt. These have been allocated to each region on the basis of suitable proxies. Company securities are examined under companies.

Use of funds. In like manner to the surpluses, where it has been possible to survey the various financial institutions as to their regional operations, and where the personal sector are involved, data have been generated.

The major item in this section is loans for house purchase. Loans by the building societies have been obtained from the Building Society Survey; those for local authorities have been taken from the regional local authority figures. Loans by banks were only available for Scotland, and Northern Ireland and loans by assurance companies were not available at all. Other items such as hire purchase debt, credit extended by retailers and identified trade credit could not be obtained directly and proxies were used for regional apportionment.

Industrial and commercial companies

Generally, the availability of data on the financial aspects of the industrial and commercial companies in the regional context is extremely poor. The main source of funds for these companies is company securities and loans. Those companies which operate in more than one region assigned to the supra-regional sector. Only those companies which operate in a single region can be classified to a particular region.

This in itself poses problems with regard to what is meant by 'operations'. With respect to productive investment, a single region company will produce in that region. However, it is more than likely that with sales effort it will transcend regional boundaries. To the extent that funds raised are solely to invest in productive capacity, the firm can be classed as to a region. However, if the funds are to mount a sales campaign can they be classified to one region? Given the methodology which has been adopted where residency for companies is based on the location of the unit of production, any flows to the company is classified to that region.

This distinction between single region and multi-region companies does not advance the collection of relevant data. Given the time available it was felt that an exercise of examining company securities and classifying the companies involved by region would not produce sufficient results to justify the time. This was also true of the purchasers of company securities. Although multi-regional financial institutions invest in company securities, the personal sector is also a considerable purchaser. A full investigation of company securities would need to relate the buyers by region as well as the companies. Again this was not possible without a major project being initiated.

A similar situation existed with the banking sector—the major supplier of loans to companies. The banking sector was approached regarding a regional analysis of their industrial loans, but it was unable to supply such an analysis. Again this distinction between single region and multi-region firms proved a practical problem.

One area of success in the company sector was in mapping the regional incidence of the special finance agencies in relation to the company sector. The special finance agencies operate in lending to or purchasing shares of companies, usually when all other sources of finance have been exhausted. In the context of the regional flows model, they can be used to portray the model to the full, because lending is to firms which are multi-regional and to firms which can safely be classified to a single region. The operations of the special finance agencies are treated separately in the appendix on the financial sector.

The successful mapping of the special finance agencies in the context of the regional model suggests that given time and the co-operation of the relevant organisations, the flow of funds to the company sector could be analysed. However, it would need to be the subject of a research effort solely devoted to the collection of the data.

The government sector

Central government. The main flows which are of direct relevance to particular regions are those between the personal sector and the government. Some of these nationally (notes and coin, government securities) are obtained as a residual and have been allocated to the regions by proxies. Others such as National Savings, have been obtained by approaching the organisations directly or by using available sample statistics.

Most of the financial transactions of the central government can be classified to flows between the supra-regional sectors and the government and assigned accordingly. Such flows are those between the overseas sector and the government: allocation of special drawing rights, official reserves, inter-government loans (net) etc.; and those which are mainly between supra-regional financial institutions and the government: treasury bills, government securities, net government indebtedness to the Bank of England, etc.

On the whole, because of the nature of the government in relation to the money flows model, and the supra-regional financial institutions with whom the government deals, the collection of data is relatively straightforward. The main problems lie with the personal sector and National Savings in particular. The part of National Savings for which the Trustee Savings Bank is responsible was obtained from the bank itself, and given continued goodwill these data should be available for future occasions. However the role of the Trustee Savings Bank changed during the period under examination, and the link with National Saving is not the same as it was in the past. This may mean that it may not be possible to separate the parts of the Trustee Savings Bank without needing greater detail. The part of National Savings for which the Department of National Savings is responsible will pose problems for future data collection. The statistics presented in the appendix are based on data produced by the now defunct voluntary savings organisations which were organised on a regional basis. Such statistics are no longer available.

In the course of collecting data on National Savings the Department for National Savings was approached, but it was unable to supply any figures. Any future collection of such data will certainly require help from this department and possibly with the increasing use of computers for the storage of raw data, the supply of statistics classified by regions may become feasible. This is something which can only be clarified by further contact with the Department of National Savings.

Other financial flows which have a regional significance are those government loans to industry and government dealings in company securities. These form part of government expenditure in the trade, industry and employment sub-programme. The regional data have been assembled as part of the public expenditure.

Local authorities. The main source of data for local authorities is the regional analysis of Local Government Financial Statistics. This allows an analysis of the financial flows relevant to local authorities by recipient region, but not from the sector or region the flow originated. Thus it is possible to get figures on the loans which local authorities in each region have obtained, but not from where and whom. Lending by local authorities for house purchase is the other major flow and these statistics are available from the same source.

Public corporations. Flows to the public corporations are in the main flows between the supra-regional sectors. Some public corporations can be assigned to particular regions (new towns and water authorities) and data can be obtained from their annual reports. In the case of the water authorities, the regional boundaries are not the same as that of the planning regions, and the outflows are considered in the financial sector as if they purchase shares and give loans (as in the case of the National Enterprise Board). These data are obtained from annual reports and assigned to the relevant region of supra-region if the recipient organisation covers more than one region.

In financial accounts, the nationalised industries are included in this sector. The financial flows associated with them can be assigned as flows between the supra-regional sectors as most of their borrowing comes from the central government or from overseas. In the financial accounts of the public sector as a whole, these are consolidated out.

The banking sector

The coverage of the banking sector's activities relevant to the region obtained for this study is poor. While much of the activities of the banking sector can be allocated to the supra-regional sector, there are considerable flows which are important in the single region context. Some data are available for Scotland and Northern Ireland directly from published sources, but nothing is presented for the English regions and Wales.

The organisations which represent the banking sector in their dealings with the central authorities were approached regarding data availability. The overall conclusion from the discussions was that data on the banking sector's operations in the regional context did not exist and a special exercise would have to be set up to obtain this information, and such a request would necessarily be judged along with the other demands for data put on the banking sector.

Other financial institutions

The 'other financial institutions' sector covers a variety of organisations which operate the different sectors. The approach to obtaining data on their regional activities was to survey the various classes of institutions. A brief account of these is given below.

Building societies: Each of the building societies was approached for data on their regional activities regarding deposits and lending. Data representing around 35 per cent of total assets were generated and the exercise suggested that the collection of data on building societies is a feasible exercise.

Assurance companies and superannuation funds: The associations which look after the general interests of the assurance companies and superannuation funds were initially approached, and eventually it was decided to survey the individual companies. This, however, did not prove successful as the vast majority of the companies could not analyse their returns on a regional basis, or did not respond. As a result, data from the *Family Expenditure Survey* was used to obtain regional figures.

Special finance agencies: The special finance agencies assist companies where for some reason they cannot obtain capital for growth, or operate in a specialist market where specialist financing is needed. The data which was generated on special finance agencies provided a good example of the money flows model operating in the regional context as the interaction between single region companies as well as larger multi-region companies and supra-regional organisations was able to be highlighted.

Other: Many of the activities of the other financial institutions sector are assigned as flows between the supra-regional sectors (purchase of company shares, government securities, etc.). Those flows which have a relevance to a single region and where no data have been generated, proxies have been used, as in the case of finance houses and leasing companies.

Overseas sector

The overseas sector interacts with the other supra-regional sectors in the main and the associated flows have been assigned to the relevant sectors.

The findings

The findings in terms of the availability of data for the various sectors are summarised in Table 1. Four categories for sources of data are considered (rows), and the major sectors form the columns. The figures show the percentage of the total which was considered from each source.

Table 1

Data availability matrix

Source sector	CSO	Published	Direct approach to producers of data	Proxy
Private	100			
Company	100			
Public Sector Expenditure				
(a) Economic category[1]		12	58	30
(b) Functional analysis[2]		11	71	18
Revenue				
Central government[3] current		72		28
Local authority current			100	
capital			100	
Financial sector[4]				
Banks				100
Building societies			100	
Special finance agencies			100	
Department for National Savings				100
Trustee Savings Bank			100	
Shares, unit trusts, etc				100
Finance houses, leasing				100
Other				100
EEC			100	

1 Wages and salaries, transfers etc.

2 Education, health, etc.

3 72% relates to adjusted published estimate.

4 Some flows in the financial sector are between supra-regional sectors and do not impinge on the regions directly (e.g. between the banking sector and government). These are not included in the matrix.

Conclusions

The impetus for this research project lay in the experience of the various regional strategies and their attempts in obtaining data on the regions, especially those relating to the public sector. The Department of the Environment, in whose domain regional strategies lay, recognised the gaps which existed in the provision of data and desired to build on the work carried out by one of the authors in the Northern Region Strategy Team. Since the commencement of the present study, the Central Statistical Office has published a *Regional Accounts Methodology,* although it had previously produced some regional statistics on special articles in *Economic Trends.* Nevertheless, gaps in regional statistics remained, and this study can be seen as complementary to the work of the CSO. Indeed, from early on in the work programme, a decision was taken to concentrate on the items where the CSO had not yet provided statistics and use the information that the CSO had already generated as and where necessary.

An initial requirement of the research was to produce a model which would describe the progress of regional money flows, but at the same time be amenable to the actual measurement of these flows in the context of the regions of the UK. This model is formulated in this main report and the data which have been generated to fit the money flows model are reported in a series of appendices.

This collection of data has in some cases managed to break new ground. This is particularly so in the financial sector where many types of financial institutions have been investigated as to the possibility of obtaining data initially; and, in some cases, data have been generated anew. However, despite this success in some areas, there have also been unsuccessful attempts. In these cases, failure may be too strong a word, because one of the initial objectives of the research was to ascertain the availability of data in the regional context. Given the right response to follow-up work, the conditions for collecting these data may be present for the future. Nevertheless, the goodwill that existed in the various financial institutions for the present study has to be retained and built upon.

The research has also managed to build on and extend the work on the public sector. Statistics on regionally relevant expenditure have been produced for a further four years up to 1977–78, making a time-series of nine years available in all. The analysis of total expenditure has also been produced for these four years. These are complemented by data on the revenues to the government from the regions, and the flows to local authorities from the central government and from rates. The production of these statistics has been made possible by the willingness of many government departments to produce data which are not produced as a matter of course. It goes without saying that gaps had to be filled by the use of proxy methods, and it is probable that some of these data could be generated within the departments concerned. Nevertheless, considerable goodwill has existed which has improved the quality of the estimates.

Finally, the report has used the CSO's work on the personal and company sector to form a basis of the data for these sectors. As such, the few limitations of the CSO data are repeated here. However, it is certain that it would have been impossible to produce the quality of these data *ab initio*, even if it had been contemplated.

As is always the case with academic research, the completion of a research project often generates many areas of further research. Gaps in the provision of regional data still exist and, as time marches on, the data generated by studies such as this become out of date. It is hoped that the impetus provided by what success this project has enjoyed will generate a more permanent data collecting base in the areas where the CSO have not yet extended their operations in the regional field. Annual updating exercises will prove easier and less costly than one-off exercises every decade or so. As well, the goodwill which is so necessary for such exercises to be successful can be built upon and not have to be regenerated every so often.

Appendix 1 The personal and company sectors

This appendix provides the data relating to the personal and company sectors. The statistics presented were all based on (and often merely repeating) the Central Statistical Office's estimates of the personal sectors flow in the regional context. This method has been adopted because it would have been a wasteful duplication of effort given the superior data gathering base of the CSO if the exercise was repeated *ab initio* to meet with the precise requirements of the money flow's model. Where any adjustments have to be made because of definitional differences, these are highlighted below. Such a strategy has allowed the major part of the research effort and data collection to be concerned with extending existing data series or breaking new ground where the CSO have not yet extended their data collection to the regional base.

The personal sector

Sources

Regionalisations of several indices of economic activity are regularly prepared by the CSO, and published in *Economic Trends,* and ultimately in *Regional Statistics.* Amongst others, these regionalisations include several components of personal sector income and expenditures. The detailed methodology pursued by the CSO has been described in *Regional Accounts* (CSO 1978).

Each June issue of *Economic Trends* presents preliminary estimates of these regional statistics relating to the calendar year before last. Improved and extended estimates appear in the subsequent November issue. Thus, there is a lag of some eighteen months in the preparation of official regional estimates, and almost two years for certain further figures.

This apparent delay is the result of preparing not only the regional estimates themselves, but also other regionalised statistical exercises and surveys upon which the regional accounts necessarily depend. For example, regional GDP estimates depend upon the availability of data on employment by industry within regions from the Annual Census of Employment. Consequently, delays in this census for 1977 have impaired the quality of regional GDP estimates which 'must therefore be interpreted with special care'.[1]

The final estimates presented in November's *Economic Trends* are consistent both in terms of conceptual definition and quantative value, with the national accounts as prepared for the *National Income and Expenditure* 'blue book'. As these national accounts are successively revised in each year's blue book, so are the regional accounts in each year's *Regional Statistics.* Due to this consistency with the national accounts, the regional estimates are imperfectly suited to the requirements of a money flow analysis. Firstly, not all the component flows are identified and secondly, there are certain conceptual inconsistencies—notably the official estimates follow the accruals conventions of national accounts, rather than the payments/receipts adopted in this study.

Not all these problems have proved possible to overcome. Nevertheless, every assistance has been provided by the CSO, consistent with departmental regulations regarding the release of data. Particularly, unpublished intermediate estimates have been made available to the project.

Overall, the analysis of the personal sector has leant heavily on the methodology and products of the CSO. The results are presented in Tables 2–13 and the particular methodology is outlined below.

Methodology

Income from employment. Personal income from employment comprises wages and salaries, earnings of HM Forces, and that share of agreed payments made by the employer on behalf of his employees towards funds conventionally considered to be the property of the personal sector—namely the National Insurance Fund, etc., and private and public superannuation schemes. Wages and salaries typically constitute 86 per cent of income from employment, earnings of HM Forces 2 per cent, and employers' contributions 12 per cent for the UK as a whole.

The regional distribution of the total income from employment, and that of wages and salaries together with HM Forces pay are to be found in *Economic Trends.* Thus, employers' contributions can be simply calculated as the remaining component of income.

The detailed methodology of producing the wage and salary estimates are presented in *Regional Accounts* (CSO 1978), and are based on information gained from the Department of Health and Social Security—taxation returns are not suitable, for despite a system of local offices, the returns reflect the location of the pay point, rather than the employment. Changes in DHSS practices have resulted in different methods since 1975, but the approach remains broadly similar, being based upon information on contributions to the National Insurance Scheme. As this information is not available for the most recent year, a stop-gap method based on employment by industry and region is employed.

The individual distribution of HM Forces pay is also calculated internally to the CSO. However, due to adjustments made to cover the special circumstances of Northern Ireland, they are grouped with the wage and salary estimate at publication. Unfortunately, the CSO was unable to furnish these particular estimates for the project.

Since 1974 when all contributions have been earnings-related, the CSO regional estimates of employers' contributions have been produced by apportioning the national totals for each industry to the regions in accordance with the distribution of the wage and salary bill for that industry amongst the regions. Prior to 1974, National Insurance Contributions also involved a flat-rate element, and this was apportioned, industry by industry, according to employment. All other earnings-related components were apportioned according to the wage and salary bill. The sum of these components produces the regional estimates of total income from employment, as published. Although estimates for employers' contributions are not explicitly published, the CSO made such estimates available to the project, disaggregated by SIC Order, or groupings of Orders for 1974 to 1976 inclusive.

In an inter-regional money flow analysis income from employment is viewed as an intra-regional flow—earned incomes received in the North, for example, are paid by employers in the North. Some cross commuting is possible at the geographical boundaries of the standard regions, and even without commuting, some employees of multi-regional companies will receive payment from outside the region of employment. However, such effects can be considered to be limited in their effect. Certainly, on the former count, the CSO estimate that for all regions other than the East Midlands, the difference between those living and working in a region is always less than 1 per cent, often greatly so, and even for the East Midlands is less than 2 per cent.

More significant are the conceptual problems. For example, the earnings of troops stationed abroad might strictly be considered a flow from the UK to the rest of the world depending upon the definition of residence, but are distributed amongst the UK regions (according to relative total population) by the CSO. Furthermore, many people receive a portion of their income in kind rather than cash. This income in kind is given monetary valuation and included in the CSO figures, both regionally and nationally. Neither of these factors has been taken into account in the tables in this appendix. (However, see the Appendix 2 for methodology on defence expenditure.)

Income from self-employment. In the national accounts, income from self-employment is grouped according to type of self-employment, namely professional persons, farmers, and, other sole traders and partnerships. However these are all treated as one in the regional accounts.

By its nature, self-employment occurs in the same region as an individual's residence, and consequently in contrast to income from employment, reservations about using local tax office information do not apply. Since 1971 the Inland Revenue is able to supply detailed figures for each standard region, broken down according to industrial classifications. These are then adjusted by the CSO to match national control totals, and also provide an industry by region matrix of such income. Final assessment of self-employed incomes for any particular year are often some two and a half years after the end of that year, and so special procedures for the latest years in the regional accounts are necessary. These assume that industrial self-employment by industry between the regions remains moderately stable in the short term, and provisional estimates are based on apportioning national control totals for each industry to the regions according to the distribution in the latest year for which firm data is available.

The CSO estimates have been used directly in the presented tables, matching the blue book national totals. As stated above, income from self-employment is essentially locally generated, and therefore, such receipts can be considered as intra-regional flows.

Rents, dividends and interest. Essentially there are two components to this form of income. Approximately one third of the total is made up from the receipts of life assurance and superannuation schemes, conventionally classed as the assets of the personal sector. Much of the rest results from rent income received on land and buildings. With some 50 per cent of all personal households living in owner-occupied property, a large portion of such rent income is merely an imputed income, but, a portion will involve actual rents paid. Similar considerations apply to the institutional private sector, again with a mix of owner-occupation and commercial property.

Thus, despite firm estimates of rents, dividends and interest appearing in the regional accounts prepared by the CSO, they do not fully meet the needs of a money flows analysis. The CSO made available the individual estimates of rent income according to sector of property for 1974,

1975 and 1976—agricultural, business, local authority, central government and private dwellings. However such estimates do not fully identify imputed rents from actual rents. One approximation would have been to subtract the private dwellings rent from the published estimate, but this would not have been possible for 1977, and would still include certain institutional and self-employed rent imputations but omit certain trade rents. Consequently, despite its imperfections, the published figures were included in the presented tables.

The non-rent components are allocated to the regions by the CSO in two ways. Receipts of life assurance and superannuation schemes are attributed in proportion to the contributions made to the schemes. The methodology used for employers' contributions has been described above and employees' contributions are allocated in the same proportion. (Non-contributory schemes are assumed to follow the same regional pattern.) The remaining portions are allocated using the Net Investment Income category in the Inland Revenue's *Survey of Personal Incomes.*

In terms of the regional flows model, rents, dividends and interest will involve both intra-regional and inter-regional flows, and for the dividends and interest component at least, will involve the financial institutions, multi-regional companies and government sectors.

Current transfers to charities from companies. In the regional accounts, these transfers are included with the much larger benefits received from the National Insurance Fund, and the like. Amounting to some £40m per annum they are identified in the national accounts, and have been separately apportioned in the current exercise because of their different nature, being flows from the company sector rather than the government administered National Insurance Fund. However, in the regional accounts, such transfers to charities are treated residually, and allocated in proportion to the total of all current grants to the personal sector. Thus, using the national totals presented in the blue book, the process was reversed, and a proportionate amount removed from the published regional estimates National Insurance Benefits, and other current grants. The larger component of these benefits are those disbursed by the DHSS to households as national insurance benefits, war pensions, family allowances and supplementary benefits. DHSS figures are used directly by the CSO. In addition, households receive rent rebates and allowances, and these are attributed to the regions using CIPFA and departmental information. Additionally, non-profit making bodies receive grants, largely in the form of grants to universities and colleges, plus maintenance grants for students. Educational statistics are used by the CSO to apportion these between the regions.

Overall, for such grants there are few conflicts between the accruals basis and a money flows analysis. The presented figures differ from the published figures only in so far as transfers to charities by companies (described above) have been separated out. In terms of money flows the remaining transfers are largely from the government to the regions, together with certain monies (such as student maintenance grants) being channelled via local authorities.

Consumers' expenditure. In the national accounts, consumers' expenditure relates to those expenditures made by UK residents, whether domestically or overseas, and excludes the expenditure in the UK by foreign residents. A similar convention is sought in the regional accounts, even though the method of achieving the estimates is somewhat different. In other words, published estimates of consumers' expenditure by region incorporate expenditures made both internal and external to the region by the residents of that region. Consequently, the inter-regional and intra-regional components are not identifiable. Also, a small element of expenditure that ought to be included as flows from the region to the rest of the world are hidden.

The CSO regional methodology leans heavily on the *Family Expenditure Survey* as an index of consumers' expenditure by region. Using information from surveys by the British and Northern Ireland Tourist Boards, national control totals are adjusted for expenditures made by foreign tourists. Because of the limited sample size for each region involved in the FES, a moving average over three successive years (with weights 1:2:1) is used for the central year of the period. Also certain items of expenditure not included in the FES are subject to special procedures to improve the quality of the results. However, the CSO is sufficiently aware of considerable margin for error in this approach, to warn against the comparison of consumers' expenditure and personal disposable income for any one region.

Transfers aborad and taxes paid abroad. The CSO publishes estimates of personal income, and personal dispersable income. These payments are a part of the differences between the two. Estimates of these adjustments, although unpublished, were provided by the CSO to the project, and these estimates are presented directly. However, there is no information on the incidence of such taxes and payments and so the CSO estimates are based solely on population. As both are paid overseas, each involves cash flows from the regions to the regions to the rest of the world. No attempt is made to separate them out, for the rest of the world is undifferentiated according to private or public sector in the money flows model. Unfortunately, the figures for transfers abroad are the net flows, with no direct information on the gross flows involved, nor whether the net flows are positive or negative.

UK taxes on income. Again, unpublished estimates were available from the CSO. These estimates result from allocations based on information included in the Inland Revenue's *Survey of Personal Income.* In a money flow analysis, these payments are simply flows between each region and the government.

National insurance contributions. The CSO estimates used for personal contributions include the contributions made by employers on behalf of their employees. These are included in the income account of the sector, and the method of regional apportionment described there. Other forms of contributions are four-fold, each individually apportioned, and then summed together to provide estimates of total regional contributions. Thus, employees' contributions are distributed according to the proportions calculated for employers' contributions, the contributions of HM Forces are allocated in proportion to Forces income, and self-employed contributions in proportion to the number of self-employed persons. The small total of non-employed contributions is distributed in proportion to all other categories. These CSO estimates are used directly in the presented tables.

Each regionalised component of personal expenditure is summed to provide the estimate for that current expenditure by region. However, this account is based almost exclusively on unpublished CSO estimates, about which they have reservations. Consequently, similar reservations must apply to the estimates of total current expenditure that results. Because the CSO exercise has yet to be completed for 1977, unpublished estimates are unavailable for this year. For completeness sake, the national totals for 1977 as published in the blue book were apportioned to the regions using 1976 distributions. Consequently, special reservations must be expressed about the presented figures for this year.

Savings. Conceptually, savings, whether negative or positive, are the balancing item between current personal income and current expenditure, and thus can be calculated as a residual. However, although acceptable for the UK as a whole, such an approach involves considerable margins of error when practiced for any region, as the income and expenditure on figures are indirectly calculated. Nevertheless, such an approach has had to be adopted as the best available, despite its shortcomings. Furthermore, because of certain accruals and imputations being excluded from the presented tables, the national total will differ from that presented in the blue book.

Capital transfers. These are similar to the current transfers described in the income account, and involve payments to the personal sector by the public sector. Largely they comprise grants to households to improve dwellings, plus certain capital payments to non-profit making institutions such as the universities. Details of such grants for each financial year were obtained from the Public Sector section (see p.84) and used to apportion national blue book totals to the regions for each calendar year. Clearly, these involve inter-regional and intra-regional flows from local and central governments to the personal sector. Together with estimates of savings, these transfers comprise the total capital receipts of the personal sector. Additions to tax reserves identified in the blue book are but an accruals/payments adjustment irrelevant to a money flow analysis, and in any case, incorporated in the different quantities classed as savings.

Gross domestic fixed capital formation. Capital investment in real assets is made by much of the personal sector. For households this takes the form of the purchase of land and buildings, whether from other sectors, or newly constructed. Of course, other segments of the personal sector are involved in such investments, and the element labelled 'by households' includes all investment in new and existing buildings and lands. The other form of fixed capital formation by the personal sector is the purchase of capital equipment by the self-employed. Neither of these investments are specifically regionalised in the CSO regional accounts, but indirect apportionments have been possible using CSO derived indices. The latter component has been attributed to the regions in proportion to income from self-employment. For the former more complex methods were necessary. Total capital formation in dwellings is identified in the national accounts, but this includes dwellings owned by the public sector, and excludes non-domestic buildings in the personal sector. An adjustment for public investment in housing is possible by subtracting public fixed capital formation on housing and community development, also identified in the regional accounts. National totals of personal fixed capital information on land and buildings were then apportioned according to the residue.

Increase in value of stocks, etc. Stockbuilding within the personal sector is almost exclusively engaged in by the self-employed. However, there is no direct information on this by region, and therefore indirect methods have to be used. For the lack of a better alternative income from self-employment is used to apportion the national totals. As with gross domestic fixed capital formation, stockbuilding is largely restricted to the region of residence of the individual or institution involved. Thus, both are essentially intra-regional money flows.

Taxes on capital. Capital assets are taxed only on transfer between persons, and when any capital gains are realised. In the period under consideration, these involved estate duties, capital transfer tax and capital gains tax. See pp.132–139 where, along with all other public sector revenues, these are described for each financial year. The national totals for the calendar years presented in the blue book are apportioned to the regions using the sum of payments of these taxes for the relevant financial year. Obviously, in terms of money flows, these represent payments by the regions to the government.

Capital transfers to public corporations. Essentially these transfers involve the charges made by public utilities for the connection of services to land and buildings. Similar transfers are identified in the company sector accounts. Due to a lack of superior information, these payments by the personal sector have been apportioned according to consumers' expenditure on housing and fuel. Any errors resulting are unlikely to have a significant effect, considering the relative contribution to total capital expenditure. Furthermore, rounding errors are proportionately that much greater.

Net acquisition of financial assets. The personal sector's dealing in financial assets is more thoroughly dealt with in the financial accounts section (see pp.161–215). However, comparison of total capital receipts and total capital expenditures permits the calculation of a residual figure of such net acquisition. Of course, the quality of such regional figures reflects the inaccuracies necessarily involved in the estimation of the other capital and current payments. In addition, the figures included here reflect the payments basis adopted, and the exclusion of certain accruals and imputations. Therefore, even the national total will not match the figures given in the blue book.

Table 2

Personal income—1974 (£m) current prices)

	North	*Yorks Humbs.*	*East Mids.*	*East Anglia*	*South-East*	*South-West*	*West Mids.*	*North-West*	*Wales*	*Scot.*	*Nrth. Ire'd.*	*UK*
Wages and salaries) Pay of HM Forces)	2413	3975	3066	1245	16400	3223	4554	5388	1940	4069	957	47230
Employers' contributions	277.0	451.9	339.1	141.6	2026.2	355.5	507.1	640.8	225.7	475.1	112.9	5552.9
Total income from employment	2690	4427	3405	1387	18426	3578	5061	6029	2166	4544	1070	52783
Income from self-employment	333	592	509	387	2535	700	580	729	355	740	217	7677
Rents, dividends and interest	309	543	440	267	3024	672	677	811	288	525	107	7663
Current transfers to charities from companies	2.5	3.7	2.5	1.2	11.9	3.3	3.7	5.4	2.5	4.1	1.2	42.0
National insutrance benefits, and other current grants from public authorities	478.5	723.3	479.5	237.8	2343.1	604.7	667.3	1014.6	436.5	792.9	221.8	8000.0
Total personal income	3813	6289	4836	2280	26340	5558	6989	8589	3248	6606	1617	76165

Table 3

Personal income—1975 (£m) (current prices)

	North	*Yorks Humbs.*	*East Mids.*	*East Anglia*	*South-East*	*South-West*	*West Mids.*	*North-West*	*Wales*	*Scot.*	*Nrth. Ire'd.*	*UK*
Wages and salaries) Pay of HM Forces)	3208	5007	3905	1649	20784	4040	5855	6882	2662	5327	1237	60556
Employers' contributions	408	638	494	196	2765	477	721	876	345	661	152	7733
Total income from employment	3616	5645	4399	1845	23549	4517	6576	7758	3007	5988	1389	68289
Income from self-employment	414	714	585	446	2773	798	671	843	423	889	265	8818
Rents, dividends and interest	365	634	543	308	3459	768	776	937	351	594	133	8868
Current transfers to charities from companies	2.5	3.7	2.5	1.3	12.1	3.3	3.7	5.4	2.1	4.2	1.2	42
National Insurance benefits and other current grants from public authorities	620.5	948.3	638.5	306.7	3043.9	807.9	884.3	1318.6	567.9	1024.8	278.8	10440
Total personal income	5015	7945	6168	2907	32837	6894	8911	10862	4351	8500	2067	96457

Table 4

Personal income—1976 (£m) (current prices)

	North	*Yorks Humbs.*	*East Mids.*	*East Anglia*	*South-East*	*South-West*	*West Mids.*	*North-West*	*Wales*	*Scot.*	*Nrth. Ire'd.*	*UK*
Wages and salaries) Pay of HM Forces)	3662	5744	4362	1900	23459	4659	6508	7853	3023	6144	1478	68789
Employers' contributions	500	789	591	243	3356	591	859	1078	420	824	193	9444
Total income from employment	4162	6533	4953	2143	26815	5247	7367	8931	3443	6968	1671	78233
Income from self-employment	488	843	698	537	3282	930	786	991	529	1075	322	10481
Rents, dividends and interest	429	773	642	365	4104	935	918	1097	408	682	146	10499
Current transfers to charities from companies	2.5	3.7	2.5	1.3	12.1	3.3	3.3	5.4	2.5	4.2	1.2	42
National Insurance benefits, and other current grants from public authorities	774.5	1183.1	783.5	378.7	3772.9	998.7	1098.7	1634.6	708.5	1279.8	349.8	12961
Total personal income	5856	9334	7079	3425	37986	8114	10173	12659	5091	10009	2490	112216

Table 5

Personal income—1977 (£m) (current prices)

	North	*Yorks Humbs.*	*East Mids.*	*East Anglia*	*South-East*	*South-West*	*West Mids.*	*North-West*	*Wales*	*Scot.*	*Nrth. Ire'd.*	*UK*
Wages and salaries)* Pay of HM Forces)	3962	6358	4869	2070	25628	5177	7227	8629	3343	6685	1571	75499
Employers' contributions*	541	873	660	265	3666	656	954	1184	464	894	205	10362
Total income from employment	4503	7231	5529	2335	29294	5833	8181	9813	3807	7559	1776	85861
Income from self-employment	548	929	767	528	3461	1238	740	1071	706	1108	465	11561
Rents, dividends and interest	481	902	719	414	4677	1068	1043	1232	463	810	162	11971
Current transfers to charities from companies	2.6	3.9	2.6	1.2	12.5	3.3	3.7	5.4	2.4	4.2	1.2	43
National Insurance benefits and other current grants from public authorities	918.4	1373.1	934.4	447.8	4466.5	1180.7	1307.3	1929.6	846.6	1499.8	430.8	15335
Total personal income	6453	10439	7952	3726	41911	9323	11275	14051	5825	10981	2835	124771

* The regional distribution of these components is not currently available for 1977. Presented figures are apportioned according to 1976 distribution, and may not sum exactly to national totals due to rounding errors.

Table 6 — *Personal expenditure–1974 (£m) (current prices)*

	North	Yorks Humbs.	East Mids.	East Anglia	South-East	South-West	West Mids.	North-West	Wales	Scot.	Nrth. Ire'd.	UK
Consumers' expenditure	2690	4076	3279	1595	18024	3599	4697	5857	2295	4591	1160	51863
Transfers abroad (net)) Taxes paid abroad)	6.8	10.6	3.8	3.8	36.6	9.1	11.2	14.2	6.0	11.3	3.3	121
UK taxes on income	490.7	842.1	625.6	330.8	3976.7	711.5	937.4	1047.5	417.0	857.8	192.9	10430
National Insurance contributions	244.8	405.9	305.1	132.4	1822.2	336.4	451.9	568.7	204.7	424.3	103.6	5000
Total current expenditure	3432.3	5334.6	4217.8	2062.0	23859.5	4656.0	6097.5	7487.4	2922.7	5884.4	1459.8	67414

Table 7 — *Personal expenditure–1975 (£m) (current prices)*

	North	Yorks Humbs.	East Mids.	East Anglia	South-East	South-West	West Mids.	North-West	Wales	Scot.	Nrth. Ire'd.	UK
Consumers' expenditure	3233	5091	4082	1930	21782	4594	5645	6982	2851	5549	1453	63192
Transfers abroad (net)) Taxes paid abroad)	8.6	13.5	10.3	4.9	46.5	11.7	14.2	18.1	7.6	14.4	4.2	154
UK taxes on income	770.6	1273.3	932.0	475.2	5538.6	1046.1	1318.2	1586.4	603.6	1275.1	279.9	15099
National Insurance contributions	354.9	562.3	435.2	179.4	2446.6	441.8	631.7	766.6	305.8	581.9	136.8	6843
Total current expenditure	4366.1	6940.1	5459.5	2589.5	29813.7	6093.6	7609.1	9353.1	3768.0	7420.4	1873.9	85288

Table 8 — *Personal expenditure–1976 (£m) (current prices)*

	North	Yorks Humbs	East Mids.	East Anglia	South-East	South-West	West Mids.	North-West	Wales	Scot.	Nrth. Ire'd.	UK
Consumers' expenditure	3780	5993	4660	2243	25304	5482	6425	8079	3381	6437	1754	73538
Transfers abroad (net)) Taxes paid abroad)	3.0	4.6	3.6	1.7	16.0	4.0	4.9	6.2	2.6	4.9	1.5	53
UK taxes on income	880.8	1454.9	1091.1	562.3	6497.7	1218.7	1553.2	1867.7	724.5	1415.5	322.4	17589
National Insurance contributions	438.2	701.0	526.2	224.2	2990.6	550.5	758.7	949.6	374.8	729.8	175.4	8419
Total current expenditure	5102.0	8153.5	6280.9	3031.2	34808.3	7255.4	8741.8	10902.5	4482.9	8587.2	2253.3	99599

Table 9

Personal expenditure–1977 (£m) (current prices)

	North	Yorks Humbs.	East Mids.	East Anglia	South-East	South-West	West Mids.	North-West	Wales	Scot.	Nrth. Ire'd.	UK
Consumers' expenditure*	4294	6807	5293	2548	28742	6227	7298	9177	3840	7311	1992	83530
Transfers abroad (net))* Taxes paid abroad)	6.5	9.9	7.7	3.7	34.4	8.6	10.5	13.3	5.6	10.5	3.2	114
UK taxes on income*	914.6	1510.7	1132.9	583.9	6747.1	1265.5	1612.8	1939.3	752.3	1469.8	334.8	18264
National Insurance contributions*	492.0	787.1	590.8	251.7	3357.9	618.1	851.9	1066.2	420.8	819.4	196.9	9453
Total current expenditure*	5707.1	9114.7	7024.4	3387.3	38881.4	8119.2	9773.2	12195.8	5018.7	9610.7	2526.9	111361

*The regional distribution of these components is not currently available for 1977. Presented figures are apportioned according to 1976 distribution, and may not sum exactly to national totals due to rounding errors.

Table 10

Personal capital account–1974 (£m) (current prices)

	North	Yorks Humbs.	East Mids.	East Anglia	South-East	South-West	West Mids.	North-West	Wales	Scot.	Nrth. Ire'd.	UK
Receipts												
Savings	380.7	954.4	618.2	218.0	2480.5	902.0	891.5	1101.6	325.3	721.6	157.2	8751
Capital transfers	12.8	17.5	23.3	19.7	174.2	27.0	30.5	47.8	25.7	80.2	6.3	465
Total	393.5	971.9	641.5	237.7	2654.7	929.0	922.0	1149.4	351.0	801.8	163.5	9216
Expenditures												
Gross domestic fixed capital formation												
–by households	46.5	92.0	93.9	92.0	167.9	150.8	96.7	79.7	67.3	104.3	18.0	1009
–other	50.0	88.9	76.4	58.1	380.7	105.1	87.1	109.5	53.3	111.1	32.6	1153
Increase in value of stock, etc	42.6	75.7	65.1	49.5	324.3	89.5	74.2	93.2	45.4	94.7	27.8	982
Taxes on capital	33.7	60.4	43.0	27.7	291.4	73.5	60.7	78.3	31.5	65.7	11.1	777
Capital transfers to public corporations	0.6	0.8	0.8	0.4	4.5	0.9	1.1	1.3	0.5	0.9	0.2	12
Net acquisition of financial assets	220.1	654.1	362.3	10.0	1485.9	509.2	602.2	787.4	153.0	425.1	73.8	5283
Total	393.5	971.9	641.5	237.7	2654.7	929.0	922.0	1149.4	351.0	801.8	163.5	9216

Table 11

Personal capital account—1975 (£m) (current prices)

	North	*Yorks Humbs.*	*East Mids.*	*East Anglia*	*South-East*	*South-West*	*West Mids.*	*North-West*	*Wales*	*Scot.*	*Nrth. Ire'd.*	*UK*
Receipts												
Savings	648.9	1004.9	708.5	317.5	3023.3	800.4	1301.9	1508.9	583.0	1079.6	193.1	11169
Capital transfers	21.5	35.8	24.8	16.6	122.0	22.2	24.5	38.3	22.3	75.6	19.5	423
Total	670.4	1040.7	733.3	334.1	3145.3	822.6	1326.4	1547.2	605.3	1155.2	212.6	11592
Expenditures												
Gross domestic fixed capital formation												
–by households	76.2	150.2	163.8	130.9	611.0	232.1	151.3	153.6	93.9	157.0	20.4	1940
–other	55.8	96.3	78.9	60.1	373.9	107.6	90.5	113.7	57.0	119.9	35.7	1189
Increase in value of stock, etc	24.2	41.9	34.3	26.1	162.6	46.8	39.3	49.4	24.8	52.1	15.5	517
Taxes on capital	31.4	56.3	41.0	26.0	261.9	65.9	54.6	71.6	29.6	58.1	11.5	708
Capital transfers to public corporations	0.9	1.4	1.2	0.6	7.1	1.5	1.7	2.1	0.7	1.4	0.3	19
Net acquisition of financial assets	481.9	694.6	414.1	90.4	1728.8	368.7	989.0	1156.8	399.9	766.7	129.2	7219
Total	670.4	1040.7	733.3	334.1	3145.3	822.6	1326.4	1547.2	605.3	1155.2	212.6	11592

Table 12

Personal capital account–1976 (£m) (current prices)

	North	*Yorks Humbs.*	*East Mids.*	*East Anglia*	*South-East*	*South-West*	*West Mids.*	*North-West*	*Wales*	*Scot.*	*Nrth. Ire'd.*	*UK*
Receipts												
Savings	754.0	1180.5	798.1	393.8	3177.7	858.6	1431.2	1756.5	608.1	1421.8	236.7	12617
Capital transfers	39.0	58.4	39.7	20.4	138.9	39.9	36.6	65.1	34.0	143.5	83.6	699
Total	793.0	1238.9	837.8	414.2	3316.6	898.5	1467.8	1821.6	642.1	1565.3	320.3	13316
Expenditures												
Gross domestic fixed capital formation												
–by households	85.4	154.4	162.6	129.7	595.9	224.4	164.7	173.9	95.7	270.7	20.6	2078
–other	66.0	114.1	94.4	72.7	440.0	125.8	106.3	134.1	71.6	145.4	43.6	1418
Increase in value of stock, etc	47.7	82.4	68.2	52.5	320.7	90.9	76.8	96.8	51.7	105.0	31.5	1024
Taxes on capital	33.6	60.1	43.9	26.4	270.8	68.5	58.8	75.1	30.6	58.1	11.2	737
Capital transfers to public corporations	1.2	1.2	1.6	0.8	9.4	2.0	2.2	2.7	1.0	1.8	0.5	25
Net acquisition of financial assets	559.1	826.0	467.1	132.1	1679.8	386.9	1059.0	1339.0	391.5	984.3	212.9	8034
Total	793.0	1238.9	837.8	414.2	3316.6	898.5	1467.8	1821.6	642.1	1565.3	320.3	13316

Table 13

Personal capital account—1977 (£m) (current prices)

	North	*Yorks Humbs.*	*East Mids.*	*East Anglia*	*South-East*	*South-West*	*West Mids.*	*North-West*	*Wales*	*Scot.*	*Nrth. Ire'd.*	*UK*
Receipts												
Savings*	745.9	1324.3	927.6	338.7	3029.6	1203.8	1501.8	1855.2	806.3	1370.3	308.1	13410
Capital transfers	130.0	56.4	39.8	24.4	130.8	47.2	38.2	62.3	39.0	179.0	96.9	844
Total	875.9	1380.7	967.4	363.1	3160.4	1251.0	1540.0	1917.5	845.3	1549.3	405.0	14254
Expenditures												
Gross domestic fixed capital formation												
–by households*	95.0	171.7	180.9	144.2	662.7	249.5	183.1	193.4	106.5	301.0	22.9	2311
–other	79.6	134.9	111.4	76.7	502.6	179.8	107.5	155.5	102.5	160.9	67.5	1679
Increase in value of stock, etc	55.6	94.3	77.9	53.6	351.5	125.7	75.1	108.8	71.7	112.5	47.2	1174
Taxes on capital*	33.5	60.3	43.9	26.6	271.0	68.4	59.1	74.9	30.6	57.6	11.2	737
Capital transfers to public corporations*	1.2	1.9	1.7	0.8	9.7	2.0	2.3	2.9	1.0	1.9	0.5	26
Net acquisition of financial assets	611.0	917.8	551.8	61.2	1362.9	625.6	1112.9	1382.0	533.0	915.4	255.7	8327
Total	875.9	1380.9	967.4	363.1	3160.4	1251.0	1540.0	1917.5	845.3	1549.3	405.0	14254

*Not all proxies used are currently available for 1977. Components marked by asterisk involve the use of 1976 proxy variables to a lesser or greater extent.

The company sector

In this section, estimates of the data concerning the company sector are presented. As with the personal sector, certain estimates are already prepared by the Central Statistics Office as part of their Regional Accounts exercise. However, these were of limited value, and generally the approach has been to seek methods of apportioning national totals to the regions, making adjustments when necessary to meet the particular needs of a money flows approach. Below, the particular sources and methods used for each component flow are detailed.

Sources

National totals for calendar years have been taken from the *National Income and Expenditure, 1967–77* blue book, and regional indices presented in *Economic Trends* in November 1978 and June 1979 have been used to apportion these amongst the regions, together with certain other sources when available. As detailed in the personal sector section, firm regional estimates have been published by the CSO in *Economic Trends* for, amongst others, 1974, 1975 and 1976. However only provisional figures are available for 1977, and in some cases, not even provisional figures. When none other are available, national totals for 1977 have been apportioned using 1976 indices. (Such components are marked by an asterisk on the relevant tables.)

The offshore oil and gas industry are providing an increasingly large contribution to the private company sector, particularly in terms of profits and investment. Because of the potentially distorting effect of such flows on the adjacent onshore regions, the activities of the offshore extractive industry are attributed to the twelfth 'region' labelled the continental shelf.

Due to a lack of information, it has not proved possible to separate out the role played by multi-regional companies. The conceptual problems referred to in the main report have not been directly encountered in the preparation of the attached estimates for CSO approach to allocate all economic activity to the regions where the production units are located has been used. As a result, due to the immense practical problems, it was impossible to enumerate all the individual flows conceptually identified.

For similar practical reasons, the trading account of the company sector is not presented. To seek to do so would involve the preparation of an inter-regional input/output analysis, for which little information is available. Consequently, the tables present a regional representation of the appropriation account and capital account of the private corporate sector.

Methodology

Gross trading profits. Regional distribution of gross trading profits are prepared by the CSO and presented in *Economic Trends.* The detailed methodology pursued by the CSO is presented in *Regional Accounts* (HMSO, 1978). This rests largely on information collected in the *Annual Census of Production* for the manufacturing industry, together with employment information for certain non-manufacturing sectors. These CSO estimates were used to apply the blue book totals between the regions, including the continental shelf. Essentially, gross trading profits are the surplus generated within the trading account of the company sector, and remain under the control of that sector until disbursed with other forms of income to the owners of the company, and others. Because of the need to omit the particular effect of the multi-regional company, by which profits generated within a region can pass to another region or a supra-regional entity before dispersal, the presented estimates of gross trading profits can be considered as intra-regional flows.

Rent and non-trading income. As a significant factor income, estimates of total rent income, are prepared by the CSO. Their approach is to build up, for each component sector (such as agriculture, business, central government, local government) separate estimates of income received from property rental. Although not published, except in aggregate, the CSO made the sectoral estimates available to the project, and national totals of rent and non-trading income were apportioned according to their estimates of business rent. While imperfect for the non-trading income component (largely interest on securities held), the two are not individually identified in the blue book, and business rent provided the best available means of apportionment. (Figures were not available for 1977, and so 1976 estimates were used for 1977 as well as for 1976.)

In a money flow analysis, both intra-regional and inter-regional flows are involved in rent income. However, information on the extent of such types of flow are not available. Similarly for non-trading income, inter-sectoral flows between the (private) company sector, and the (public) government sector can be envisaged.

Income from abroad. The sum of gross trading profits, and rent and non-trading income for each region provides the estimates of total UK derived income. Many companies benefit from income earned overseas, either from the profits of non-resident trading subsidiaries and branches, or as returns on portfolio investments made in overseas enterprises and the like. Unfortunately, little information on the regional incidence of such income is available, and so, national totals derived from the blue book have been apportioned according to the CSO estimates of gross trading profits. In a money flow analysis, these receipts of income constitute flows from the rest of the world, to the various regions, and, if identified, the multi-regional corporate sector.

These estimates have been added to the UK originating sources of incomes to provide regionalised estimates of total current receipts by the company sector—these do not sum to the national total presented in the blue book, as stock appreciation has been excluded from this analysis for it constitutes an imputed rather than cash receipt.

Dividends and interest. Payments are made to each of the various creditors of the company, both stockholder and money lender. In the blue book, the payments made to each type of interest held in the company are separately enumerated. Little information is available on the regional dimension of such payments, and so they have been attributed, in aggregate, according to the CSO estimates of gross trading profits, to which many but not all are intimately related. Clearly, ownership of loan stock and share capital can cross regional boundaries, and thus such disbursements will involve inter-regional payments. Similarly, many financial institutions will be represented, and thus the supra-regional entities should also be involved.

In the blue book, an element 'additions to divident reserves' is recorded to cover the difference between accruals and payments within a particular year. In a money flow analysis such differences would not exist, and thus this element is excluded from the presented tables.

Current transfers to charities. This payment is the direct analogue of the item included under current income of the personal sector, as 'current transfers to charities from companies'. Consequently, the estimates prepared for the personal sector have been transferred directly.

Profits due abroad. In the same way in which domestic companies receive income from abroad, a portion of domestic profits must be remitted overseas to non-residents owning an interest in domestic industry. As with corporate income from abroad, no direct information is available at a regional scale, and the gross trading profits proxy has been used. Once again, these payments involve flows between the UK regions and the rest of the world sector.

Taxes paid abroad. These payments are very similar to profits due abroad, though made to overseas governments rather than overseas private residents. A similar approach, using CSO gross trading profits estimates has been used.

Undistributed income. The balance between total income and the sum of disbursements described above constitute that portion of income not distributed by the company but 'saved' for internal uses. In the same manner by which personal savings form a part of the personal capital accounts, this undistributed income is a major component of corporate capital receipts. In the national accounts, this is calculated as residual. However, for the regional estimates it was felt more suitable to allocate it according to gross trading profits, due to the rather indirect manner in which most other current payments had been apportioned. Consequently, for any one region total receipts do not match total payments. Furthermore, because certain accruals and imputations have been omitted from the money flows analysis, the national total of undistributed income exceeds the accruals based figure in the blue book.

Capital transfers. The other component of capital receipts are the grants of one form or another received by the company sector. Largely these are the investment grants made by government in pursuit of its regional and industrial strategies. National totals from the blue book have been apportioned to the regions according to figures of such payments gleaned from the public sector sections of this appendix. Clearly, the vase majority of these payments are flows from government to the regions. Added to undistributed profits, these make up the total capital receipts relevant to a money flow analysis. The additions to tax and dividend reserves enumerated in the blue book result from the accruals basis of the national accounts, and are incorporated in the higher estimates for undistributed income.

Gross domestic fixed capital formation. A major element of capital expenditures is to establish fixed investments of one kind or another. Such expenditures within the regions are calculated in the regional accounts, largely based on information in the *Annual Census of Production,* complemented by other sources for agriculture, forestry and fishing, extractive industry, and communications. These include an element of investment made in the public sector. Nevertheless, they present the best information available, and were used to apportion national totals to the regions and the continental shelf.

Increase in value of stocks and work in progress. Physical increases in the amount of stocks of components and partly finished products also constitute a form of investment, and are included in the capital account. Once again CSO estimates were available to apportion national totals to the regions.

Taxes on capital. Companies are not liable to either capital gains tax nor capital transfer tax, the prime taxes on capital facing the personal sector. However, capital gains can be enjoyed, merely increasing trading surplus, and thus liability for corporation tax. The national figure is therefore an estimate of the capital component of corporation tax paid. Along with all other public revenues, corporation tax is analysed elsewhere (see p.134) but for financial years, not calendar years. However, the regional incidence presented there is the product of allocating national receipts according to gross trading profits, as the best indicator of the regional incidence of the tax base. Thus, once again this component has been attributed to the regions, for each calendar year, according to the CSO estimates of gross trading profits.

Capital transfers to public corporations. This small element of company capital expenditures largely involves payments for the connection of public utilities to buildings and land. Little information is at hand to identify the regional pattern of such payments, and once again, national totals were apportioned according to gross trading profits. The small aggregate size means that any distortions will have little real effect upon total capital payments.

Net acquisition of financial assets. If capital expenditures exceed capital receipts, then the company sector must borrow funds from other sources. These transactions are presented in greater detail in the financial accounts section (see pp.161–215). The figures presented here are but a residual balancing item, and therefore reflect the accuracy, or otherwise of the several components of the capital account for each region.

Overall, the analysis of the company sector at the regional scale is very imperfect, reflecting both the difficulties in measuring specially the impact of such a disaggregate sector, and the paucity of hard information already available. The majority of transactions involving the company sector will be intra-sectoral, as traditionally represented in an input/output format. Many such transactions will be inter-regional due to the considerable spatial specialisation and yet integration of the UK economy. As a result, the extent to which money is channelled between the regions by the company sector cannot be readily gauged.

Table 14

Company sector: Appropriation account–1974 (£m) (current prices)

	North	Yorks Humbs.	East Mids.	East Anglia	South-East	South-West	West Mids.	North-West	Wales	Scot.	Nrth. Ire'd.	Cont. Shelf	UK
Gross trading profits	311.1	448.5	288.9	138.7	1359.3	282.4	454.3	613.4	282.8	452.7	110.1	–23.9	4718
Rent and non-trading income	146.2	252.7	199.9	116.0	2997.5	285.6	334.9	415.4	121.1	272.6	128.1	–	5270
Total UK income	457.3	701.2	488.8	254.7	4356.8	568.0	789.2	1028.8	403.9	725.3	238.2	–23.9	9988
Income from abroad	176.1	254.0	163.7	78.5	770.0	159.9	257.3	347.5	160.2	256.4	62.4	–	2686
Total	633.4	955.2	625.5	333.2	5126.2	727.9	1046.5	1376.3	564.1	981.7	300.6	–23.9	12674
Dividends and interest	383.8	553.5	356.6	171.2	1677.8	348.5	560.7	757.1	349.0	558.8	135.9	–	5853
Current transfers to charities	2.5	3.7	2.5	1.2	11.9	3.3	3.7	5.4	2.5	4.1	1.2	–	42
Profits due abroad	43.0	61.9	39.9	19.2	187.8	39.0	62.7	84.7	39.1	62.5	15.2	–	655
UK taxes on income	157.7	227.5	146.5	70.3	689.4	143.2	230.4	311.1	143.4	229.6	55.8	–	2405
Taxes paid abroad	26.9	38.8	25.0	12.0	117.5	24.4	39.3	53.0	24.4	39.1	9.5	–	410
Undistributed income	217.0	312.9	201.6	96.8	948.5	197.0	317.0	428.0	197.3	315.9	76.8	–	3309
Total	830.9	1198.3	772.1	370.7	3632.9	755.4	1213.8	1639.3	755.7	1210.0	294.4	–	12674

Table 15

Company sector: Appropriation account–1975 (£m) (current prices)

	North	Yorks Humbs.	East Mids.	East Anglia	South-East	South-West	West Mids.	North-West.	Wales	Scot.	Nrth. Ire'd.	Cont. Shelf	UK
Gross trading profits	363.2	497.1	375.1	174.6	1626.1	347.5	495.4	718.3	254.7	553.1	119.1	–1.3	5523
Rent and non-trading income	156.7	272.8	218.1	126.9	3182.3	308.4	362.3	445.3	129.3	291.0	136.8	–	5630
Total UK income	519.9	769.9	593.2	301.5	4808.4	655.9	857.7	1163.6	384.0	844.1	255.9	–1.3	11153
Income from abroad	154.2	211.0	159.2	74.1	690.2	147.5	210.3	304.9	108.1	234.8	50.1	–	2345
Total	674.1	980.9	752.4	375.6	5498.6	803.4	1068.0	1468.5	492.1	1078.9	306.0	–1.3	13498
Dividends and interest	403.6	552.4	416.8	194.0	1807.1	386.2	550.1	798.3	283.0	614.6	132.3	–	6139
Current transfers to charities	2.5	3.7	2.5	1.3	12.1	3.3	3.7	5.4	2.1	4.2	1.2	–	42
Profits due abroad	40.9	56.0	42.2	19.7	183.1	39.1	55.8	80.9	28.7	62.3	13.4	–	622
UK taxes on income	115.3	157.7	119.0	55.4	516.0	110.3	157.2	228.0	80.8	175.5	37.8	–	1753
Taxes paid abroad	33.0	45.2	34.1	15.9	147.8	31.6	45.0	65.3	23.1	50.3	10.8	–	502
Undistributed income	291.9	399.5	301.4	140.3	1307.0	279.3	398.2	577.4	204.7	444.5	95.7	–	4440
Total	887.2	1214.5	916.0	426.6	3973.1	849.8	1210.0	1755.3	622.4	1351.4	291.2	–	13498

Table 16

Company sector: Appropriation account—1976 (£m) (current prices)

	North	Yorks Humbs.	East Mids.	East Anglia	South-East	South-West	West Mids.	North-West	Wales	Scot.	Nrth. Ire'd.	Cont. Shelf	UK
Gross trading profits	464.5	668.7	490.8	224.1	2052.3	446.4	658.8	952.3	361.3	734.3	152.8	201.6	7408
Rent and non-trading income	191.9	332.8	267.3	157.0	3804.0	376.7	441.3	540.0	155.2	352.5	162.3	–	6781
Total UK income	656.4	1001.5	758.1	381.1	5856.3	823.1	1100.1	1492.3	516.5	1086.8	315.1	201.6	14189
Income from abroad	213.3	307.0	225.3	102.9	942.2	204.9	302.4	437.2	165.9	337.1	70.2	92.5	3401
Total	869.7	1308.5	983.4	484.0	6798.6	1028.0	1402.5	1929.5	682.4	1423.9	385.3	294.1	17590
Dividends and interest	424.0	610.4	448.0	204.5	1873.3	407.5	601.3	869.3	329.8	670.3	139.5	184.0	6762
Current transfers to charities	2.5	3.7	2.5	1.3	12.1	3.3	3.3	5.4	2.5	4.2	1.2	–	42
Profits due abroad	61.3	88.2	64.7	29.5	270.7	58.9	86.9	125.6	47.7	96.8	20.2	26.6	977
UK taxes on income	101.1	145.6	106.8	48.8	446.9	97.2	143.4	207.4	78.7	159.9	33.3	43.9	1613
Taxes paid abroad	29.8	42.8	31.5	14.4	131.6	28.6	42.2	61.1	23.2	47.1	9.8	12.9	475
Undistributed income	484.1	697.0	511.6	233.5	2139.0	465.2	686.6	992.6	376.6	765.4	159.3	210.1	7721
Total	1102.8	1587.7	1165.1	532.0	4873.6	1060.1	1563.7	2261.4	858.5	1743.7	2107.0	477.5	17590

Table 17

Company sector: Appropriation account—1977 (£m) (current prices)

	North	Yorks Humbs.	East Mids.	East Anglia	South-East	South-West	West Mids.	North-West	Wales	Scot.	Nrth. Ire'd.	Cont. Shelf	UK
Gross trading profits	600.5	932.7	661.8	296.9	2863.6	612.0	883.9	1317.3	491.5	988.8	210.2	907.8	10767
Rent and non-trading income*	206.2	357.6	287.2	168.7	4087.3	404.8	474.2	580.2	166.7	378.8	174.4	–	7286
Total UK income	806.7	1290.3	949.0	465.6	6950.9	1016.8	1358.1	1397.5	658.2	1367.6	384.7	907.8	18053
Income from abroad	190.1	295.2	209.5	94.0	906.4	193.7	280.0	417.0	155.6	313.0	66.5	287.3	3408
Total	996.8	1585.5	1158.5	559.6	7857.3	1210.5	1638.1	2314.5	813.8	1680.6	451.2	1195.1	21461
Dividends and interest	412.1	640.0	454.2	203.7	1965.2	420.0	606.6	904.0	337.3	678.6	144.3	623.0	7389
Current transfers to charities	2.6	3.9	2.6	1.2	18.5	3.3	3.7	5.4	2.4	4.2	1.2	–	43
Profits due abroad	97.4	151.3	107.3	48.1	464.4	99.2	143.3	213.6	79.7	160.3	34.1	147.2	1746
UK taxes on income	156.4	243.0	172.4	77.3	746.0	159.4	230.2	343.2	128.1	257.6	54.8	236.5	2805
Taxes paid abroad	21.0	32.6	23.1	10.4	100.0	21.4	30.9	46.0	17.2	34.5	7.3	31.7	376
Undistributed income	507.7	788.5	559.4	251.0	2420.7	517.3	747.2	1113.6	415.5	835.9	177.7	767.4	9102
Total	1197.2	1859.3	1319.0	591.7	5708.8	1220.6	1761.9	2625.8	980.2	1971.1	419.4	1805.8	21461

*The proxy used for this component is not currently available for 1977, and so the 1976 proxy has been used.

Table 18

Company sector: Capital account–1974 (£m) (current prices)

	North	Yorks Humbs.	East Mids.	East Anglia	South-East	South-West	West Mids.	North-West	Wales	Scot.	Nrth. Ire'd.	Cont. Shelf	UK
Receipts													
Undistributed profits	217.0	312.9	201.6	96.8	948.5	197.0	317.0	428.0	197.3	315.9	76.8	–	3309
Capital transfers	62.5	22.8	6.0	3.5	52.2	12.9	16.5	53.7	45.6	66.4	24.8	–	367
Total	279.5	335.7	207.6	100.3	1000.7	209.9	333.5	481.7	242.9	382.3	101.6	–	3676
Expenditures													
Gross domestic fixed capital formation	498.4	590.9	438.6	253.1	2159.1	509.1	598.6	767.5	371.6	829.1	208.0	301.1	7525
Increase in value of stocks, etc.	359.0	536.6	380.6	212.9	1825.6	364.9	626.8	755.4	349.2	526.8	149.1	–	6087
Taxes on capital	5.4	7.8	5.1	2.4	23.8	4.9	8.0	10.7	4.9	7.9	1.9	–	83
Capital transfers to public corporations	1.2	1.7	1.1	0.5	5.2	1.1	1.7	2.3	1.1	1.7	0.4	–	18
Net acquisition of financial assets	- 584.5	- 801.3	- 617.8	- 368.6	- 3013.0	- 670.1	- 901.6	- 1054.2	- 483.9	- 983.2	- 257.8	- 301.1	- 10037
Total	279.5	335.7	207.6	100.3	1000.7	209.9	333.5	481.7	242.9	382.3	101.6	–	3676

Table 19

Company sector: Capital account–1975 (£m) (current prices)

	North	Yorks Humbs.	East Mids.	East Anglia	South-East	South-West	West Mids.	North West	Wales	Scot.	Nrth. Ire'd.	Cont. Shelf	UK
Receipts													
Undistributed profits	291.9	399.5	301.4	140.3	1307.0	279.3	398.2	577.4	204.7	444.5	95.7	–	4440
Capital transfers	153.4	29.9	6.6	2.3	26.1	10.4	8.2	61.5	67.3	114.2	52.0	–	532
Total	445.3	429.4	308.0	142.6	1333.1	289.7	406.4	638.9	272.0	558.7	147.7	–	4972
Expenditures													
Gross domestic fixed capital formation	620.5	640.9	478.8	253.0	2342.0	516.2	654.8	753.8	444.0	996.6	245.5	784.8	8731
Increase in value of stocks, etc.	131.4	183.6	138.2	78.5	623.0	128.4	210.7	262.5	80.7	187.0	48.8	–	2073
Taxes on capital	8.0	10.9	8.2	3.8	35.5	7.6	10.9	15.7	5.6	12.1	2.6	–	121
Capital transfers to public corporations	1.4	2.0	1.5	0.7	6.5	1.4	2.0	2.9	1.0	2.2	0.5	–	22
Net acquisition of financial assets	- 316.0	- 408.0	- 318.7	- 193.4	- 1673.9	- 363.9	- 472.0	- 396.0	- 259.3	- 639.2	- 149.7	- 748.8	- 5975
Total	445.3	429.4	308.0	142.6	1333.1	289.7	406.4	638.9	272.0	558.7	147.7	–	4972

Table 20

Company sector: Capital account—1976 (£m) (current prices)

	North	Yorks Humbs.	East Mids.	East Anglia	South-East	South-West	West Mids.	North West	Wales	Scot.	Nrth. Ire'd.	Cont. Shelf	UK
Receipts													
Undistributed profits	484.1	697.0	511.6	233.5	2139.0	465.2	686.6	992.6	376.6	765.4	159.3	210.1	7721
Capital transfers	121.2	22.0	3.6	1.1	12.4	6.7	4.0	52.9	50.6	89.0	41.3	–	405
Total	605.3	719.0	515.2	234.6	2151.4	471.9	690.6	1045.5	427.2	854.4	200.6	210.1	8126
Expenditures													
Gross domestic fixed capital formation	674.8	754.6	568.7	276.8	2652.0	570.9	733.6	868.7	550.4	1090.6	280.6	1084.2	10106
Increase in value of stocks, etc.	308.6	446.9	341.5	192.5	1416.3	325.4	506.5	647.8	254.4	499.6	121.4	–	5061
Taxes on capital	9.3	13.4	9.8	4.5	41.0	8.9	13.2	19.0	7.2	14.7	3.1	4.0	148
Capital transfers to public corporation	1.8	2.5	1.9	0.8	7.8	1.7	2.5	3.6	1.4	2.8	0.6	0.8	28
Net acquisition of financial assets	- 398.2	- 498.4	- 406.7	- 240.0	- 1965.7	- 435.0	- 565.2	- 493.6	- 386.2	- 753.3	- 205.1	- 878.9	- 7217
Total	605.3	719.0	515.2	234.6	2151.4	471.9	690.6	1045.5	427.2	854.4	200.6	210.1	8126

Table 21

Company sector: Capital account—1977 (£m) (current prices)

	North	Yorks Humbs.	East Mids.	East Anglia	South-East	South-West	West Mids.	North-West	Wales	Scot.	Nrth. Ire'd.	Cont. Shelf	UK
Receipts													
Undistributed profits	507.7	788.5	559.4	251.0	2420.7	517.3	747.2	1113.6	415.5	835.9	177.7	767.4	9102
Capital transfers	96.0	16.0	1.3	0.1	1.7	5.4	0.5	35.3	49.3	73.3	36.2	–	315
Total	603.7	804.5	560.7	251.1	2422.4	522.7	747.7	1148.9	464.8	909.2	213.9	767.4	9417
Expenditures													
Gross domestic fixed capital formation*	797.3	891.5	672.0	327.1	3133.3	674.5	866.7	1026.4	650.3	1288.6	331.5	1280.9	11940
Increase in value of stocks, etc.*	305.0	441.7	337.5	190.3	1399.8	321.6	500.6	640.3	251.4	493.8	120.0	–	5002
Taxes on capital	9.5	14.7	10.4	4.7	45.2	9.7	14.0	20.8	7.8	15.6	3.3	14.3	170
Capital transfers to public corporations	2.1	3.2	2.2	1.0	9.8	2.1	3.0	4.5	1.7	3.4	0.7	3.1	37
Net acquisition of financial assets	- 510.2	- 546.6	- 461.4	- 272.0	- 2165.7	- 485.2	- 636.6	- 543.1	- 446.4	- 892.2	- 241.6	- 530.9	- 7732
Total	603.7	804.5	560.7	251.1	2422.4	522.7	747.7	1148.9	464.8	909.2	213.9	767.4	9417

* The proxy used for this component is not currently available for 1977, and so the 1976 proxy has been used.

Appendix 2 The general government sector and public corporations (other than nationalised industries)

The flows associated with the general government sector (the central government and local authorities) and public corporations (other than the nationalised industries) are the subject of this appendix.

The first part of the appendix deals with the expenditures of the three separate groups. Within this section, the data on regionally relevant expenditures classified by spending programme are presented, followed by an examination of total spending by each spending agency in the regions. This is followed by a section relating to the financing of these expenditures.

Public expenditure

The two different ways of analysing public expenditure in the regional context has been outlined in Chapter 3. This distinction was made between the actual money flows emanating from general government on the one hand and the location of the services (or programmes) to which the money flows relate. As well, the distinction was made between the services which could be considered to be regional in character and those which are indivisible with respect to regions and the services which are provided.

The sources and methods employed in producing the data on the central government's regionally relevant expenditure by programmes and total money flows by economic category is presented first, followed by a similar exposition for local authorities and public corporations in that order.

The data are presented in terms of each authorities' current and capital account for each regionally relevant spending programme, and the whole of the general governments' total spending by economic category for each year for the period 1974–75 to 1977–78 inclusive.

Agriculture, fisheries, food and forestry

Data on the regional incidence of expenditure in the agriculture, fisheries, food and forestry programme have been assembled from a variety of sources. In some sub-programmes no regional data were available and proxies were assembled to allocate the national control totals to obtain regional figures. The sources and methods in each of the sub-programmes are discussed in detail below

Market regulation and production support

Market regulation under Common Agriculture Policy (CAP) of the European Economic Community (EEC). The expenditures made under this sub-programme cover policies on intervention buying and other general intervention measures for the whole of the UK. These can be attributed to a producers subsidy where stock have been withheld from the market to ensure higher prices for the produce or in some cases, a consumer subsidy where the expenditure has been used to keep prices down through price equalisation policies or supporting inter-community trade or third country trade/non EEC. No direct data on the regional incidence of this programme were available.

The national control totals in this section (and the further breakdown by commodity) were obtained from the *Appropriation Accounts.* Moneys from the EEC to support this sub-programme are not included under this heading so the only receipts in the *Appropriation Account* that have to be netted off are receipts, sales and fees.

The individual items involved and the method of allocation are as follows:

Sugar (equalisation arrangements) was treated as a consumer subsidy and each region's consumption of sugar was used to allocate the total.

Meat (withholding stocks) was treated as a producer's subsidy and the total livestock (cattle, sheep and pigs) on agriculture holdings, in each region, was used as a proxy.

Butter (withholding stocks) was treated as a producer's subsidy and the cows in milk in each region was used as a proxy.

Aids to animal feeds was treated as a producer's subsidy and total livestock on agriculture holdings in each region was used as a proxy.

Intra-community and third country trade expenditure was treated as a consumer subsidy (cf. cmnd 6393 *Public Expenditure to 1979–80,* page 26) and allocated by population in each region.

Production subsidies were allocated according to each region's agriculture area.

Special import subsidy for sugar was treated as a consumer subsidy and allocated according to each region's consumption of sugar.

Beef premium expenditure was treated as a producer's subsidy and allocated using the stock of cattle (not in milk or calf, or bulls for service) in each region.

Skimmed milk expenditure was treated as a producer's subsidy and allocated by the number of cows in milk in each region.

Price guarantees on products supported by the CAP

The expenditure on this programme was on wheat, barley, oats and mixed corn and the production of these crops by region was used as a proxy. Expenditure for Scotland was obtained directly from the *Appropriation Accounts.*

The subsidy on eggs related to the UK and the number of fowl producing eggs in each region was used as a proxy.

Price guarantees on other products

Sheep. The stock of sheep in each region (England and Wales) was used as a proxy. Expenditure in Scotland was obtained directly from the *Appropriation Accounts.*

Wool. The stock of sheep in each region (UK) was used as a proxy.

Potatoes. The production of potatoes in each region (UK) was used as a proxy.

Production grants and subsidies

Figures on production grants and subsidies for each region of England and Wales, were supplied by the Ministry of Agriculture, Fisheries and Food (MAFF) except for lime, fertiliser and calf subsidies. The regional distribution of arable land was used to allocate the lime and fertiliser subsidy, and each region's stock of calves to allocate the calf subsidy. Figures for Scotland were obtained from the *Appropriation Accounts.*

Support for capital and other improvements

Figures for the regions of England and Wales were supplied by MAFF. Figures for Scotland were obtained from the *Appropriation Accounts.*

Other assistance to agriculture production, food processing and marketing

Figures for Scotland were obtained from the appropriation accounts. No direct data for the English regions, and Wales, were available. Control totals for England and Wales were obtained from the *Appropriation Accounts* and were allocated as follows:

Education, advisory and research and development services: Each region's share of population was used as a proxy.

Livestock services: Slaughter of diseased animals: each region's share of livestock was used as a proxy. Brucellosis eradication payments: each region's share of cattle was used as a proxy.

Food services: Payments to sugar producers to keep down the price to the consumer was treated as consumer subsidy and allocated according to each region's (UK) consumption of sugar.

Other: Each region's share of agricultural land was used as a proxy.

Food subsidies: Expenditure on food subsidies was allocated by the regional consumption of the various products which were subsidised: milk, breadflour, butter, cheese, tea, household flour and beef. Control totals were obtained from the *Appropriation Accounts.*

Central and miscellaneous services: Figures for the regions of England and Wales were obtained from MAFF. Expenditure on Kew Gardens was obtained from the *Appropriation Accounts.* Figures for Scotland were obtained from the *Appropriation Accounts.*

Support for fishing: Central government expenditure was allocated by employees in employment in fishing.

Forestry: Forestry expenditure was allocated according to regional figures on new planting and stocking in the relevant year taken from regional statistics.

Trade, industry and employment

Data on the regional incidence of expenditure in the trade, industry and employment programme have been assembled from a variety of sources. In some sub-programmes no regional data were available and proxies were assembled to allocate the national control totals to obtain regional figures. The sources and methods in each sub-programme are discussed in detail below.

Regional development grants

Figures on regional development grants are taken from the *Report of the 1972 Industry Act*, annually.

Provision of land and building

Figures on offers of assistance for land and buildings are given in the *Report of the 1972 Industry Act*, annually, for each development area, and intermediate area by country. The English intermediate area figures were distributed to the regions using employees in employment. These total regional offers were used as a proxy to distribute actual payments between regions.

Selective assistance to industry in assisted areas

Figures on selective assistance to industry in assisted areas are available from the *Report of the 1972 Industry Act*, annually.

Other regional support

This comprises expenditures by the Development Commission (including Council for Small Industries in Rural Areas (CoSira); aid to regional promotional bodies, (North of England Development Council); the Highlands and Islands Development Board and the Development Board for Rural Wales. Figures for the Development Commission were taken from its annual statement of accounts (CoSira supplied a regional analysis of their expenditure). The remainder of the data were taken from the *Appropriation Accounts.*

Regional employment premium

These figures were taken from *Regional Statistics.*

Residual expenditure under the repealed section of LEA 1972

These are included in the Provision of Land and Building above.

Scottish and Welsh development agencies

Figures for the SDA and WDA were taken from the *Appropriation Accounts.*

General industrial research and development

Figures for 1974–75 were supplied by the departments responsible for the expenditure. Figures for the North and West Midlands were similarly supplied for 1975–76 and 1976–77. The figures for the remainder of the regions were obtained by applying the 1974–75 distribution (less the North and West Midlands) to the national figure (less the North and West Midlands).

Technological and industrial sponsorship

The same method as for general industrial research and development was used.

Aircraft and aerospace general research and development

The Department of Industry supplied partial figures for 1974–75 (the amount spent in the South-East, the remainder being unallocated). Figures for the remaining regions were obtained by applying the 1973–74 distribution (less the South-East) to the national total (less the South-East). The 1973–74 figures were obtained from NRST Report No.12, op.cit. The distribution which resulted in 1974–75 was used to allocate the national total to the regions for the other years.

Concorde

The figures in NRST Report No.12, op.cit. for 1973–74 were used to allocate the national totals.

RB 211

The Department of Industry supplied figures for 1974–75 for all regions and for the North and West Midlands for 1975–76 and 1976–77. The 1974–75 distribution (minus the North and West Midlands) was used to allocate the national total (less the North and West Midlands).

Other aircraft and aeroengine projects and assistance

The same method used for the RB 211 was adopted.

Space

The same method used for the RB 211 was adopted.

Nuclear

The figures were supplied by the UK Atomic Energy Authority.

National Enterprise Board

Expenditure on individual companies were obtained from the Annual Report of the National Enterprise Board. Where the company is located in a single region, the expenditure is attributed to that region. Where the company is located in more than one region, the company was asked to provide regional figures of where the NEB assistance was used. British Leyland the main recipient of NEB aid in the period considered, was unable to do so, and their total was distributed according to employees in employment in the motor vehicle industry in the regions where BL operated. NEB expenditure in a company, irrespective of the method (share or loan) was allocated to that company as the aim of the expenditure is to provide the NEB with an interest in the company. This is so in the case where the NEB purchases shares from a third party and does not necessarily contribute directly to the finances of the company.

Selective assistance to individual industries, firms and undertakings

Included in this sub-programme are the schemes to help individual industries, or help selected industries to accelerate investment expenditures. Payments by region under these schemes are available from the report of the 1972 Industry Act, annually. Added to these are the expenditures made to individual undertakings.The problems which arise with the National Enterprise Board in the regional context appear here. The solution outlined under the NEB is adopted here. The source of data on aid to individual firms is the report of the 1972 Industry Act, and the appropriation accounts for the Department of Energy.

Promotion of tourism

Data on aid to the regional tourist boards are available for the English regions from the English Tourist Board annual report. Data for Scotland and Wales are available from the Supply Estimates.

Refinancing of home shipbuilding lending

The Department of Industry refinances a proportion of the credit provided by the clearing banks available for the purchase of ships built in this country. This stimulates output and employment in the shipyards. The regional distribution of employees in employment in shipbuilding and marine engineering, has been used as a proxy to apportion the total.

Interest support costs

These are the costs of interest support for fixed rate home shipbuilding lending. They are distributed according to employees in employment in shipbuilding and marine engineering.

Assistance to shipbuilding industry

This comprises construction grants to shipbuilders, the figures are from the Industry Act report, annually. Other expenditure includes aid to individual companies; these data are taken from the *Appropriation Accounts* and the Industry Act Report and assigned to the region where the shipbuilders are located.

Other support services

Figures for 1974–75 were supplied by the relevant departments and were used to allocate the other years.

Investment grants

Figures on investment grants made in Wales, Scotland, by development areas and non-development areas, are available from the report of the 1972 Industry Act, annually. The figures for the English development areas were allocated to these respective regions by their relative labour force. The figures for the English non-development areas were also allocated according to their respective labour force.

Compensation for price restraint

These refer to payments made by the government to the electricity and gas industries, and the Post Office for losses which resulted from prices charged to the consumer being kept below the level which they might have been if the industries had been allowed a free hand in pricing. They are treated as a consumer subsidy. For the electricity industry, the amounts paid to the area boards were allocated to the regions with which boards were associated. The payments to CEGB were allocated according to regional sales. Payment to the gas industry was allocated to the regions according to sales by region. Payments to the Post Office were allocated according to the expenditure by region on postage and telephone from the family expenditure survey.

Assistance to the coal industry

Figures for 1974–75 were supplied by the Department of Energy. Figures for 1975–76 comprise two elements:

1 Expenditure under the Coal Industry Act; these figures were based on data on regional grants and grants per output by mining area taken from the Annual Report of the National Coal Board. The mining areas were updated to the respective standard planning regions.
2 Expenditure made under the Penumoconiosis Scheme. National figures were allocated according to regional employment in coal mining. For 1976–77 and 1977–78, the figures were obtained as in 1.

Other compensation

Figures for 1974–75 were supplied by the relevant departments; for 1975–76 and 1976–77 figures for the North and West Midlands were supplied. The remainder were obtained by applying the 1974–75 regional distribution (less the North and West Midlands) to the national total (less the North and West Midlands).

International trade

Export promotion and trade co-operation. The majority of this sub-programme is spent overseas.

Refinancing of fixed rate export credits. These cover a proportion of the fixed rate sterling credits provided by the clearing banks as aid to exporters. Regional GDP has been used as a proxy for regional exports to apportion the total.

Interest support for fixed rate export credits. These are additional cost to the government in allowing banks a commercial rate of return on sterling and foreign currency credits for exporters as well as the net cost of borrowing for refinancing sterling credits for exporters. Regional GDP has been used as a proxy for regional exports to apportion the total.

Employment services and employment rehabilitation

No direct data on expenditure in this programme were available. The services covered relate to the expenditures on the Employment Service Agency, Professional Employment Registry, Transference Scheme and Industrial Rehabilitation. As these expenditures are related to finding the unemployed employment, the regional distribution of those unemployed was used as a proxy.

Industrial training

No direct data were available. The regional distribution of those serving apprenticeships and receiving industrial training was used as a proxy (Regional Statistics).

Redundancy and maternity fund payments

No direct data on the regional distribution were available and the regional distribution of the increase in the numbers unemployed in the relevant year was used as a proxy.

Industrial relations and other labour market services

This includes the costs of the Department of Employment staff engaged on general manpower, economic policy, the conciliation and arbitration service, industrial tribunals and the Industrial Arbitration Board. Employment was used as a proxy for regional apportionment. Also included are the measures to alleviate unemployment such as Job Creation, Community Industry Scheme and Temporary Employment Subsidy. These data were supplied by the Department of Employment, apart from the Job Creation Scheme, the numbers involved in each region in this scheme was used to apportion the national total.

Health and safety at work

No direct data were available. Population was used as a proxy to allocate to regions.

Regulation of domestic trade and industry and consumer protection

Figures for 1974–75 were supplied by the relevant departments. These were used to allocate the national totals for the other years.

Central and miscellaneous services

Figures for the Departments of Industry, Energy, Prices and Consumer Protection, and Trade, were supplied by the departments for 1974–75. Administrative expenditures by the Department of the Employment were not available but were allocated to the regions on the basis of the other departments. The expenditure in the South-East included national expenditures so the figures for the South-East were reduced to allow for this. The ratio of South-East population to national population, was used to obtain a figure for the South-East. This distribution was used to allocate the expenditures for the other years. Added to these are the Department of Employment's grant to Remploy which was allocated by population.

Roads and transport

The sources for data on the regional distribution of public expenditure in the roads and transport programme are varied. In some sub-programmes direct data are available; in others, proxies have to be used to allocate national totals. The methods and the sources used are as follows:

Motorways and trunk roads

New construction and improvement expenditure is available for each region, from Transport Statistics, annually. Maintenance expenditure includes public lighting on trunk roads as well as maintenance and cleansing.

Central government subsidies

British Rail

Passenger subsidies: For 1974–75 the government subsidy was in two forms:

1 Grants for unremunerative passenger services.
2 A special grant to meet British Rail's cash flow shortfall.

For 1 the 1974 annual report of British Rail provided the amount for the services which obtained the grant for the calendar 1974. Services which operated wholly within a region were allocated to that region; for services operating across regional boundaries, the subsidies were allocated to the relevant regions on a track mileage basis. For 2 the percentage distribution of miles travelled by train by residents of each region (from the National Travel Survey) was used as a proxy to allocate the national total.

In 1975–76 the method of supporting British Rail was changed. Instead of a cash deficiency grant and a grant for unremunerative services, the government provided support in respect of public service obligation for the whole of the rail passenger sector. The total was distributed to the regions according to the percentage distribution of miles travelled by train, taken from the National Travel Survey. After 1974–75 there were also additional payments to British Rail.

Grants for rail freight and parcels. These were allocated according to regional GDP.

Pension funding and superannuation fund. These were allocated according to regional population.

Level-crossing and infrastructure grants. These were allocated by regional capital expenditure in transport and communications.

Scottish Transport Group

Figures were taken directly from the PESC exercise.

New bus grants

Figures were allocated according to employees in employment in MLH 702 in each region: Road Passenger Transport.

Ports and shipping

Ports. This item covers loans to ports in the private sector and loans were obtained directly from the Department of the Environment.

Shipping. Expenditure on shipping services by region was obtained from the Department of Trade in 1974–75. The regional distribution in 1974–75 was used to obtain the figures for the other years.

Other civil aviation services. Figures for 1974–75 were obtained directly from the Department of Trade; these were used to obtain the figures for the other years.

Other transport services

No direct data were available and population was used as a proxy for regional apportionment.

Housing

Statistics on housing expenditure for the standard planning regions for 1974–75, and 1975–76, have been assembled from a variety of sources. Detailed sources and methods for the individual sub-programmes are as follows.

Central government expenditure on subsidies, rent rebates and rent allowances to local authorities and new towns, and contributions from the rate fund by local authorities, and local authority administration

Central government subsidies to local authorities have been included in local authority expenditure. For the new towns, figures were taken from the annual reports of the new towns. For the Scottish Special Housing Association (SSHA), the figure was obtained as a residual subtracting total government subsidies to new towns from total subsidies to new towns and Scottish Special Housing Association.

Housing association deficit grants

The figures are based on statistics on deficit grants paid to housing associations classified by the location of their headquarters from 1974–75 to 1976–77, supplied by the Department of the Environment. Grants to associations which operated in more than one region were distributed according to regional allocation of grants to single region associations. This 1974–75 to 1976–77 accumulated total was then allocated to each year in the ratio of the national total in each year to the accumulated national total over the period.

Option mortgages

Expenditure in Scotland and Wales were obtained from the appropriation accounts. Estimates of expenditure in the English regions were obtained by dividing the annual total on the basis of information on the number of mortages in each quarter, the percentage of these which option mortages and the average value of mortgage advanced in each region.

Administration

Figures for Scotland were available from the appropriation accounts. No direct data were available for the regions of England and Wales, and the national totals were distributed on the basis of population.

Loans and grants to housing associations

Capital grants by central government. Figures for Scotland and Wales were obtained from Identifiable Public Expenditure in Scotland and Wales. The figures for the English regions were built up using a proxy of the volume of activity by the Housing Corporation in their own regions. Where the Housing Corporation's own region differed from the Standard Planning Regions, population was used to adjust the Housing Corporation's regions to Standard Planning Regions. The volume of activity used was the number of dwellings under approval at the end of each financial year.

Other environmental services

British Waterways Board

Expenditure was allocated according to employees in employment in MLH 706 in each region: Port and Inland Water Transport (except in the Northern Region where the British Waterways Board do not operate).

Royal palaces and royal parks

Expenditure on individual palaces and parks were obtained from the Supply Estimates, annually, and were allocated to the regions in which they are situated.

Historic buildings and ancient monuments

Expenditure on historic buildings in England is available from the annual report of the Historic Buildings Council and allocated to the region in which they are located. No data are available on historic monuments and population was used as a proxy. Figures for Scotland and Wales were obtained from the *Appropriation Accounts*, annually.

Environmental research

This covers research work carried out at the Transport and Road Research Laboratory, the Building Research Establishment and the Hydraulic Research Station. Other expenditures have not been identified and are not included.

Central and miscellaneous services

No direct data are available and population was used as a proxy for regional apportionment.

Law, order and protective services

Public expenditure on the law, order and protective services programme for the regions have been assembled from a variety of sources, using proxies for central government expenditure.

No direct data were available for the English regions and Wales; for Scotland, the *Appropriation Accounts* provided expenditure on courts, legal aid, civil defence and other expenditure under this programme.

For England and Wales the following proxies were used to allocate the various sub-programmes.

Crown courts

Persons found guilty of indictable offences at the Crown Court by region.

Legal Aid

Numbers granted legal aid in Magistrates Courts classified by county and numbers granted legal aid in Crown Courts by division (geographic). These were allocated to their respective regions and the percentage distribution was applied to the control total for England and Wales.

Residual

This covers civil defence, control of immigration/nationality, other protective services, community services, central and miscellaneous services, and civil emergencies.

Regional distribution of population was used as proxy in the absence of any other suitable one.

Education and libraries, science and arts

Sources for the regional apportionment of public expenditure in the education and libraries, science and arts programme are varied. Sources and methods for each of the groupings of sub-programmes used are as follows.

Education

Schools: capital and current. Figures for the English regions and Wales were obtained by applying the regional distribution of teachers in maintained and direct grant schools (the recipients of the grants). Figures for Scotland were taken from the *Appropriation Accounts.*

Universities. Figures for each university were obtained from the *Appropriation Accounts.* These represent the grants to universities from the University Grants Committee. Open University expenditure has been allocated to the regions on the basis of residency of Open University students. Student grants in England and Wales are awarded by local authorities and are included under local authorities. In Scotland student grants are administered by the Scottish Education Department and are included under government spending. These are included here.

Further education. Government grants to voluntary colleges of education in England and Wales are based on the 1973–74 distribution to individual colleges, aggregated to form regions. Figures for Scotland are obtained from the *Appropriation Accounts.* As with university expenditure, student grants are included in the figure for Scotland. Also the colleges of education in Scotland are under central government control (unlike in England and Wales) and these account for the much higher spending in Scotland. The figures for Scotland and the other regions are not comparable as a result.

Miscellaneous educational services, research and administration. No direct data were available for the English regions and Wales. Population was used as a proxy. Figures for Scotland were taken from the *Appropriation Accounts.*

Central government libraries

Figures were taken from the *Appropriation Accounts.*

Research Councils

These figures are those which relate to each research council's own units classified according to the region in which it is located. Grants to universities for research or to students are not included. The figures have been taken from the *Appropriation Accounts.*

Arts

National museums and galleries. Figures of the individual museums were obtained from the *Appropriation Accounts* and are aggregated to their respective regions.

Arts Council and other arts. Figures for Scotland and Wales were obtained from the *Appropriation Accounts* for England, some projects were identified and allocated to the respective region (e.g. National Theatre); the remainder was allocated on a population basis.

Health and personal social services

Health

Hospital and community services and family practitioners. Figures for the English Standard Planning Regions, current and capital expenditure, were obtained from the Department of Health and Social Security. Figures for Scotland and Wales were taken from Health Services in Scotland (annual report) and National Health Service Acts Accounts, (annual) respectively.

Other health services: (current and capital). Figures for Scotland were obtained from the Health Services in Scotland (annual report). Figures for the regions of England and Wales, were not available and were obtained by applying population in each area to the national total (less Scotland.

Personal social services

Central government. Figures for Scotland and Wales were taken from the *Appropriation Accounts*, annually. Figures for the English regions were not available and were obtained by applying population in each area to the national total (less Scotland and Wales).

Central and miscellaneous services. Figures for Scotland were obtained from Health Services in Scotland (annual report). Figures for the regions of England, and Wales, were obtained by applying population to the national totals (less expenditure on central administration which was treated as national in character, and less Scotland's figures).

Social security

Figures on the individual sub-programme for the regions of England, Wales and Scotland have been taken from *Regional Statistics* except where noted below. Total expenditure for Northern Ireland are taken directly from the PESC exercise.

Lump sum payments to pensions

Regional figures are not available directly. They were obtained by allocating total by the regional distribution of retirement pensions.

Administration and miscellaneous services

Wages and salaries of those engaged in the Department of Health and Social Security administration were made available by the Department. Only the regional organisation, i.e. non-headquarter expenditure, is included here. These wages and salaries were provided for the DHSS regions which join the East Midlands and East Anglia standard planning regions together. Population was used to divide this total to get the two planning regions. The resultant regional distribution of wages and salaries in the planning regions was used to allocate the non-wages and salaries component of total administrative expenses (less those allocated to headquarters on a similar basis) to obtain the total administrative and miscellaneous figures.

Public expenditure by economic category

The analysis of central government expenditure with respect to the total expenditures can conveniently be divided into two parts: regionally relevant expenditure and national expenditures. As far as the categories of expenditure classified in these divisions is concerned it is reasonable to assume that wages and salaries and transfer payments paid by the central government in each region accrue to that region. Any leakages in the first round are likely to apply to the purchases of goods and non-labour services, plant, machinery and vehicles. In order to ascertain the regional incidence of these items, an analysis of each programme for the wages and salaries and transfers items is to be undertaken, while the purchase of non-labour goods and services is to be treated as a whole.

Regionally relevant expenditures

The objective here is to classify the central government's expenditure in each programme by region into economic categories. From the knowledge of economic categories of each sub-programme nationally, it is possible to assign sub-programmes to economic categories. For example, if all of sub-programme X is transfer payments nationally, then it must be all transfer payments in each region. Obviously where a programme nationally consists of more than one economic category, the problem becomes more difficult. However, there is further information on the relative size of the economic categories nationally, and this can be used for further classification regionally. In all then, although it cannot be assumed that total central government spending in a region can be classified into economic categories using the national breakdown, it is reasonable to assume that the economic categories nationally in a sub-programme may apply in a region where the sub-programme exists. The classification of regionally relevant expenditure into economic categories is carried out in four stages:

1 An examination of each region's regionally relevant expenditures in each sub-programme along with the national proportions of current economic goods and services, and transfers for current expenditure, and gross domestic fixed capital formation (gdfcf) and other capital for capital expenditure, provided a breakdown of each region's regionally relevant expenditure by these four categories.

2 The current economic goods and services (cegs) was then examined as to their distribution between wages and salaries and 'other payments'. For each programme these were available nationally. Each programme was examined separately and the cegs were apportioned according to the national ratios of wages and salaries in these programmes. In all but two programmes, it was considered likely the 'other' payments were related to the day to day operations of the employees carrying out the programme (post, postage, heating and general administration). These are likely to be purchased locally. Of the two other programmes, cegs in trade, industry and employment were all allocated to the region to which the regionally relevant expenditure was attributed. The non-wages and salaries element: spending on Concorde, nuclear, space, RB 211, etc. were assumed, in the first round, to be spent in the region in

which the contract was placed.

In the second such programme, health and personal social services, this assumption is not likely to be correct. An analysis of regional and area health authorities expenditure by wages and salaries and other payments and a list of items which were bought centrally and then distributed to the health authorities to use, provided information on: (a) the ratio of wages and salaries to total current expenditures, (b) the ratio of goods bought by centrally placed contracts and (c) the ratio of goods bought locally. These ratios were applied to each region's spending on current economic goods and services in hospitals and gave figures for wages and salaries and goods purchased locally which were assumed to apply to the region in which they were made. However, for goods purchased by contract centrally, it was necessary to estimate each region's production of these goods. Regional GDP was used as a proxy.

Aggregating across all programmes, an estimate for current economic goods and services purchased in each region was obtained.

3 A similar method was used for gross domestic fixed capital formation. From 1 above, gdfcf by region was obtained for each programme. Nationally the split between construction, and plant and machinery, and vehicles is available for each programme. Applying these ratios to the regions' gdfcf, a figure for expenditure on construction which is assumed to enter directly into the regions was obtained. For vehicles, and plant and machinery, the amount spent in each region was obtained by applying regional GDP (as a proxy) to the national total because it was assumed that these would be bought centrally rather than in the region in which they were to be used.

4 Capital grants and loans in each region were allocated to the region in the same way as current transfers. This is because it is only the first round effects which are being measured. The regional distribution of how these grants and loans are to be used would be picked up in the secondary and subsequent flows.

'National' expenditures

The method of allocating the 'national' expenditures by region for each of the programmes is as follows.

Current expenditure

Defence. For defence expenditure the regional impact relates to where the forces and the Ministry of Defence civil servants are located geographically, and where defence equipment is purchased. The wages and salaries category is made up of three items: forces pay, civilians pay and pensions. For the first two, the regional distribution of forces and civilians (including overseas) was used. For pensions, the regional distribution of population was thought to be a more realistic proxy. The control totals were obtained from the *Appropriation Accounts.* For the non-wages and salaries items, there are a variety of categories. By far the largest item is the centrally procured equipment (Procurement Executive). There is also the locally purchased items at the various defence bases; and the expenditure associated with the accommodation of the forces and civil servants. These were allocated to the regions thus. The regional distribution of defence contracts was obtained directly from the Procurement Executive. The locally purchased items were allocated on the basis of the regional distribution of forces. New furniture and works for accommodation were allocated according to the regional distribution of personnel. The control totals were obtained from the *Appropriation Accounts* . See Short (1981b) for more detail on defence expenditure.

Overseas services. Headquarter expenditure was attributed to the South-East. The remainder was allocated to overseas.

Social security. The wages and salaries of headquarter staff by region, were obtained from DHSS. The associated administration costs were allocated in proportion to wages and salaries and attributed directly to the region concerned.

Prisons. The prison population in each region (aggregating the prisons in each region) was used as a proxy to allocate prison expenditure. It was assumed that the non-wages element would be procured locally.

Other public services and common services. The sub-programmes in these two programmes were examined as to regional incidence. (Parliament, government actuary, Paymaster General.) The remainder were allocated by regional GDP.

Debt interest. Debt interest paid to the holders of debt in each region is relevant in the context of this section. After deducting payments to abroad (estimated as one-seventh of total debt payments), the regional distribution of net investment income was used as proxy for regional apportionment.

Capital expenditure

Prisons. The prison population in each region was used as a proxy.

Defence, common services and other public services. The regional distribution of gross domestic capital formation in defence and other general administration was used to allocate capital expenditure (mainly construction) in these programmes.

Local authorities

Statistics on local authority expenditure are presented in two ways reflecting the adopted methodology. The first is concerned with the regionally relevant expenditures of local authorities in each region on the programmes which are supplied by the local authorities and consumed by the residents of each region. The second is concerned with the region where the local authorities purchase the goods and services which are consumed in the programmes they supply. These are the expenditures relating to what a region produces for its own local authorities and for other region's local authorities in the first instance.

Data on local authority expenditure and income in the regions are available from the same inputs which go to produce the national figures. This is, for the English regions and Wales, the statutory returns made for the Department of the Environment and Welsh Office by each of the local authorities which are published for the nation in Local Government Financial Statistics (LGFS). For Scotland, similar returns are made to the Scottish Office and are published as Local Financial Returns (Scotland).

Although these data are available on an annual basis, there was a hiatus resulting from the local government reorganisation of April 1974. Figures for 1974–75 for the English regions were not available from the normal source. Apart from that year, however, the quality of information on local authority operations in the region matches that of the national data and this can be expected of the future. However, the local authority reorganisation in Scotland has resulted in a considerable delay in the production of Local Financial Returns (Scotland) and at present only the 1974–75 edition is published.This has necessitated estimation of local authority expenditures for Scotland using the identifiable public expenditure published in *Abstract of Scottish Statistics* and the estimates of central government and public corporation expenditure.

Regionally relevant expenditure. Revenue account. The data presented here are classified by the PESC programme headings. However, the detail provided in Local Government Financial Statistics is available also at the regional level.

As mentioned, the figures for 1974–75 were not produced in the normal manner for the English regions. An alternative source of information was adopted to obtain these data produced here. The Chartered Institute of Public Finance and Accountancy (CIPFA) produces the returns of rates which gives details of spending in each local authority of the country. CIPFA were also faced with some authorities not producing figures for 1974–75; however it was possible to generate estimates for those non-responding authorities based on their 1975–76/1977–78 returns using the average growth rates of similar authorities, shire county (district), metropolitan county (district). Each region's authorities were aggregated across the region to form the regional total.

For 1975–76 to 1977–78 the LGFS figures were used to produce the data in the tables. These figures are in line with the national accounts definition of local authority spending, i.e. fees and charges form part of personal sector spending and are netted off total expenditure in each services. Debt repayments is considered in total and is also not analysed by individual service.

Capital account. No data are available for 1974–75 for the English regions because of the problems involved with reorganisations. The solution adopted for the revenue account was not possible because CIPFA does not produce figures on the capital account. While the Society of County Treasurers produces figures for each shire county's capital expenditure, the omissions of districts' capital spending means that the source cannot be used. The pragmatic solution is to use the average capital spending by programme in the 1975–76 to 1977–78 period in each region to allocate the totals for 1974–75. The LGFS source was adopted for this period and the figures are in line with the National Accounts conventions; sales and repayments are netted off total capital expenditure to form local authority capital expenditure.

Local authority expenditure by economic category. The presentation of local authority expenditure by function shows the amounts spent by the local authorities in the regions on services: however this does not give the final destination of the expenditure. To provide the services, local authorities may have to import goods and services from outside their own particular area, or buy goods produced in the local authority's own locality.

What is of concern in this section is firstly, the amount produced and consumed in the region itself, and secondly, each region's exports of goods and services to be consumed by local authorities elsewhere. Two sets of figures, the amount consumed in a region (in relation to local authorities, the value of services shown in the previous section) and the amount produced and consumed in each region in relation to these services will provide the amount for imports of goods and services to be consumed as local authority services. The difference between total expenditure in a region resulting from all local authorities and the expenditure of providing services by each region's local authorities will show whether a particular region is a net importer or exporter of goods for local authorities services.

In attempting to assess the amounts which are imported by local authorities to provide their various services, it is necessary first of all to examine the methodology involved. What is being examined is the analysis of expenditure in the purchase of goods and services which are being consumed as local authority services; these are the labour, the equipment, etc. which contribute to the service, transfer payments to residents etc.

One problem arises in relation to the measurement of the expenditures in this section. Because of public expenditure is measured net of fees and charges and is only concerned with the tax on rate-payers' contributions on the current account, or borrowing grants on the capital account, it is impossible to say if the total wages and salaries have been met from rates or government grants rather than fees and charges. Whereas it is possible to measure the exchequer contribution to spending in a service in a particular region, it is still not possible to analyse the public spending part in terms of wages and salaries, etc., exactly. It is only possible to analyse the gross total in terms of wages and salaries, etc.

A second problem arises in that it is not possible to obtain the breakdown of local authority expenditure into its component economic categories for the English regions. However the national figures can be used as it is unlikely that a region will differ greatly from the national ratio. Current and capital expenditure will be examined separately.

Local authority current expenditure. For the country as a whole, the percentage breakdown of regionally relevant expenditure is as follows:

	% of total		
	Expenditure on goods and services	Grants to persons	Subsidies
1974–75	91.32	4.39	4.29
1975–76	90.71	4.68	4.61
1976–77	90.71	5.29	4.0
1977–78	89.06	10.4	

Wages and salaries account for roughly 82 percent of expenditure on on the four years. This assumes that fees and charges have been netted off total gross expenditures to obtain net expenditures and have financed non-wages and salaries items. Assuming national percentages, around 91 per cent of current expenditure by local authorities is on wages and salaries, grants to persons and subsidies. These are further assumed to accrue in the region in which they have been made in the programme sense. The remaining 10 per cent or so cannot be assumed to accrue to the region which has consumed the services as they may have been imported.

Debt interest has not been included in the percentages given above. The payment of debt interest in the case of local authorities is for the most part to the Public Works Loans Board, and in terms of the overall regional model, a flow to a supra-regional sector.

Local authority capital expenditure. A similar problem as to the treatment of income in the current account arises in the capital account. The income from sales of assets is netted off gross expenditures. However, these sales are classified according to the broad economic categories and can be related to the item.

Although the source of data on local authority capital expenditure permit a breakdown by economic category, the national percentages are used here for illustration.

	Percentage distribution			
	Purchase of land and buildings, new dwellings and new construction	Vehicles	Plant and machinery	Capital grants and net lending
1974–75	76.4	1.9	3.4	18.7
1975–76	80.5	2.7	3.8	13.0
1976–77	88.0	3.5	3.9	4.6
1977–78		96.5		3.5

The purchase of land, much of new construction of new dwellings and other construction are likely to be made in the region where the service is being provided. Similarly with capital grants and net lending. Local authorities do not advance money either in the form of grants or lending outside of their boundary. However money spent on vehicles, plant and machinery cannot be assumed to accrue to the region in which the purchaser is located as local authorities do not necessarily have to purchase in their own region or may not find suppliers in their own region. Similarly a local authority may not necessarily purchase the materials it uses in the building of houses or roads, etc. in its own locality. It would appear that the main direct leakage from a region is in their types of goods and not in the wages and salaries of those engaged in capital projects and capital transfers.

In order to establish these patterns of spending by geographical area, an analysis of four local authorities payments was carried out. The payment schedule of cheques categorised by value and address of recipient of four local authorities: a metropolitan district and a shire county in the Northern region; and a metropolitan district and metropolitan county in the West Midlands were examined for a representative month of the year (May 1978).

The percentage of breakdown of payments by region is as follows:

	N	YH	EM	EA	SE	SW	WM	NW	W	S	NI	O'seas
Northern county	72.01	6.60	2.72	0.88	10.10	0.31	3.51	3.17	0.07	0.62	..	..
Northern met. district	79.93	5.20	0.52	0.39	9.23	1.02	1.35	1.90	0.03	0.41	..	0.01
West Mids. counties	1.09	1.59	0.62	0.03	6.95	0.49	86.53	2.09	0.21	0.18	..	0.15
West Mids. met. district	0.01	0.71	0.90	0.06	3.94	0.12	92.04	0.97	0.03	0.26	0.79	..

..: negligible

This shows that the leakage from the region due to direct purchases outside of the region is considerably smaller than the retained spending. This is as expected. Much of the purchases are of day to day items: food for school meals, fuel for heating, etc. Note, however, that this does not say anything about the origin of manufacture of the goods bought. A local authority is likely to buy cars from a local car dealer rather than purchase directly from the manufacturer. These subsequent effects are beyond this analysis.

There is also a second important factor to be considered in relation to income generation in this context. Although the four regions in which the local authorities are situated do not receive 100 per cent of their local authorities spending, they do receive spending from other regions' local authorities. It is the total effect of local authorities spend-in a region which is of interest.

The limited figures above suggest that regions such as the South-East, West Midlands, North-West and Yorkshire and Humberside are likely to receive more from other regions than the others. This could be greater than the leakages from their own local authorities. However, it would be necessary to carry out this exercise for each region to verify this.

Given the relative size of the figures to other expenditures, such as on wages and salaries, it would not alter the total picture unduly if the assumption were made that each region obtained from other regions an amount roughly equivalent to the leakage from its own local authorities. The net effect would be zero, and the total spending on goods and services, plant, machinery and vehicles, etc., by the local authorities in each region, would provide a fair approximation to the spending generated in a region as a result of total local authority spending in the nation as a whole.

As the other classes of expenditure, wages and salaries, grants, subsidies, construction, etc. were assumed to be accruing directly to the region in which the local authority was situated without any leakage, total spending by each region's local authorities is therefore assumed to represent the contribution to the regions' first round income as a result of local authorities expenditure.

Public corporations

The public corporations covered here are the new towns, regional water authorities, housing corporation, Scottish Special Housing Corporation, Covent Garden Market Authority and the Public Trust Ports.

Statistics on the capital expenditure of these various organisations have been provided by the organisations themselves, the government departments under which their expenditure comes, or from published sources. While the Regional Water Authorities are organised on a regional basis, their areal coverage does not coincide with the standard planning regions. Each of the authorities was approached for details of their capital spending so that capital spending by standard planning region could be computed by 'shifting' parts of water authorities together. Details of spending by the new towns in England were obtained from the Department of the Environment, while figures for the Scottish and Welsh new towns were obtained from the annual reports. Details of expenditure by the Scottish Special Housing Association and the Covent Garden Market Authority were taken from the public expenditure analysis from PESC. Information on the Public Trust Ports was obtained from the Department of Transport. No information was available on the regional distribution of the Housing Corporations spending and the national total was allocated by using a proxy. This proxy was based on the volume of new approvals in each of the Housing Corporations regions, adjusted to the standard planning regions where necessary using population.

The financing of this expenditure by these public corporations is in the main by loans from the Public Works Loan Board and closely corresponds to the capital expenditure. Details of annual loans can be found in the *Annual Accounts* of the Public Works Loan Board.

With respect to the analysis of the economic categories of public expenditure, the amounts entering each region's economy in the first round is unlikely to differ greatly from the totals shown here as the majority of these expenditures are on construction and are likely to adopt a similar pattern to the local authority expenditure.

Table 22 *Central government: regionally relevant current expenditure—1974–75: (£m) (current prices)*

	North	*Yorks Humbs.*	*East Mids.*	*East Anglia*	*South-East*	*South-West*	*West Mids.*	*North-West*	*Wales*	*Scot.*	*Nrth. Ire'd.*	*UK*
Agriculture, fisheries and forestry	73.2	88.7	72.7	41.3	295.1	104.0	97.1	107.2	88.7	170.9	69.9	1208.8
Trade, industry and employment	151.2	129.1	142.4	47.9	386.8	133.6	118.1	181.9	102.6	196.5	74.0	1664.1
Roads and transport	21.5	34.7	20.6	13.9	238.9	26.9	25.7	40.1	21.5	60.2	27.7	531.7
Housing	13.2	8.3	8.7	2.9	28.8	8.5	10.9	12.3	1.6	17.5	38.2	150.9
Other environmental services	2.6	6.6	3.3	1.6	31.3	4.6	5.2	5.3	0.3	1.6	16.5	78.9
Law, order and protective services	7.3	13.1	8.2	3.4	40.2	8.3	10.9	16.7	6.1	12.2	66.4	192.8
Education, libraries, science and arts	23.0	49.6	23.9	27.8	254.5	32.2	37.8	67.0	31.5	122.3	88.3	757.9
Health and personal social services	202.7	308.8	207.8	108.8	1309.4	287.0	311.3	444.2	200.2	417.0	135.4	3932.6
Social security	432.2	627.5	427.7	200.2	1960.6	545.2	572.3	890.0	366.9	670.5	214.3	6907.4
Total	926.9	1266.4	915.3	447.8	4545.6	1150.3	1189.3	1764.7	819.4	1668.7	730.7	15425.1

Subsidies to local authorities are included under local authority expenditure (except for Northern Ireland).

Table 23 *Central government: regionally relevant capital expenditure–1974–75: (£m) (current prices)*

	North	*Yorks Humbs.*	*East Mids.*	*East Anglia*	*South-East*	*South-West*	*West Mids.*	*North-West*	*Wales*	*Scot.*	*Nrth. Ire'd.*	*UK*
Agriculture, fisheries and forestry	8.2	12.2	6.4	7.5	12.2	13.7	6.4	6.2	12.4	23.2	17.2	125.6
Trade, industry and employment	146.0	73.1	54.9	18.1	199.5	60.8	79.9	139.9	84.8	165.8	112.5	1135.3
Roads and transport	16.4	23.4	7.6	15.4	87.0	39.1	17.1	36.8	19.5	31.1	23.0	316.4
Housing	..	..	..	..	..	..	..	..	..	..	0.6	0.6
Other environmental services	0.4	0.7	0.4	0.3	3.2	0.5	0.7	0.8	..	0.2	15.9	23.1
Law, order and protective services	1.0	1.7	1.1	0.4	5.2	1.1	1.4	1.9	0.7	2.3	2.5	19.3
Education, libraries, science and arts	6.0	11.5	9.4	5.3	56.8	7.1	7.3	16.6	6.1	21.0	11.4	158.5
Health and personal social services	16.6	27.1	25.7	11.5	104.8	23.1	28.6	35.9	15.8	32.8	11.2	333.1
Social security												
Total	194.6	149.7	105.5	58.5	468.7	145.4	141.4	238.1	139.3	276.4	194.3	2111.9

.. negligible

Table 24 *Local authority regionally relevant current expenditure—1974–75: (£m) (current prices)*

	North	Yorks Humbs.	East Mids.	East Anglia	South-East	South-West	West Mids.	North-West	Wales	Scot.	Nrth. Ire'd.	UK
Agriculture, forestry and fishing[1]												
Trade, industry and employment[2]									1.3	..	0.1	1.4
Roads and transport	48.3	67.5	44.4	20.9	214.7	60.0	65.3	78.0	36.7	59.3	-0.1	695.0
Housing[3]	54.7	64.2	36.3	15.9	369.6	34.2	67.2	90.6	41.3	155.0		929.0
Other environmental services	84.3	107.6	71.6	32.8	398.7	92.8	108.8	121.5	40.5	105.4	15.2	179.2
Law, order and protective services	44.8	59.8	43.9	20.0	301.4	51.5	61.5	74.2	33.9	77.8	36.0	804.8
Education, libraries, science and arts	243.2	345.2	259.9	118.3	1285.1	272.4	371.5	380.2	226.5	430.5	50.2	3983.0
Health and person social services	35.7	48.9	33.9	14.6	221.2	36.2	45.8	55.5	27.9	66.8		586.5
Social security												
Total	511.0	693.2	490.0	222.5	2790.7	547.1	720.1	800.0	408.1	894.8	101.4	8178.9

1, 2: Included in other environmental services.
3 Includes central government housing subsidies to local authorities.

Table 25

Local authority: regionally relevant capital expenditure—1974–75: (£m) (current prices)

	North	*Yorks Humbs.*	*East Mids.*	*East Anglia*	*South-East*	*South-West*	*West Mids.*	*North-West*	*Wales*	*Scot.*	*Nrth. Ire'd.*	*UK*
Agriculture, fishing and forestry[1]											0.2	0.2
Trade, industry and employment	0.1	..	..	..	0.2	0.1	..	0.1	0.1	..	1.1	1.7
Roads and transport	57.7	35.1	20.5	10.7	160.4	26.4	55.7	46.0	24.5	51.5		488.5
Housing	166.1	187.3	189.6	73.2	1103.7	119.4	222.7	272.7	132.6	232.9	1.6	2701.8
Other environmental services	30.7	32.3	23.1	9.2	170.6	24.7	42.8	42.9	25.0	101.2	3.6	506.1
Law, order and protective services	1.5	4.9	3.8	3.3	25.6	2.7	3.7	5.7	2.5	6.7	3.4	63.8
Education, libraries, science and arts	29.9	51.4	40.9	18.2	158.1	32.6	47.3	55.6	24.5	65.0	17.7	541.2
Health and personal social services	6.5	8.9	5.0	1.9	27.5	3.2	7.1	8.4	3.7	7.4		79.6
Social security												
Total	292.5	319.9	282.9	116.5	1646.1	209.1	379.3	431.4	212.9	464.7	27.6	4382.9

1: Included in other environmental services.

Table 26

Public corporations regionally relevant capital expenditure—1974—75 (£m) (current prices)

	North	Yorks Humbs.	East Mids.	East Anglia	South-East	South-West	West Mids.	North-West	Wales	Scot.	Nrth. Ire'd.	UK
Agriculture, forestry and fishing					-0.2							-0.2
Trade, industry and employment												
Roads and transport	3.1		1.3	2.2	7.5		2.5	4.6	0.4	22.8		44.4
Housing	16.8	9.1	21.2	17.7	88.2	9.8	33.1	50.9	10.8	51.8	46.2	355.5
Other environmental services	33.4	42.0	47.7	32.0	109.7	47.1	58.1	53.4	41.0	6.3		470.7
Law, order and protective services												
Education, libraries, science and arts												
Health and personal social services												
Social security												
Total	53.3	51.1	70.1	51.9	205.2	56.9	93.7	108.9	52.2	80.9	46.2	870.4

Table 27

Total public expenditure 'in' the regions of the UK—1974—75 (£m) (current prices)

	North	Yorks Humbs.	East Mids.	East Anglia	South-East	South-West	West Mids.	North-West	Wales	Scot.	Nrth. Ire'd.	UK
Current economic goods and services	861.4	1228.3	1116.1	483.1	5793.9	1545.7	1315.8	1505.6	784.6	1492.5	525.0	16652.0
Current transfers	775.2	1034.8	713.0	357.7	3624.3	872.6	954.8	1413.2	649.6	1379.6	445.1	12219.9
Gross domestic fixed capital formation	331.2	366.0	333.6	173.5	1774.8	296.7	443.2	537.2	270.4	552.6	136.4	5215.6
Capital transfers	217.1	165.1	133.6	56.6	605.2	129.4	180.5	248.8	140.6	284.6	139.2	2300.7
Total	2184.9	2794.2	2296.3	1070.9	11798.2	2844.4	2894.3	3704.8	1845.2	3709.3	1245.7	36388.2

Table 28 *Central government: regionally relevant current expenditure—1975—76: (£m) (current prices)*

	North	*Yorks Humbs.*	*East Mids.*	*East Anglia*	*South-East*	*South-West*	*West Mids.*	*North-West*	*Wales*	*Scot.*	*Nrth. Ire'd.*	*UK*
Agriculture, forestry and fisheries	90.7	119.3	93.2	52.1	360.6	129.0	124.1	140.5	104.4	193.6	75.4	1482.9
Trade, industry and employment	152.0	94.0	87.9	23.0	270.6	92.2	108.8	192.0	106.6	232.9	89.3	1449.3
Roads and transport	31.1	48.1	34.3	17.4	302.2	37.3	42.4	55.8	28.9	67.2	32.1	696.8
Housing[1]	14.3	11.9	12.8	3.7	38.7	13.2	14.4	16.9	2.3	23.6	40.0	191.8
Other environmental services	3.8	9.7	4.5	2.3	41.3	6.3	7.1	7.1	1.1	1.8	21.3	106.3
Law, order and protective services	10.1	18.2	11.7	4.7	60.3	11.6	15.3	23.1	6.7	15.8	88.2	265.7
Education, libraries, sciences and arts	28.2	61.4	31.0	34.6	322.6	40.8	43.7	83.5	40.8	153.6	117.4	957.6
Health and personal social services	262.3	399.6	274.1	142.3	1689.2	379.1	409.1	571.2	256.3	552.0	190.8	5126.0
Social security	578.6	846.1	586.8	270.1	2673.9	750.9	800.8	1211.2	528.2	912.1	283.5	9442.2
Total	1171.1	1608.3	1136.3	550.2	5759.4	1460.4	1565.7	2301.3	1075.3	2152.6	938.0	19718.6

1: Subsidies to local authorities are included under local authority expenditure (except for Northern Ireland).

Table 29

Central government: regionally relevant capital expenditure–1975–76: (£m) (current prices)

	North	*Yorks Humbs.*	*East Mids.*	*East Anglia*	*South-East*	*South-West*	*West Mids.*	*North-West*	*Wales*	*Scot.*	*Nrth. Ire'd.*	*UK*
Agriculture, fisheries and forestry	8.5	12.5	5.0	6.1	9.3	10.0	4.8	5.1	9.3	37.8	15.9	124.3
Trade, industry and employment	198.3	87.9	77.6	19.7	296.1	94.3	193.9	217.6	91.9	246.6	147.7	1671.6
Roads and transport	33.0	29.7	11.7	13.0	114.6	63.8	31.1	39.7	44.0	42.7	33.0	456.3
Housing	7.0	10.2	11.5	5.1	47.8	11.3	17.9	19.2	5.5	1.2	0.5	137.2
Other environmental services	0.4	0.7	0.6	0.2	3.7	0.7	0.9	1.1	0.2	0.2	25.4	34.1
Law, order and protective services	1.0	1.9	1.3	0.5	5.8	1.2	1.6	2.1	1.0	1.0	9.3	26.7
Education, libraries, science and arts	5.2	14.5	11.0	6.4	67.9	6.1	9.4	19.8	6.8	24.8	15.7	187.6
Health and personal social services	19.3	37.6	34.6	14.4	127.4	24.2	33.6	47.6	23.5	42.7	15.6	420.5
Social security												
Total	272.7	195.0	153.3	65.4	672.6	211.6	293.2	352.2	182.2	397.0	263.1	3058.3

Table 30 *Local authority regionally relevant current expenditure—1975—76: (£m) (current prices)*

	North	Yorks Humbs.	East Mids.	East Anglia	South-East	South-West	West Mids.	North-West	Wales	Scot.	Nrth. Ire'd.	UK
Agriculture, forestry and fishing[1]												
Trade, industry and employment	1.8	3.3	1.6	2.3	8.9	2.3	2.9	3.5	2.5	1		29.1
Roads and transport	48.4	70.4	44.2	20.4	317.3	53.1	76.5	112.6	49.1	99.7	-0.1	891.6
Housing[2]	75.3	81.5	51.3	25.3	488.9	44.6	85.1	126.3	51.8	188.8		1218.9
Other environmental services	55.8	87.7	57.3	25.9	365.7	52.3	88.9	144.3	69.8	184.2	18.9	1150.8
Law, order and protective services	64.1	103.6	66.1	29.1	491.6	77.3	95.4	142.0	53.8	105.9	48.9	1277.8
Education, libraries, sciences and arts	280.3	500.4	366.5	154.6	1790.0	379.6	524.9	682.4	295.8	561.9	78.7	5615.1
Health and personal social services	48.8	72.2	50.0	19.9	308.4	52.4	65.2	108.2	40.5	103.4		869.0
Social security												
Total	574.5	919.1	637.0	277.5	3770.8	661.6	938.9	1319.3	563.3	1243.9	146.4	11052.3
Debt interest	79.3	96.8	69.1	34.4	527.7	87.2	112.6	149.2	74.0			

1: Included in other environmental services

2: Includes central government housing subsidies to local authorities.

Table 31 — *Local authorities regionally relevant capital expenditure—1975–76: (£m) (current prices)*

	North	*Yorks Humbs.*	*East Mids.*	*East Anglia*	*South-East*	*South-West*	*West Mids.*	*North-West*	*Wales*	*Scot.*	*Nrth. Ire'd.*	*UK*
Agriculture, forestry and fishing[1]											0.1	0.1
Trade, industry and employment	0.3	0.1	..	..	0.2	..	0.1	..	0.1	..	1.3	2.1
Roads and transport	46.5	35.4	21.8	10.6	146.8	33.4	34.1	46.9	24.1	74.7	0.1	474.4
Housing	157.2	154.0	189.2	83.3	1046.9	99.6	190.4	268.0	121.3	246.0	1.4	2557.3
Other environmental services	27.7	30.7	26.6	11.7	173.8	24.0	57.2	43.9	30.8	141.0	5.3	572.7
Law, order and protective services	2.0	4.4	3.6	3.7	28.4	4.5	5.2	4.5	4.0	11.6	4.1	76.0
Education, libraries, science and arts	30.1	51.8	41.2	18.3	159.4	32.9	47.7	56.0	28.8	60.9	21.2	548.3
Health and personal social services	6.4	9.2	5.6	2.3	29.2	3.3	8.1	8.8	4.6	9.2		86.7
Social security												
Total	270.2	285.6	288.0	129.9	1584.7	197.7	342.8	428.1	213.7	543.4	33.5	4317.6

1: Included in other environmental services.

..: Less than 0.1.

Table 32 *Public corporations: regionally relevant capital expenditure—1975–76: (£m) (current prices)*

	North	*Yorks Humbs.*	*East Mids.*	*East Anglia*	*South-East*	*South-West*	*West Mids.*	*North-West*	*Wales*	*Scot.*	*Nrth. Ire'd.*	*UK*
Agriculture, forestry and fishing					5.2							5.2
Trade, industry and employment												
Roads and transport	4.6		1.6	4.7	10.5		3.3	5.9	0.8	22.1	0.1	53.6
Housing	18.2	7.0	29.0	19.4	85.4	7.8	41.8	45.9	12.3	81.4	75.4	423.6
Other environmental services	48.7	51.2	41.5	53.0	151.7	54.3	60.2	70.0	43.9	3.6	0.2	578.3
Law, order and protective services												
Education, libraries, science and arts												
Health and personal social services												
Social security												
Total	71.5	58.2	72.1	77.1	252.8	62.1	105.3	121.8	57.0	107.1	75.7	1060.7

Table 33 *Total public expenditure 'in' the regions of the UK–1975–76: (£m) (current prices)*

	North	*Yorks Humbs.*	*East Mids.*	*East Anglia*	*South-East*	*South-West*	*West Mids.*	*North-West*	*Wales*	*Scot.*	*Nrth. Ire'd.*	*UK*
Current economic goods and services	1071.6	1612.7	1321.7	625.2	7660.9	1990.4	1679.3	2335.3	1003.1	2127.9	692.8	22120.9
Current transfer	973.8	1311.8	919.5	437.2	4492.5	1107.8	1227.3	1770.1	828.0	1627.1	546.4	15241.6
Gross domestic fixed capital formation	365.0	385.5	373.2	220.7	1953.2	341.8	474.8	596.1	304.5	699.8	208.7	5959.3
Capital transfers	259.3	166.2	149.3	57.1	650.6	153.2	280.6	327.0	138.3	368.0	183.3	2732.9
Total	2669.7	3476.2	2763.7	1340.2	14757.2	3593.2	3662.0	5028.6	2309.9	4822.8	1631.2	46054.7

Table 34 *Central government: regionally relevant current expenditure–1976–77 (£m) (current prices)*

	North	*Yorks Humbs.*	*East Mids.*	*East Anglia*	*South-East*	*South-West*	*West Mids.*	*North-West*	*Wales*	*Scot.*	*Nrth. Ire'd.*	*UK*
Agriculture, fishing and forestry	57.9	71.8	53.6	34.6	223.8	71.7	72.1	84.1	66.3	169.1	71.1	976.1
Trade, industry and employment	185.6	100.5	94.5	28.5	329.3	109.1	94.1	200.6	110.1	325.4	86.1	1663.8
Roads and transport	25.8	40.7	28.7	16.5	278.6	32.0	38.8	66.8	26.2	53.6	37.0	664.7
Housing	25.9	15.8	24.2	10.5	76.2	17.6	29.9	35.0	6.1	37.4	66.3	344.9
Other environmental services	3.8	11.2	4.7	2.6	56.0	7.3	7.5	10.3	1.9	2.9	24.4	132.6
Law, order and protective services	10.9	19.7	12.7	5.1	65.3	12.6	16.6	25.0	7.3	16.5	94.5	286.2
Education, libraries, science and arts	34.0	73.0	37.5	44.5	417.6	49.8	55.9	101.3	51.6	182.6	132.9	1180.7
Health and personal social services	301.2	468.2	323.3	167.9	1939.9	431.0	474.0	662.5	287.5	622.9	222.1	5900.5
Social security	687.4	1006.9	692.4	321.3	3141.8	885.3	960.5	1435.6	646.3	1109.3	340.8	11227.6
Total	1332.5	1807.8	1271.6	631.5	6528.5	1616.4	1749.4	2621.2	1203.3	2519.7	1075.2	22357.1

Table 35

Central government: regionally relevant capital expenditure: 1976–77 (£m) (current prices)

	North	*Yorks Humbs.*	*East Mids.*	*East Anglia*	*South-East*	*South-West*	*West Mids.*	*North-West*	*Wales*	*Scot.*	*Nrth. Ire'd.*	*UK*
Agriculture, fishing and forestry	6.8	7.0	4.0	4.6	7.4	8.0	4.1	3.6	7.3	36.5	13.2	102.5
Trade, industry and employment	214.9	82.7	70.7	22.6	231.0	59.8	73.8	136.5	97.4	207.1	134.3	1330.8
Roads and transport	27.8	27.5	22.4	18.9	114.6	54.2	28.2	47.5	59.9	47.3	35.9	484.2
Housing	16.4	19.7	24.1	20.2	189.5	14.9	40.2	54.0	9.5	10.3	0.7	399.5
Other environmental services	0.4	0.7	0.5	0.3	5.7	0.6	0.8	1.0	0.2	0.4	23.4	34.0
Law, order and protective services	1.2	2.3	1.6	0.6	7.1	5.1	2.0	2.6	1.2	1.0	9.6	34.3
Education, libraries, science and arts	8.0	16.3	10.5	3.5	44.3	7.5	8.7	20.9	6.7	25.2	13.5	165.1
Health and personal social services	25.0	26.7	42.1	12.8	113.3	35.8	28.1	50.6	18.4	37.0	17.9	407.7
Social security	..	..	..	..	..	..	..	..	..	..	0.1	0.1
Total	300.5	182.9	175.9	83.5	712.9	185.9	185.9	316.7	200.6	364.8	248.6	2958.2

.. : Negligible

Table 36

Local authority regionally relevant current expenditure—1976–77 (£m) (current prices)

	North	Yorks Humbs.	East Mids.	East Anglia	South-East	South-West	West Mids.	North-West	Wales	Scot.	Nrth Ire'd.	UK
Agriculture, forestry and fishing[1]											-0.1	-0.1
Trade, industry and employment	2.3	4.0	2.0	0.9	10.8	2.7	3.4	4.2	2.5	1	0.2	33.0
Roads and transport	59.8	86.4	51.9	20.3	310.2	58.4	80.4	125.3	56.7	103.7	-0.1	953.0
Housing[2]	84.9	90.8	65.3	29.5	644.0	54.0	101.5	138.5	62.4	235.6		1506.5
Other environmental services	62.4	78.7	56.7	26.6	400.6	61.7	87.6	147.2	78.7	207.0	21.6	1228.8
Law, order and protective services	76.4	113.2	77.7	35.2	501.3	90.4	111.7	160.4	62.7	121.9	61.0	1411.9
Education, libraries, science and arts	375.3	599.3	418.1	179.6	2014.5	429.5	591.7	770.9	335.2	610.0	91.4	6385.5
Health and personal social services	57.5	85.1	58.3	23.7	369.0	60.5	75.5	126.7	46.8	133.9		1037.0
Social security												
Total	718.6	1057.5	730.0	315.8	4250.4	757.2	1051.8	1473.2	645.0	1412.1	174.0	12585.6
Debt interest	90.9	119.2	83.8	41.3	625.9	104.9	132.0	177.7	84.4			

1 Included in other environmental services

2 Includes central government housing subsidies to local authorities

Table 37 *Local authorities regionally relevant capital expenditure 1976–77 (£m) (current prices)*

	North	*Yorks Humbs.*	*East Mids.*	*East Anglia*	*South-East*	*South-West*	*West Mids.*	*North-West*	*Wales*	*Scot.*	*Nrth. Ire'd.*	*UK*
Agriculture, forestry and fishing[1]											0.1	0.1
Trade, industry and employment	0.2	0.1	0.1	..	0.3	0.2	0.2	..	..	..	1.0	2.1
Roads and transport	46.3	30.6	20.3	10.4	141.6	27.5	38.4	43.8	23.7	84.5	0.2	467.3
Housing	149.8	176.0	172.8	61.8	950.7	110.2	208.8	236.7	120.4	243.5	1.4	2432.1
Other environmental services	29.8	32.6	23.1	9.3	167.2	22.9	38.9	39.2	27.9	129.0	5.1	525.0
Law, order and protective services	1.9	5.7	4.0	3.5	26.2	2.2	3.4	8.0	2.5	10.9	5.6	73.9
Education, libraries, science and arts	26.7	45.6	36.8	14.5	150.8	30.3	42.8	55.1	26.2	80.0	24.2	533.0
Health and personal social services	5.1	8.6	3.8	1.5	24.2	2.9	6.2	7.0	4.8	13.0		77.1
Social security												
Total	259.8	299.2	260.9	101.0	1461.0	196.2	338.7	389.8	205.5	560.9	37.6	4110.6

1 : Included in other environmental services

.. : Negligible

Table 38 *Public corporations: regionally relevant capital expenditure—1976–77 (£m) (current prices)*

	North	Yorks Humbs.	East Mids.	East Anglia	South-East	South-West	West Mids.	North-West	Wales	Scot.	Nrth. Ire'd.	UK
Agriculture, forestry and fishing					4.3							4.3
Trade, industry and employment												
Roads and transport	6.2		1.1	4.6	17.0	0.3	6.7	10.6	1.0	18.3		65.8
Housing	14.5	2.3	19.8	21.3	88.7	1.7	34.2	41.3	7.2	62.2	107.4	400.6
Other environmental services	68.1	49.5	41.8	36.9	162.5	32.1	58.7	85.9	32.3	11.6	0.2	579.6
Law, order and protective services												
Education, libraries, science and arts												
Health and personal social services												
Social security												
Total	88.8	51.8	62.7	62.8	272.5	34.1	99.6	137.8	40.5	92.1	107.6	1050.3

Table 39 *Total public expenditure 'in' the regions of the UK—1976–77 (£m) (current prices)*

	North	Yorks Humbs.	East Mids.	East Anglia	South-East	South-West	West Mids.	North-West	Wales	Scot.	Nrth. Ire'd.	UK
Current economic goods and services	1454.0	1868.5	1352.6	729.5	8881.1	2020.9	1950.1	2885.1	1164.8	2445.0	788.3	25539.9
Current transfers	1105.2	1462.3	1018.7	507.9	5350.1	1285.1	1403.2	2085.3	947.5	2061.9	643.0	17870.2
Gross domestic fixed capital formation	407.7	409.8	382.9	195.9	1992.9	333.2	493.9	628.0	324.9	742.3	240.9	6152.4
Capital transfers	248.5	139.4	123.6	57.4	550.4	98.8	146.1	236.7	131.1	299.3	166.1	2197.4
Total	3215.4	3880.0	2877.8	1490.7	16774.5	3738.0	3993.3	5835.1	2568.3	5548.5	1838.3	52759.9

Table 40 *Central government: regionally relevant current expenditure–1977–78 (£m) (current prices)*

	North	*Yorks Humbs.*	*East Mids.*	*East Anglia*	*South-East*	*South-West*	*West Mids.*	*North-West*	*Wales*	*Scot.*	*Nrth. Ire'd.*	*UK*
Agriculture, fishing and forestry	55.7	62.7	49.0	34.7	188.6	71.5	64.0	71.2	65.9	184.6	97.3	945.2
Trade, industry and employment	140.1	141.5	100.2	25.0	321.9	97.8	112.2	226.8	113.9	223.3	96.0	1598.7
Roads and transport	29.5	43.9	31.7	17.5	320.0	35.6	42.6	71.2	29.7	58.6	44.7	725.0
Housing	28.5	17.0	27.8	12.3	88.9	19.0	34.4	41.0	6.3	50.7	54.8	380.7
Other environmental services	4.1	12.1	5.2	2.9	60.8	8.0	8.3	11.9	2.3	3.6	27.2	146.4
Law, order and protective services	12.1	21.8	14.1	5.6	72.3	14.0	18.4	27.7	8.1	20.4	87.4	301.9
Education, libraries, science and arts	30.1	64.9	34.0	40.9	407.0	44.2	49.4	92.5	50.7	188.1	141.9	1143.7
Health and personal social services	338.7	525.6	363.2	190.9	2156.4	482.7	531.9	748.9	325.6	705.4	251.5	6620.8
Social security	823.5	1205.2	830.8	383.8	3771.2	1064.9	1152.5	1721.3	774.7	1325.4	405.7	13459.0
Total	1462.3	2094.7	1456.0	713.6	7387.1	1837.7	2013.7	3012.5	1377.2	2706.1	1206.5	25321.4

Table 41 *Central government: regionally relevant capital expenditure–1977–78 (£m) (current prices)*

	North	*Yorks Humbs.*	*East Mids.*	*East Anglia*	*South-East*	*South-West*	*West Mids.*	*North-West*	*Wales*	*Scot.*	*Nrth. Ire'd.*	*UK*
Agriculture, fishing and forestry	8.8	8.4	5.6	5.9	10.5	11.0	5.6	4.8	10.2	45.4	14.7	130.9
Trade, industry and employment	118.7	16.6	- 6.2	- 4.7	- 35.7	- 11.1	38.5	64.3	87.0	133.6	99.3	560.3
Roads and transport	11.3	49.0	12.9	27.7	77.8	32.7	13.3	33.0	46.4	63.4	40.9	408.4
Housing	34.5	46.3	23.6	16.1	178.2	24.8	80.8	69.0	16.0	20.3	0.6	510.2
Other environmental services	0.5	0.8	0.6	0.3	5.3	0.7	0.8	1.0	0.2	0.2	26.3	36.7
Law, order and protective services	0.8	1.7	1.1	0.4	5.2	1.1	1.5	1.9	0.9	0.9	8.6	23.2
Education, libraries, science and arts	5.3	12.5	8.7	3.2	38.1	6.5	7.6	17.6	4.1	22.5	13.8	139.9
Health and personal social services	22.5	25.3	46.0	13.0	97.4	34.2	22.3	55.2	20.3	38.1	18.2	392.5
Social security	..	..	..	..	..	..	..	..	..	..	0.1	0.1
Total	202.4	160.6	92.3	61.9	376.8	99.9	170.4	246.8	185.1	324.4	222.5	2143.1

.. : Negligible

Table 42

Local authority regional relevant current expenditure—1977–78 (£m) (current prices)

	North	*Yorks Humbs.*	*East Mids.*	*East Anglia*	*South-East*	*South-West*	*West Mids.*	*North-West*	*Wales*	*Scot.*	*Nrth. Ire'd.*	*UK*
Agriculture, forestry and fishing[1]											-0.2	-0.2
Trade, industry and employment	2.2	4.5	2.3	0.9	12.2	3.3	3.9	4.6	2.6	[1]	0.2	36.7
Roads and transport	66.5	110.2	58.7	24.1	307.1	64.7	84.0	131.5	63.8	118.4	0.2	1029.2
Housing[2]	97.6	105.7	76.6	34.1	656.7	63.2	115.3	161.0	68.7	212.5	0.3	1591.7
Other environmental services	78.7	107.4	68.0	34.3	472.9	80.6	112.3	168.6	86.7	266.2	24.9	1500.6
Law, order and protective services	81.8	121.1	84.9	38.1	544.9	113.3	122.5	177.9	68.0	131.3	75.1	1558.9
Education, libraries, science and arts	409.2	621.8	453.3	196.3	2195.0	473.3	606.2	842.4	367.6	679.5	106.2	6950.8
Health and personal social services	67.6	94.5	64.7	26.4	401.1	68.5	87.4	140.0	52.0	150.2		1152.4
Social security												
Total	803.6	1165.2	808.5	354.2	4589.9	866.9	1131.6	1626.0	709.4	1558.1	206.7	13820.1
Debt interest	94.2	118.5	80.8	39.4	636.6	98.2	135.6	178.3	67.7			

1: Included in other environmental services

2: Includes central government housing subsidies to local authorities.

Table 43 *Local authorities: regionally relevant capital expenditure—1977—78 (£m) (current prices)*

	North	Yorks Humbs.	East Mids.	East Anglia	South-East	South-West	West Mids.	North-West	Wales	Scot.	Nrth. Ire'd.	UK
Agriculture, forestry and fishing [1]											1.6	1.6
Trade, industry and employment	0.4	0.1	0.1	..	1.1	0.2	0.3	0.1	0.1		1.3	3.7
Roads and transport	55.9	24.5	10.6	6.5	124.8	7.1	30.9	27.7	21.8	78.7	0.2	388.7
Housing [2]	147.3	182.3	164.6	55.2	1022.0	116.6	210.0	241.3	99.3	215.9	0.9	2455.4
Other environmental services	29.8	28.5	16.0	5.1	144.3	23.3	25.8	38.9	20.4	107.0	3.9	443.0
Law, order and protective services	1.1	6.5	5.2	4.1	30.9	2.5	3.9	6.9	3.1	11.6	7.2	83.0
Education, libraries, science and arts	23.8	41.0	32.1	16.2	115.9	24.7	37.0	38.6	21.0	74.8	30.5	455.6
Health and personal social services	4.5	4.3	3.0	1.0	14.8	1.7	3.3	5.1	3.7	14.6		56.0
Social security												
Total	262.8	287.2	231.6	88.1	1453.8	176.1	311.2	358.6	169.4	502.6	45.6	3887.0

1: Included in other environmental services
2: Includes other trading
.. : Less than 0.1

Table 44

Public corporations: regionally relevant capital expenditure—1977—78 (£m) (current prices)

	North	*Yorks Humbs.*	*East Mids.*	*East Anglia*	*South-East*	*South-West*	*West Mids.*	*North-West*	*Wales*	*Scot.*	*Nrth. Ire'd.*	*UK*
Agriculture, forestry and fishing					- 0.2							- 0.2
Trade, industry and employment												
Roads and transport	7.7		1.5	5.7	22.7	0.2	13.8	9.2	0.6	13.6	1.1	76.1
Housing	12.0	- 1.6	4.8	16.1	46.2	- 0.9	18.9	34.9	1.9	75.4	115.0	322.7
Other environmental services	73.8	53.1	39.3	34.4	145.9	30.2	61.2	84.3	37.6	12.7	0.5	573.0
Law, order and protective services												
Education, libraries, science and arts												
Health and personal social services												
Social security												
Total	93.5	51.5	45.6	56.2	214.6	29.5	93.9	128.4	40.1	101.7	116.6	971.6

Table 45

Total public expenditure 'in' the regions of the UK—1977—78 (£m) (current prices)

	North	*Yorks Humbs.*	*East Mids.*	*East Anglia*	*South-East*	*South-West*	*West Mids.*	*North-West*	*Wales*	*Scot.*	*Nrth. Ire'd.*	*UK*
Current economic goods and services	1506.3	2031.8	1646.8	845.9	9716.6	2584.2	2017.4	2938.4	1248.6	2788.0	887.2	28211.2
Current transfers	1229.2	1741.0	1248.3	599.5	6141.6	1541.6	1650.6	2448.9	1126.4	3368.0	732.6	20727.2
Gross domestic fixed capital formation	402.1	422.9	336.0	189.4	1919.7	291.7	453.3	588.9	282.1	709.2	253.2	5848.5
Capital transfers	164.0	91.8	39.5	22.5	224.5	33.5	139.9	165.9	121.6	233.9	145.6	1382.7
Total	3301.6	4287.5	3270.6	1657.3	18001.9	4451.0	4261.2	6142.1	2778.7	5999.1	2018.6	56169.6

Tax revenues

A significant element of inter-regional money flows are the revenues raised to finance central government expenditures. This section, is concerned specifically with these revenues.

Due to the largely unitary political and economic structure of the UK few tax rates or tax structures vary between the regions, and taxes are collected by national organisations, namely HM Customs and Excise, and the Board of the Inland Revenue. Currently, few if any taxes have an explicit regional policy function. The sources of national total revenues for taxes are the annual *Reports* of the Departments responsible for the actual collection of the revenues. The *Reports* are superior to the blue book in that they enumerate actual receipts of tax in a particular year, rather than the tax liabilities accruing in that year, and are in line with the money flow conventions adopted. Furthermore, they are on a financial year basis.

The component revenues of Inland Revenue (together with Motor Vehicle Duties) and Customs and Excise Duties are individually considered. The analysis leans heavily on the methodology pursued by the Central Statistical Office in its annual *Regional Statistics* exercise of estimating the incidence of indirect taxation. Whenever feasible, use is made of other official regionalisations of taxation, such as the Inland Revenue's *Survey of Personal Income.* However, the basic methodology is to consider each form of taxation in turn, and relate the revenue generated to the regions. Often the results of direct survey can be used, in other cases, indirect surrogate variables are employed to apportion national totals.

The data for the four financial years 1974–75, to 1977–78 are provided, while national total revenues were available for 1977–78, the surveys or proxies use to apportion them were not always available beyond 1976. Consequently certain component revenues for 1977–78 were apportioned according to the regional weightings used for 1976–77, and thus, such results presented for 1977–78 must be used cautiously.

The quality of the results reflect the quality of the methods used, but despite imperfections, it is felt that the results give a representation of the relative positions of the various sources of revenue in the regions. Fortunately, most of the major taxes can be apportioned to the regions using the results of surveys, or according to the relative distribution of the tax base. In this way, the significance of using less direct methods for minor sources of revenues is considerably reduced.

Regional apportionment of inland revenues

The Board of the Inland Revenue produces an annual *Report* on the activities in the current and recent past financial years, containing statistics on the actual monies received in each financial year. This emphasis on actual receipts rather than accruing tax liabilities, means that certain obsolete taxes, such as surtax and estate duties, are encountered, as the tax liabilities of previous years are finally settled.

The Board operates through a series of local offices, and consequently can provide some regional breakdowns of national statistics according to locality of collection. However, these administrative conventions may not necessarily make economic sense, since formal incidence (even of those so-called 'direct' taxes) will not always reflect the final economic burden of the tax. Each of the taxes received by the Inland Revenue between 1974–75 and 1977–78, are discussed below in terms of the methodology used to apportion the national statistics between the regions. The national figures have been taken from Table 1 of the *121st Report of the Board of the Inland Revenue* (1979).

Income tax

Currently, income tax is payable on personal incomes, net of certain allowances and exemptions, but no longer on corporate incomes. Each year, a *Survey of Personal Incomes* is undertaken from a sample of the records held by local offices. Amongst other things, this survey considers the regional distribution of the various components of personal taxable incomes—earned and unearned, from employment and self-employment—and the direct taxes paid out of that income. The CSO confirms in its study of *Regional Accounts* (1978) that there is an effective coincidence of workplace and residence at the regional scale and so the figures in the survey can be used to apportion the national totals of income tax.

In the survey the income of civil servants serving abroad, the armed forces, and the merchant navy are not included in the regions, but are included in the sub-total for England and the total of UK. Accordingly, home-based armed forces were allocated to the regions according to statistics in *Regional Statistics* as these are relevant to the money flows model.

The method used to estimate the regional figures was to apportion the national total of income tax received by the Inland Revenue in each financial year using the adjusted survey of personal incomes figures of taxes paid out of regional incomes.

Surtax

Surtax has been replaced by the higher rates of income tax, and so the sums under consideration were not great. Like income tax, surtax was payable on personal incomes, and the same method of apportioning between the regions was used.

Corporation tax, and other taxes on profits

Corporation Tax is by far the larger of these two elements and, as they are both taxes on corporate profits, they can be conveniently considered together. Due to the role of the multi-regional company in the UK, and the tendency for head offices to be geographically distant from the production units, direct information of the sort used to apportion personal taxation would show a disproportionate amount of tax revenue originating in London and the Home Counties. Consequently, other measures must be used. In this case, total tax payments were apportioned according to the regional distribution of gross trading profits and surpluses, as presented in *Regional Statistics.*

Because of the increasing returns from the North Sea oil and gas industry, the CSO procedure is followed to identify a twelfth quasi-region, the continental shelf. Only in the two later years has this been a source of corporation tax.

Capital gains tax

Capital gains tax is levied on any realised increase in value of assets owned by the personal sector; though with certain exemptions, such as owner-occupied housing. Capital gains enjoyed by the corporate sector are not subject to this tax. The prime source of taxable capital gains are financial assets of one sort or another and that a suitable proxy would be the regional distribution of unearned income. Estimates of total personal investment income were used to apportion this tax between the regions (from the *Survey of Personal Incomes).*

Estate duties

Until 1974–75, duty was payable on the estates of deceased persons. Whilst now replaced in principle by capital transfer tax, estate duties continue to be received, as the settlements of many estates stretch over a period of more than one year. As no direct data are available, the apportionment of these receipts to the regions requires some measure of the incidence of deaths, weighted according to the size of the estate at death. As 1974–75 was the last year in which estate duties were applied, the number of deaths occurring in the regions in that year was taken as the base. This was weighted by the average *per capita* earnings for each region, in that year, in an attempt to reflect the undoubted regional variations in wealth at death.

Capital transfer tax

This tax replaced estate duties. However, the same method of apportionment is not suitable as this tax concerns all transfers of wealth between persons. The incidence of taxable transfers is almost certainly linked to personal wealth. However, only at the national scale have attempts been made to estimate personal wealth holding (*Economic Trends,* January 1978). Consequently, it has been apportioned to the regions according to the level of personal income, as identified by the *Survey of Personal Incomes.*

Stamp duties

Stamp duties are payable on a series of legal and financial documents. The great proportion of duties result from the activities of the London Stock Market. However, as the Stock Market serves much of the UK, it would be a distortion of the incidence of stamp duties to attempt to allocate them to the region in which they are received by the Inland Revenue. There seems to be no perfect solution to this problem, and so stamp duties were apportioned in proportion to the estimates of regional gross domestic product, as presented in *Regional Statistics.*

Development land tax

Development land tax seeks to reap some of the increase in value of land resulting from its change in use. Predominantly, such increases in value of land result from a change from non-urban to urban uses due to the construction of buildings. Thus it seems reasonable to apportion such a tax according to the value of new orders received by contractors in the construction industry *(Regional Statistics).*

Petroleum revenue tax. This is payable on the production of petroleum in the UK. The majority of this production will come from the continental shelf, but none was payable during the period under consideration.

Motor vehicle duties. All motor vehicles (with few exceptions) that are used on public highways are required to be licenced. These include motor cycles, private motor cars and various types of commercial vehicle, each bearing different rates of duty. However, the regional distribution of the several classes of vehicle are quite similar (*Regional Statistics*) and these duties were apportioned in aggregate according to the number of all licenced vehicles in each region.

Regional apportionment of customs and excise duties

Statistics on the total monies collected by HM Customs and Excise are contained in their annual *Report.* Whilst details are given for certain breakdowns according to category, there is no information according to locality of collection. However, since many such duties are collected at the point of production or wholesale distribution, such information would not be too relevant to a regional analysis of the taxation. By their nature most indirect taxes are passed on to the final consumer, who may well be resident in a different region.

Consequently, to allocate customs and excise duties to the regions, secondary sources must be used to apportion the national totals, which have been taken from the *69th Report of the Commissioners of HM Customs and Excise* (1979).

Value added tax and purchase tax. In 1973–74, purchase tax was abolished and replaced by value added tax. However, during the period under consideration a small amount (approximately £1m per annum) of purchase tax was collected in arrears. Due to its small absolute quantity and similar nature to VAT, it was apportioned at the same time and in the same manner as VAT.

VAT is levied on all purchases of liable goods and services, but since all registered traders can offset the VAT on their purchases against that in their sales, VAT effectively falls upon the final consumer. The rate of tax varies according to the type of goods and services (exempt, zero-rated, basic-rated and higher-rated) and through time. Thus the process of apportionment is complicated.

The *Family Expenditure Survey* (FES) provides estimates, *inter alia*, of the spending patterns of a sample of households in each of the regions. From the FES, expenditure on each category of VAT rated goods and services by the average household in each region was calculated for each year, weighted by the appropriate VAT rate (0, 8, 12½ or 25 per cent). These were then grossed up to total regional expenditures according to the actual number of households in each region and the resultant index was then used to apportion the total VAT receipts for each financial year.

To raise the sample size within the regions, the published FES tables are the amalgamated results of two consecutive years' survey. This meant, for example, that VAT for 1975–76 was apportioned according to survey results for the two years 1975 and 1976.

Car tax. Car tax was introduced at the same time as VAT, and replaced the higher levels of purchase tax on cars. Currently it is charged on the purchase of new cars, in addition to VAT. Consequently, car tax was apportioned to the regions according to the number of new car registrations, as found in *Regional Statistics.*

Tax on hydrocarbon oils. The amounts of duty raised on the different types of hydrocarbon oil are provided in the annual *Report.* These figures, together with estimates of the inland deliveries of the major types of oil subject to duty in *Regional Statistics,* permitted a regional apportionment of the UK figures, by category. These were then summed to produce the final estimates of the incidence of the tax on all hydrocarbon oils.

Tax on tobacco. This tax is collected from the importers and manufacturers of tobacco products, the distribution of which is more concentrated than that of the consumers. The *Family Expenditure Survey* records family expenditure on such products, in each region. However, expenditure on tobacco is notoriously under-enumerated by the FES, compared with figures for total sales of tobacco. When FES average household estimates are grossed up by the number of households to actual expenditure by the whole regional population, there is a shortfall for the nation as a whole. One alternative approach would be to apportion tax on tobacco according to the distribution of adult population in the regions. This makes the heroic assumption that *per capita* consumption varies little between regions. On balance, it would seem better to use the FES-based estimates of expenditure as indices of actual expenditure, or in other words to assume that the degree of under-recording of such expenditures is uniform for all regions.

Taxes on alcohol. As with the tax on hydrocarbon oils, a sub-division of these taxes according to the type of product is presented by the annual *Report.* However, as with tobacco duties, these taxes are collected at the point of production or import, not point of sale. Furthermore, the *Family Expenditure Survey,* whilst recording such expenditures by households, categorises them differently, and so this extra detail cannot readily be utilised.

The reservations about using FES information to apportion the tax on tobacco also apply to taxes on alcohol. Thus, all taxes on alcohol, grouped together, were apportioned using the same method as for taxes on tobacco.

Betting and gaming taxes. In total some five separate taxes are levied on betting and gaming activities, each as a proportion of 'turnover'; whether stakes, winnings or an assessment of rateable value of the licenced premises. Clearly, certain of these taxes are very locally orientated in their point of collection, but others, such as that on pool betting, is geographically very concentrated. Thus any directly available figures would have to be qualified before use. No information on the regional incidence of betting and gaming is readily available. Consequently, the total UK revenues have been apportioned in proportion to regional shares of total adult population.

Tax on matches and mechanical lighters. Both domestically produced and imported matches and mechanical lighters are subject to tax. Unfortunately there is no specific information on the purchase of these items in the *Family Expenditure Survey.* Whilst recognising that they can be used for other purposes, matches and mechanical lighters are used predominantly by smokers, and might well be considered as a complementary good of tobacco. For this reason, these taxes were apportioned by the same indices as taxes on tobacco. As total revenues do not exceed £10m per annum, any distortions so resulting will not have a significant effect upon any estimate for the total regional tax apportionments.

Protective duties and customs duties. During the transitional period of membership of the EEC, the old customs duties have gradually been replaced by protective duties. These have the same effect, namely offering some degree of preferential treatment for domestic industry in the UK market, and both are applied, in a similar manner, to imports of products. The major change has been a change in the countries affected by the protection these duties offer—away from the Commonwealth, EFTA and Sterling area countries, and increasingly in favour of the EEC member countries.

In the annual *Report,* these duties are considered together, but broken down according to category of products. To apportion them between the regions, these categories were approximately grouped into food, raw materials and semi-manufactures, and manufactured goods. Each of these groups was then apportioned to the regions according to the regional variations in the expenditure on food, drink and tobacco; regional gross domestic product resulting from manufacturing; and expenditure on manufactured products, respectively. (All from *Regional Statistics).* This method is superior to estimates based on the import figures for each region from the rest of the world, which would discriminate against those regions without major world ports.

Agricultural levies. These are another component of the UK membership of the EEC, and are levied on imports of food from countries outside the EEC. The FES regional estimates, of household purchases of food grossed up by the number of households in each region were used as an index of contribution to these levies.

Shipbuilders' rebate. Export orders of ships necessarily incorporate goods and services on which have been paid certain indirect taxes, for which HM Customs and Excise make a rebate to the manufacturers and builders. These rebates also include vehicle licence duties collected by the Department of Environment and Transport, who make a partly offsetting payment to HM Customs and Excise.

The net rebate from HM Customs and Excise has been allocated according to the regional distribution of employment in shipbuilding and marine engineering, from the Annual Census of Employment, as presented periodically in the *Department of Employment Gazette.*

Miscellaneous taxes. Comprising several sources of revenue, these never exceeded £10m per annum during the period under consideration. The least distorting method of apportionment is in proportion to all other taxes.

Table 46

Inland revenue receipts—1974–75 (£m) (current prices)

	North	Yorks Humbs	East Mids.	East Anglia	South-East	South-West	West Mids.	North-West	Wales	Scot.	Nrth. Ire'd.	Cont. Shelf	R. of World	Total
Income tax	473.4	819.3	609.5	326.0	3882.6	710.1	909.5	1011.8	404.9	835.0	195.1	–	93.6	10270.9
Surtax	8.6	14.9	11.0	5.8	70.5	12.9	16.6	18.4	7.3	15.1	3.5	–	1.7	186.3
Corporation tax and other taxes or profit	185.9	268.2	172.8	82.9	812.9	168.9	271.6	366.8	169.1	270.1	65.8	–	–	2835.5
Capital gains tax	13.4	28.3	18.6	15.7	153.4	41.9	28.2	33.2	13.3	30.8	4.7	–	–	381.6
Estate duties	17.8	27.7	21.3	10.0	116.8	26.2	28.1	39.4	15.9	30.1	5.6	–	–	338.9
Capital transfer tax	–	–	–	–	–	–	–	–	–	–	–	–	–	–
Stamp duties	10.2	16.4	12.6	5.8	68.5	13.9	18.3	22.4	8.5	17.4	4.1	–	–	198.0
Development land tax	–	–	–	–	–	–	–	–	–	–	–	–	–	–
Total inland revenue	709.3	1174.8	845.8	446.2	5104.6	973.9	1272.3	1492.0	619.0	1198.5	278.8	–	95.3	14210.2
Motor vehicle duties	25.5	41.0	35.1	21.8	180.4	46.8	51.1	54.3	26.1	38.3	11.7	–	–	532.2

The regional components have been independently rounded and sometimes the sum of regions differs from the total

Table 47

Customs and excise duties—1974–75 (£m) (current prices)

	North	Yorks Humbs.	East Mids.	East Anglia	South-East	South-West	West Mids.	North-West	Wales	Scot.	Nrth. Ire'd.	UK
VAT and purchase tax	121.9	194.4	161.6	77.0	905.7	183.0	235.2	264.7	108.0	206.5	52.6	2510.6
Car tax	5.5	10.5	7.1	4.3	43.4	7.9	12.6	12.2	4.8	10.2	3.8	122.3
Hydrocarbon oil	77.8	125.5	106.2	61.4	461.1	146.6	143.7	166.6	90.9	131.4	38.2	1549.1
Tobacco	80.4	123.2	89.7	30.8	383.1	80.4	128.6	168.8	65.6	150.0	37.5	1339.5
Alcohol	67.8	101.1	78.7	26.9	349.3	68.7	112.0	139.3	54.4	117.6	18.9	1134.3
Betting and gamind	13.3	20.1	15.8	7.6	73.4	18.3	21.8	27.9	11.8	21.8	6.1	238.5
Matches and mech.lighters	0.5	0.8	0.6	0.2	2.5	0.5	0.8	1.1	0.4	1.0	0.2	8.7
Protective/customs duties	26.0	40.4	32.0	15.3	171.3	33.5	47.4	57.3	22.2	44.1	11.6	501.0
Agriculture levies (EEC)	1.4	2.1	1.6	0.8	8.1	1.8	2.3	2.8	1.2	2.3	0.6	25.2
Shipbuilders rebate (Net)	- 1.3	- 0.2	–	- 0.1	- 1.0	- 0.6	–	- 0.3	–	- 1.1	- 0.3	- 4.9
Miscellaneous	0.1	0.1	0.1	–	0.4	0.1	0.1	0.1	0.1	0.1	–	1.1
Total customs and excise duties	393.4	618.0	493.4	224.2	2397.3	540.2	704.5	840.5	359.4	683.9	169.2	7425.5

The regional components have been independently rounded and sometimes the sum of regions differs from the UK figure

Table 48

Inland Revenue receipts–1975–76 (£m) (current prices)

	North	Yorks Humbs.	Eastq Mids.	East Anglia	South-East	South-West	West Mids.	North-West	Wales	Scot.	Nrth. Ire'd.	Cont. Shelf	R. of World	Total
Income tax	749.5	1250.4	917.4	473.7	5464.8	1055.2	1292.6	1540.2	591.9	1254.1	286.1	–	165.1	15040.8
Surtax	5.5	9.0	6.6	3.5	39.5	7.6	9.4	11.1	4.2	9.0	2.1	–	1.2	108.7
Corporation tax and other taxes or profit	129.7	177.5	133.9	62.3	580.6	124.1	176.9	256.5	90.9	197.5	42.5	–	–	1972.4
Capital gains tax	14.4	29.3	20.6	16.3	151.4	41.9	26.9	34.9	15.2	30.0	5.8	–	–	386.7
Estate duties	11.2	17.3	13.3	6.3	73.2	16.4	17.6	24.7	9.9	18.9	3.5	–	–	212.3
Capital transfer tax	6.2	10.4	7.6	3.7	40.5	8.4	10.8	12.9	4.9	9.9	2.3	–	–	117.6
Stamp duties	14.9	23.0	18.1	8.3	96.1	19.4	25.9	31.6	12.5	25.1	5.9	–	–	280.8
Development land tax	–	–	–	–	–	–	–	–	–	–	–	–	–	–
Total Inland Revenue	931.4	1516.9	1117.5	574.1	6446.1	1273.0	1560.1	1911.9	729.5	1544.5	348.2	–	166.3	18119.3
Motor vehicle duties	35.4	62.1	55.8	32.2	263.5	72.4	74.7	78.7	37.8	57.4	17.3	–	–	786.5

The regional components have been independently rounded and sometimes the sum of the regions differs from the total

Table 49

Customs and excise duties–1975–76 (£m) (current prices)

	North	Yorks Humbs.	East Mids.	East Anglia	South-East	South-West	West Mids.	North-West	Wales	Scot.	Nrth. Ire'd.	UK
VAT and purchase tax	182.0	284.1	227.4	105.3	1200.2	264.9	307.2	371.8	154.9	285.1	73.3	3456.2
Car tax	8.8	15.8	10.4	6.1	60.7	12.1	17.5	18.4	7.2	16.4	6.7	180.0
Hydrocarbon oil	77.3	121.7	105.1	62.5	464.9	148.4	141.6	158.1	89.6	133.6	40.1	1541.9
Tobacco	100.8	151.1	109.2	42.0	470.2	105.8	161.2	211.6	90.7	194.8	40.3	1679.3
Alcohol	97.4	138.8	108.5	36.6	486.4	96.1	144.8	185.9	80.0	159.8	28.7	1563.0
Betting and gaming	14.8	23.1	17.6	8.5	81.3	20.4	24.2	30.9	13.2	24.3	6.8	265.0
Matches and mech.lighters	0.5	0.7	0.5	0.2	2.3	0.5	0.8	1.0	0.4	0.9	0.2	8.1
Protective/customs duties	26.5	41.8	33.2	15.5	174.8	36.2	47.4	57.3	23.3	45.1	12.3	513.3
Agriculture levies (EEC)	2.4	3.8	3.0	1.4	14.5	3.3	4.1	5.6	2.3	4.2	1.2	45.2
Shipbuilders rebate (Net)	- 1.4	- 0.2	–	- 0.1	- 1.1	- 0.6	–	- 0.3	–	- 1.2	- 0.3	- 5.3
Miscellaneous	0.3	0.4	0.3	0.2	1.6	0.4	0.5	0.6	0.2	0.5	0.1	5.0
Total customs and excise duties	509.4	781.1	615.2	278.2	2955.7	687.5	849.3	1040.9	461.8	863.5	209.4	9251.7

The regional components have been independently rounded and sometimes the sum of the regions differs from the UK figure

Table 50 *Inland Revenue receipts—1976–77 (£m) (current prices)*

	North	Yorks Humbs.	East Mids.	East Anglia	South-East	South-West	West Mids.	North-West	Wales	Scot.	Nrth. Ire'd.	Cont.	R. of World	Total
Income tax	835.0	1386.8	1041.2	545.2	6237.2	1203.8	1475.0	1766.7	692.0	1362.6	317.7	–	150.5	17013.7
Surtax	3.0	5.0	3.8	2.0	22.7	4.4	5.4	6.5	2.6	5.0	1.2	–	0.6	62.2
Corporation tax and other taxes or profit	165.2	237.8	174.6	79.7	729.9	158.8	234.3	338.7	128.5	261.2	54.5	71.7	–	2634.5
Capital gains tax	12.0	25.3	17.6	13.3	126.9	37.4	22.4	28.6	12.3	23.7	3.7	–	–	323.4
Estate duties	6.6	10.2	7.8	3.7	42.9	9.6	10.3	14.5	5.8	11.1	2.1	–	–	124.4
Capital transfer tax	13.6	22.2	16.7	8.3	90.0	18.7	23.7	29.0	11.3	20.9	4.9	–	–	259.2
Stamp duties	14.4	22.5	17.3	8.2	92.5	18.8	24.7	30.7	12.2	24.6	5.8	–	–	271.6
Development land tax	0.1	0.1	0.1	0.1	0.3	0.1	0.1	0.1	0.1	0.1	–	–	–	1.1
Total Inland Revenue	1049.9	1709.9	1279.1	660.5	7342.4	1451.6	1795.9	2214.8	864.8	1709.2	389.9	71.7	151.1	20690.1
Motor vehicle duties	37.5	65.3	57.1	33.4	270.0	74.2	76.7	84.8	39.2	58.7	17.9	–	–	815.7

The regional components have been independently rounded and sometimes the sum of regions differs from the total

Table 51 *Customs and excise duties—1976–77 (£m) (current prices)*

	North	Yorks Humbs.	East Mids.	East Anglia	South-East	South-West	West Mids.	North-West	Wales	Scot.	Nrth. Ire'd.	UK
VAT and purchase tax	197.5	307.4	235.8	115.1	1302.2	287.0	326.9	405.5	193.6	317.6	81.7	3770.3
Car tax	10.7	19.2	13.1	7.4	72.6	14.4	20.9	22.9	8.5	19.6	8.7	218.0
Hydrocarbon oil	97.7	165.2	136.5	85.6	628.5	211.9	184.0	211.8	117.7	174.7	54.9	2067.3
Tobacco	123.3	176.7	121.4	50.4	516.0	118.7	164.5	239.7	95.0	222.1	47.3	1874.9
Alcohol	125.3	174.7	130.5	47.1	594.8	131.1	180.2	236.6	93.0	198.0	34.3	1945.6
Betting and gaming	15.8	24.8	19.0	9.3	86.9	22.2	26.0	33.0	14.1	26.1	7.3	284.3
Matches and mech.lighters	0.5	0.8	0.5	0.2	2.2	0.5	0.7	1.0	0.4	0.9	0.2	7.9
Protective/customs duties	35.4	56.2	42.8	20.4	228.0	48.7	61.1	75.2	31.6	59.9	16.6	675.8
Agriculture levies (EEC)	2.8	4.4	3.4	1.6	16.9	3.9	4.7	5.9	2.7	4.8	1.4	52.7
Shipbuilders rebate (Net)	-1.8	-0.2	-0.1	-0.1	-1.4	-0.8	-0.1	-0.4	–	-1.5	-0.4	-6.8
Miscellaneous	-0.2	-0.2	-0.2	-0.1	-1.2	-0.3	-0.3	-0.4	-0.2	-0.4	-0.1	-3.8
Total customs and excise duties	607.0	929.0	702.7	336.9	3445.5	837.1	968.6	1230.8	556.4	1021.8	251.9	10886.2

The regional components have been independently rounded and sometimes the sum of regions differs from the UK figures

Table 52 *Inland Revenue receipts—1977–78 (£m) (current prices)*

	North	*Yorks Humbs.*	*East Mids.*	*East Anglia*	*South-East*	*South-West*	*West Mids.*	*North-West*	*Wales*	*Scot.*	*Nrth. Ire'd.*	*Cont. Shelf*	*R. of World*	*Total*
Income tax	854.9	1419.9	1066.0	558.2	6386.0	1232.5	1510.2	1808.9	708.5	1395.1	325.3	–	154.1	17419.7
Surtax	1.4	2.4	1.8	1.0	10.9	2.1	2.6	3.2	1.3	2.4	0.6	–	0.3	30.0
Corporation tax and other taxes or profits	186.0	288.9	205.0	92.0	887.1	189.6	273.8	408.1	152.3	306.3	65.1	281.2	–	3335.5
Capital gains tax	12.6	26.6	18.5	14.0	133.4	39.3	23.5	30.1	12.9	24.9	3.9	–	–	339.9
Estate duties	4.6	7.1	5.4	2.6	29.9	6.7	7.2	10.1	4.1	7.7	1.4	–	–	86.7
Capital transfer tax	16.3	26.7	20.1	10.0	108.1	22.5	28.5	34.8	13.6	25.1	5.9	–	–	311.2
Stamp duties	19.7	31.5	24.2	11.1	126.9	26.9	34.1	42.7	17.3	33.6	8.2	–	–	376.3
Development land tax	0.4	0.5	0.4	0.3	2.1	0.4	0.6	0.6	0.3	0.8	0.2	–	–	6.8
Petroleum revenue duty	–	–	–	–	–	–	–	–	–	–	–	–	–	–
Total Inland Revenue	1095.9	1803.6	1341.4	689.2	7684.4	1520.0	1880.5	2338.5	910.3	1795.9	410.6	281.2	154.4	21906.1
Motor vehicle duties	47.2	82.8	72.3	43.0	349.1	96.5	99.6	108.0	49.3	76.5	24.1	–	–	1048.4

The regional components have been independently rounded and sometimes the sum of the regions differs from the total.

Table 53 *Customs and excise duties–1977–78 (£m) (current prices)*

	North	*Yorks Humbs.*	*East Mids.*	*East Anglia*	*South-East*	*South-West*	*West Mids.*	*North-West*	*Wales*	*Scot.*	*Nrth. Ire'd.*	*UK*
VAT and purchase tax	221.8	345.3	264.9	129.3	1462.7	322.4	367.2	455.5	217.5	356.7	91.8	4235.0
Car tax	13.4	24.3	18.3	9.7	97.5	19.2	28.0	29.7	10.9	24.3	10.9	285.9
Hydrocarbon oil	117.9	203.9	154.5	101.1	730.1	241.7	219.5	268.1	146.2	212.7	65.3	2460.0
Tobacco	135.3	193.9	133.2	55.3	566.3	130.3	180.5	263.1	104.3	243.7	51.9	2057.6
Alcohol	132.9	185.2	138.4	49.9	630.7	139.0	191.1	250.9	98.6	209.9	36.4	2062.9
Betting and gaming	17.9	28.0	21.5	10.5	96.6	24.6	29.6	37.4	15.9	29.8	8.8	320.5
Matches and mech. lighters	0.6	0.8	0.6	0.2	2.4	0.5	0.8	1.1	0.4	1.0	0.2	8.6
Protective/customs duties	35.7	56.7	43.2	20.6	230.1	49.1	61.7	75.9	31.9	60.4	16.7	681.9
Agriculture levies (EEC)	9.5	14.9	11.5	5.4	57.1	13.2	15.9	20.0	9.1	16.2	4.7	178.2
Shipbuilders rebate (net)	- 2.9	- 0.3	- 0.2	- 0.2	- 2.2	- 1.3	- 0.2	- 0.6	—	- 2.4	- 0.6	- 10.8
Miscellaneous	0.4	0.7	0.5	0.2	2.4	0.6	0.7	0.9	0.4	0.7	0.2	7.7
Total customs and excise duties	682.5	1053.4	786.4	382.0	3873.7	939.3	1094.8	1402.0	635.2	1153.0	286.3	12287.4

The regional components have been independently rounded and sometimes the sum of regions differs from the UK total

National Insurance, etc., contributions

National insurance contributions and the like, are very similar to several forms of taxation, being obligatory payments into a government administered fund. Certainly, the burden of the employers' National Insurance Contributions is no different to that of an *ad valorem* payroll tax. The analysis of the inter-regional redistribution effects of the individual National Insurance funds is further complicated by the maintenance of separate funds for Northern Ireland and for the UK. The fund of each 'country' is operated independently, but each year adjustments are made between them. The effect of this is similar to the manner in which any one region within the UK will not receive benefits from the Fund in absolute proportion to its contributions that year. Similar circumstances apply to the Redundancy Funds, which are also operated independently for Northern Ireland and the UK.

Since April 1975 the structure of the several Funds have been changed. Under section 33 of the Social Security Act, 1973, the Industrial Injuries Fund, and the National Insurance (Reserve) Fund were wound up, and their assets passed to the National Insurance Fund. Thus, during 1974–75, contributions were made to the Industrial Injuries Fund, and in the analysis below these are included with the National Insurance Fund contributions for that year. The National Insurance (Reserve) Fund did not involve the making of contributions and so does not affect this analysis. The National Insurance Contributions now incorporate a number of once separate schemes. Similarly, the National Health Service benefits from these contributions, although no separate Fund exists. However, the value of such contributions to the National Health Service can be identified in published statistics. For example, in 1975–76, out of total National Insurance contributions of £6184m made in the UK, some £416m accrued to the National Health Service. Finally a Maternity Fund has been recently established, and since 1977–78, employers have been required to make payments towards it in addition to the Redundancy Fund. Due to the similar nature and purpose between these two funds, they have been grouped together in the analysis below.

National Insurance Fund. Figures are provided by the *Annual Report* of the National Insurance Fund presented to Parliament, for the UK only, with the necessary additional details for Northern Ireland found in the *Northern Ireland Digest of Statistics,* published quarterly. However, no published regionalisation of these contributions are available. The CSO *Regional Accounts* estimate the distribution of such contributions in each calendar year as a component of total income from employment, and, as one of the differences between personal income and personal disposable income. Whilst employers' and employees' contributions are separately attributed to the regions, they are each based on the distribution of wages and salaries received. The resulting estimates, for 1974 to 1976 inclusive, although not published, were made available by the CSO.

A similar methodology was adopted in this analysis. The Northern Ireland figures are as presented in the *Northern Ireland Direst of Statistics,* and the estimates for the regions of the UK are the national totals apportioned according to total income from employment, as found in *Regional Accounts.* According to the Department of Health and Social Security, those whose earnings are such to require contributions to be made under the National Insurance Acts are as below:

Employed	23.26
Self-employed	1.73
Non-employed	0.19
Total	25.18 millions

These figures, taken from the *Annual Abstract of Statistics,* apply to 1974, the last year for which they are currently available. Nevertheless, they do indicate the overwhelming majority of contributions are likely to come as employees' contributions or employers' contributions. Consequently, any distortions in apportioning all National Insurance contributions in aggregate are unlikely to be serious. Similarly, the use of an income from *employment* proxy can be defended. (Regional estimates of wages and salaries are not yet available for 1977, and so income from employment was used on the grounds of consistency.)

Redundancy fund. Redundancy fund payments are currently levied at a rate equivalent to 0.2 per cent of those earnings of a company's employees on which the employer is required to make National Insurance contributions. The same methodology as that used to apportion the National Insurance contributions can be employed. As with the National Insurance Fund, UK totals can be found in an *Annual Report* as presented to Parliament, and details of the separate Northern Ireland Fund were obtained from the *Northern Ireland Digest of Statistics.* For 1977–78 these figures included the payments made by employers to the recently established Maternity Fund.

Local authorities income

The sources for the data on income flow to local authorities are the same as for the expenditure. As with the expenditure, data were unavailable for 1974–75 from *Local Government Financial Statistics,* and

Table 54

National Insurance, etc., contributions (£m) (current prices)

	North	*Yorks Humbs.*	*East Mids.*	*East Anglia*	*South-East*	*South-West*	*West Mids.*	*North-West*	*Wales*	*Scot.*	*Nrth. Ire'd.*	*UK*
1974–75												
National Insurance†	269.3	443.3	340.9	138.9	1845.0	358.3	506.7	603.7	216.9	455.0	79.3	5257.2
Redundancy Fund	2.6	4.3	3.3	1.3	17.8	3.5	4.9	5.8	2.1	4.4	1.3	51.4
Total	271.9	447.6	344.2	140.2	1862.8	361.8	511.6	609.5	219.0	459.4	180.6	5308.6
1975–76												
National Insurance	334.2	521.7	406.6	170.5	2176.7	417.5	607.8	717.1	277.9	553.5	140.0	6323.7
Redundancy Fund	4.9	7.6	5.9	2.5	31.6	6.2	8.9	10.5	4.1	8.1	2.3	90.6
Total	339.1	529.3	412.5	173.0	2208.3	423.7	616.7	727.6	282.0	261.6	142.3	6414.3
1976–77												
National Insurance	420.1	659.6	500.1	216.3	2707.1	529.8	743.8	901.6	347.6	703.5	175.0	7904.4
Redundancy Fund	6.2	9.8	7.4	3.2	39.9	7.9	11.1	13.4	5.1	10.5	2.3	116.9
Total	426.3	669.4	507.5	219.5	2747.0	537.7	754.9	915.0	352.7	714.0	177.3	8021.3
1977–78												
National Insurance	458.4	736.1	562.8	237.7	2981.9	593.8	832.8	998.9	387.5	769.4	211.2	8770.5
Redundancy Fund*	8.2	13.2	10.1	4.3	53.3	10.6	14.9	17.9	6.9	13.8	2.8	155.8
Total	456.6	749.3	572.9	242.0	3035.2	604.4	847.7	1016.8	394.4	783.2	214.0	8926.3

†Includes contributions to Industrial Injuries Fund

*Includes contributions to Maternity Fund

The regional components have been independently rounded and sometimes the sum of regions differs from the UK total

Table 55

Local authority: funding of current expenditure (£m) (current prices)

	North	Yorks Humbs.	East Mids.	East Anglia	South-East	South-West	West Mids.	North-West	Wales	Scot.	Nrth. Ire'd.
1974–75											
Government grants	175.1	311.7	255.3	112.0	1350.5	263.4	353.7	406.2	395.1	724.9	56.6
Rates	163.8	219.6	177.7	91.2	1307.2	202.0	291.6	354.8	119.5	304.5	51.3
1975–76											
Government grants	581.1	835.8	563.0	222.6	2553.5	573.4	750.7	1076.4	525.9	923.7	84.4
Rates	196.7	265.5	218.9	115.0	1813.6	250.4	361.2	432.4	149.0	385.1	88.4
1976–77											
Government grants	634.2	929.2	587.9	248.4	3016.6	682.3	843.1	1216.3	589.1	1128.5	98.1
Rates	220.2	291.2	245.5	121.8	1959.3	270.7	388.3	470.4	173.1	442.7	76.4
1977–78											
Government grants	675.4	981.9	652.4	274.0	3065 1	651.0	885.2	1287.7	601.0	1223.3	121.2
Rates	246.6	336.0	277.2	145.1	2214.1	310.9	441.2	531.7	185.3	523.0	88.3

Table 56 *Local authority: funding of capital expenditure (£m) (current prices)*

	North	Yorks Humbs.	East Mids.	East Anglia	South-East	South-West	West Mids.	North-West	Wales	Scot.	Nrth. Ire'd.
1974–75											
Loans									168.7	426.8	
Grants									11.9	28.9	19.6
1975–76											
Loans	232.9	256.6	239.7	97.2	1483.5	204.7	324.0	409.5	172.9		
Grants	30.1	3.0	8.3	6.3	82.4	11.4	16.0	20.3	15.2		9.3
1976–77											
Loans	222.2	273.1	237.6	89.2	1406.3	194.6	307.9	367.5	160.5		
Grants	28.9	7.2	14.4	9.2	137.9	14.5	14.8	30.5	21.0		19.4
1977–78											
Loans	194.2	251.2	206.4	77.3	1224.4	170.2	272.0	328.0	133.9		
Grants	48.0	10.3	4.9	9.5	131.1	8.4	19.1	32.8	22.3		17.2

specific government grants and rate support grant were obtained using the CIPFA publications. Rates were taken from the rateable value in England and Wales publication.

For 1975–76 to 1977–78 the LGFS figures are used. Specific government grants can be classified according to the PESC programmes, and rate support grant which are received by the authorities to finance their overall expenditure, cannot be assigned to any particular programme.

On the capital account, figures for Scotland and Wales are presented for 1974–75. For the years 1975–76 to 1977–78 figures for the English regions and Wales on loans and government grants are available by programme. The Scottish figures are not as yet available due to the delay in the publication of *Local Financial Returns* (Scotland). (See Short and Nichols (1980) for details of grants by programme.)

The European Communities

The European Communities have played an increasing role in the economy of the UK since its accession in 1973. As a result, the Com munities' institutions cannot be ignored in an analysis of the money flows between the regions of the UK. Not only does the UK make contributions to the Community budget, but also receives not inconsiderable disbursements from the several Community Funds. Several of these Funds have a distinct regional bias, and so, like all other intermediary institutions, the Community has the scope for redistributing resources between the regions of the UK.

Membership contributions take three forms. The Common Agricultural Policy involves certain levies on agricultural produce. These levies accrue not to the national government but to the Community. In the UK these levies, like certain other forms of indirect taxation, are collected by HM Customs and Excise who receive a percentage of such receipts to cover collection costs. All other receipts pass directly to the Community rather than the Exchequer. Similarly, certain customs duties charged under the Common Customs Tarriff but collected by HM Customs and Excise pass directly to the Community. Finally, it has been agreed by the Council of the European Communities, that the equivalent yield from a rate of VAT, not exceeding 1 per cent, applied to a harmonised tax base should also accrue to the Community automatically. However, such procedures were not complied with in the period currently under consideration (1974–75 to 1977–78), and indeed by the programmed starting rate of 1st January 1978 only the UK and Belgium had harmonised their VAT tax base, causing a postponement. In the interim, transfers have been made between national exchequers and the Community, calculated according to the relative size of national GNP.

Thus, in a money flows analysis, these contributions can be seen as transfers between UK residents or UK government and the Community institutions. The government component is included in the government sector accounts, and the residents' component is part of total public revenues as described in the taxation section. This section therefore concentrates on the disbursements made by the European Community, and seeks to present the regional dimension of these monies.

Annual reports published by the Community in Brussels are one source of information of these disbursements, but do not always provide a regional disaggregation of national rceipts. Furthermore, all monetary quantities are expressed in 'Units of Account'. Whilst this avoids the problems of handling concurrently nine different national currencies, it provides problems at a national scale. The rate of exchange between sterling and the Unit of Account varies through time, often changing within a year. Thus, year-end accounts cannot readily be converted into sterling without information on the time profile of payments through the year. For this reason, the analysis presented here rests heavily on the regular English language editions of the *Press Releases* and *Background Reports* published by the Commission of the European Communities, supplemented by other sources where necessary.

In preparing a regional flows analysis there are certain difficulties which have to be overcome if comprehensive estimates are to be achieved, without double-counting flows enumerated elsewhere. Both in making applications, and receiving any disbursements, UK residents are usually required to operate via national government departments or agencies. The former point has little significance to the money flows analysis, however the latter point seriously complicates the process of identifying flows at the regional level. Certain national agencies (such as the Training Services Agency, or the Water Council) can put up projects for assistance from the Community. Many of these projects will have a specific and identifiable regional dimension (such as the improvement of water supply within a region), and so few problems are presented. In other cases, the project is national in its organisation (such as the retraining programme of Skill Centres) the regional incidence of which cannot be matched to Community support, though necessarily there is an implicit regional incidence of this support. In other cases, a discrete project may gain Community support. In other cases, a discrete project may gain Community support, applying to one or more regions but not the whole country, but on which no further details are available. For these reasons it is necessary to deal with twelve UK regions, including a quasi-region which receives non-allocable funds on behalf of the UK as a whole.

Not all assistance provided by the Community is passed on to the originator of the project. This is particularly so with industrial projects receiving assistance from the European Regional Development Fund. To be eligible to receive ERDF support, the project must also be eligible for national regional policy, and, all industrial applications to the ERDF are made via the Department of Industry. However all such ERDF monies received are not passed to the enterprise concerned with the project, rather they are kept to boost the total resources available for national regional policy assistance. Whilst it is possible to defend this practice at a national level, and similarly consider that the 'additionality' criteria are being complied with, this is not necessarily so for each individual region. At a practical level, such declared regional 'receipts' are something of a fiction in the UK context, and should not be incorporated in the money flows analysis. Funds 'awarded' to particular regions go no further than the national fund, and will be enumerated as part of the total expenditures of the national Regional Development Grant scheme of the Department of Industry. To include both would involve double-counting, and therefore ERDF infrastructure monies must be separated from the ERDF industrial monies.

In addition to making non-repayable grants, the Community also offers considerable quantities of loans, particularly the European Investment Bank. Ideally, the repayments of such loans ought to be specifically identified, but these are picked up in the financial sector analysis, along with all other capital transfers out of the UK. Another complication is that money loans are made in instalments over a period of time, and thus do not apply solely to the year in which they are announced. However, details of such staged payments expressed in sterling, are hard to come by.

Bearing in mind these considerations, the receipts by UK residents from each of the Community 'funds' are outlined in turn, below. Generally all fund dispersals are presented, and the 'fictional' regionalisations are clearly identified, but for some funds, paucity of data prevents a full regionalisation of national receipts.

Overall, the process of preparing consistent and comparable statistics of the operations of the European Community within the UK is fraught with practical difficulties. Different sources of national statistics are seldom comparable–*Hansard* and (ISEC/B25/79) shows an analysis by the European Commission marked inconsistencies, despite a very similar time period under consideration.

	Hansard (Jan. 1973–Sept. 1978) £m	ISEC/B25/79 (Jan. 1973–Dec. 1978) £m
ESF	134.1	283.2
ERDF	112.1	268.7
FEOGA (Guidance)	66.3	56.6
EIB	1005.6	1169.3
ECSC (Loans)	491.5	930.1
ECSC (Grants)	28.0	70.0

Due to the problems over the varying 'rate of exchange' between national currencies and the Unit of Account, the inconsistencies are greater if statistics denominated in Units of Account are also consulted.

Using the *Press Release* and *Background Report* analysis is also imperfect. Not only is the coverage incomplete, but it begs the question of when the payments are actually made, for announcements concerning a particular budget (i.e. calendar) year are often made well into the subsequent calendar year. Thus, probably 'awards' aggregate for each budget are more likely accruals based on the annual budget appropriation than actual cash payments in that year.

These observations, together with reservations concerning the relationship of many of the cash flows to national public expenditures, suggest that all the figures presented herewith must be used with extreme caution. For similar reasons, an aggregated picture of total flows to the regions from the European Community cannot be assembled from these sources.

The European Social Fund (ESF)

The objective of the Social Fund is to improve the employment opportunities for workers within the Community by increasing their geographical and occupational mobility. In policy terms, this is reflected in support for schemes for training, retraining and resettling the unemployed and under employed.

Within the UK the majority of the grants received have been for training and retraining of the unemployed, and work preparation for school leavers. For example, the Training Opportunities Scheme and the Work Experience Programme organised by the Manpower Services Commission, plus projects provided by industrial training schemes, nationalised industries, and private firms. Because of the larger schemes especially those nationally organised, and operated by national agencies, the particular regional dimension cannot be separated from the other operations of such agencies. Due to its devolved administrative structure,

Northern Ireland is more identifiable than the regions of the UK for, ESF applications are made independently for Northern Ireland.

Other applications for aid in the UK are made through the Department of Employment, and so the great majority of disbursements made do not pass directly to the regions, but are included in the operations of central government. A further complication to the analysis is that since 1977, certain allocations made have been for operations phased over a number of years, but are budgeted for in the years approved. In other words, any available figures since then will be a mixture of accruals and payments. However, even enquiries to the Department of Employment could not produce sound figures for the regional incidence of the Social Fund. The Department stressed that much of the money received is for national policies pursued by central agencies, usually to general regions. Indeed, serious doubt has been raised concerning the validity of regionalisations prepared and published by the European Commission—and even these attribute some 70 per cent of national receipts to multi-regional projects! Consequently, it is impossible to provide any regionalisation of the effects of the European Social Fund. Total national receipts for the individual calendar years, as supplied by the Department of Employment are:

	1974	1975	1976	1977
£m	25.9	45.9	44.1	85.1

Because of the reservations expressed by the Department concerning European Commission figures, no attempt has been made to apportion these to the regions according to the relative incidence presented in the ISEC/B25/79 *Background Report.* However, the vast majority can be considered as flows from the European Community to central government.

Since 1978, the ESF has been operated with a specific regional dimension, whereby projects in specially disadvantaged regions receive a greater percentage support from the Fund. Perhaps as a result of this innovation, the distinct lack of regional information may be remedied in the future.

European Agricultural Guidance and Guarantee Fund (FEOGA)

There are two separate sections to the Agricultural Fund. The larger by far is the Guarantee Section, concerned with the price support mechanisms of the Community's Common Agricultural Policy. Within the UK this role is performed by the Intervention Board for Agricultural Products and its operations are considered part of public expenditures, although the great majority of its activities are financed directly from Community resources. Consequently, its operations are considered in detail in the section dealing with public expenditures.

Nevertheless, this non-domestic funding clearly represents a money flow to the central government from the European Community. For completeness sake, the total annual sums involved are presented below, as taken from successive annual reports regularly presented to Parliament:

	1974	1975	1976	1977	1978
£m	118.8	339.6	195.4	146.4	420.1

For the whole European Community, the Guarantee section of the Agricultural Fund is responsible for something like 65 per cent of the annual total budget.

The Guidance section of the fund seeks to help in the restructuring and improvement of the Communities' food production industry including fishing and food processing, through the provision of percentage grants to cover approved costs. All applications pass through the Ministry of Agriculture, and care must be exercised to avoid double-counting of Community measures and similar national supportive schemes. The estimates presented concern the actual disbursements of the Guidance section of the Fund, as announced in the Commission's *Press Releases* and *Background Reports.* In some cases projects approved for support are to do with more than one region, reflecting the increasingly corporate structure of the food production industry. Such indivisible grants have been grouped under a multi-regional heading.

The European Regional Development Fund (ERDF)

In the period under consideration, the ERDF has been operated on a strict quota system. Each member state has been allocated a proportion of the total Fund over a period of years, but has to present individual cases meriting aid from the Fund to receive its quota. For example, the UK was entitled to 27.03 per cent of the total resources attributed to the ERDF. (A smaller non-quota section, limited to 5 per cent of the total ERDF resources was introduced from 1977 onwards, but a method of disbursing this section is till to be agreed, and therefore, the non-quota section has been held over for future years.)

Each individual project seeking ERDF support must also be eligible for support from the national governments regional policy aid, thus industrial schemes must be eligible for Regional Development Grant in the UK. All such industrial schemes must apply to the ERDF via the Department of Industry, and ERDF grants received for industrial schemes do not pass to the industrial enterprise concerned—it receives only the RDG—but is used by the Department of Industry to boost the resources available for RDG. Consequently, although the individual projects successfully submitted for ERDF support are published, and indeed regionalised, the payments made do not involve flows from the Community to the individual regions. Rather they are supra-regional flows from the European Community to the central government.

Another aspect of the ERDF are the grants in support of infrastructural improvements made by public authorities as part of the process of regional development. Such applications also are not made directly to the ERDF, and must pass through the Department of the Environment. However, the monies are received by the executive authorities involved in the infrastructural improvements, and thus can be considered as truly regional receipts, passing from the European Community to the public sector in the region concerned. The source of the figures presented are the several *Press Releases* and *Background Reports* issued by the Commission of the European Community, detailing each tranche as it is allocated. Further details are available in the regular *Annual Reports* of the ERDF, but most monetary values are expressed in units of account to make cross-national comparisons, and thus of less value to a purely national analysis. No figures are presented for 1974 as the Fund was not established until 1975. Similarly, not all regions are represented, since not all regions contain Assisted Areas. Finally, these figures represent total allocation as announced. Due to certain grants not being taken up despite being approved, or underspending, the actual receipts are less than those presented. Such adjustments or 'decommitments' took place in 1977 but apply also to 1975 and 1976. The *net* sum received by all regions in 1977 was £55.3m rather than £60.8m.

The European Coal and Steel Community (ECSC)

The ECSC provides both loans and non-repayable grants to the coal and steel industries in the UK to, and in support of, new investments, industrial reconversion and towards the improvement of workers' housing. Unlike the disbursements of the ERDF, these payments are not enumerated in detail in the *Press Releases*, and suchlike, of the European Commission. The UK Office of the Commission has provided regionalised details of ECSC payments for the period 1973–78 as a whole, but could not provide annual estimates. The annual *Financial Report* of the ECSC presents national total receipts for each calendar year, but in units of accounts. The usual problems of conversion into national currencies is further complicated by the fact that the individual ECSC loans are denominated in a variety of currencies (such as US dollars, Swiss francs, Dutch guilders, sterling, etc.), each of which fluctuates against the unit of account through time.

Hansard (1 Dec. 1978) details the individual loans made to both the National Coal Board, and the British Steel Corporation between 1973 and mid-1978, together with the sterling equivalent of the loan at the time it was made. The aggregate annual receipts are

(£m)	1974	1975	1976	1977	Total
BSC	42.0	37.4	207.3	120.4	407.1
NCB	18.0	7.1	89.8	61.0	239.9
Total	60.0	108.5	297.1	181.4	647.0

For the NCB, further details of the purposes of the loans are provided, but the great majority involve collieries in more than one region, and so these national totals cannot be directly identified with individual regions. The BSC negotiates its loans solely on a national basis, and no further detail is offered. The best available regionalisation of ECSC loans is presented in the European Commission's *Background Report* (ISEC/B25/79). Considering, in aggregate, the loans and grants for the period 1973–1978 inclusive, this analysis involved some £930m worth of loans, of which some 30 per cent were attributed to the UK as a whole. Nevertheless, it provides an order of relative significance for the regions on this count, and consequently was used to apportion the national totals identified in *Hansard* for each of the calendar years 1974–1977.

Despite the difficulties involved in converting units of account to sterling, the statistics presented in the ECSC *Financial Report* are of value. Amongst other things, they show that for 1974, 1975 and 1976 at at least, no loan repayments had been made by the UK recipients of ECSC loans. Thus, the national figures shown in *Hansard* can be taken as both net and gross flows of funds with the UK.

Grants made by the ECSC are of smaller individual size than loans, and no individual details are presented in *Hansard*, nor are annual figures presented, merely the 1973 to mid-1978 totals:

	£m
BSC	2.2
NCB	25.8
	28.0

Furthermore, the *Background Report* (ISEL/B25/79) does not offer any regional breakdown of the national totals, and consequently, no regionalisation is attempted in the present analysis.

The European Investment Bank

The EIB provides loans, or guarantees, towards the capital cost of major projects in the Community, with an emphasis on the less favoured regions and modernisation of industries. Smaller schemes are also aided, by the means of 'global' sums put at the disposal of national agencies, such as ICFC finance for small businesses. Major loans are negotiated directly with the EIB, and so can be considered as flows from the Community to the regions. However, this is often complicated by organisations, such as British Rail, British Steel, or the Water Council who receive support for multi-regional projects. The 'global' sums are administered by the Department of Industry, once again introducing complications of separating Community disbursements from public expenditures.

Loans require repayment, and in a true regional flows analysis, these repayments ought also to be identified and attributed to regions. Similarly, payment of the loan principle is often staged over a number of years. However, details of both of these aspects are imperfectly available. Consequently, presented figures are gross loans made by the EIB, and for any one year are a mixture of accruals and actual payments.

The presented estimates were taken from *Hansard*, 1 Dec. 1978) and identifies each particular loan made since 1973.

Table 57 *European Regional Development Fund (£m)*

	North	Yorks Humbs.	East Mids.	East Anglia	South-East	South-West	West Mids.	North-West	Wales	Scot.	Nrth. Ire'd.	UK
1975												
Infrastructure	5.5	1.0	0.1			0.4	..	2.6	5.8	6.0	2.2	23.6
Industrial	1.7					0.4		0.4	0.4	3.8	5.6	12.2
Total	7.2	1.0	0.1			0.8	..	3.0	6.2	9.8	7.8	35.8
1976												
Infrastructure	9.9	0.9	0.2			0.6	..	4.4	4.5	10.3	5.2	36.0
Industrial	9.0	1.2	0.1			0.2		2.5	3.9	4.3	2.0	23.2
Total	18.9	2.1	0.3			0.8	..	6.9	8.4	14.6	7.2	59.2
1977												
Infrastructure	10.4	2.1	0.3			0.5		2.3	5.5	8.8	4.9	34.8
Industrial	8.8	0.5						3.2	1.6	7.4	4.5	26.0
Total	19.2	2.6	0.3			0.5		5.5	7.1	16.2	9.4	60.8

The regional components have been independently rounded and sometimes the sum of regions differs from the total.
..: Negligible

Table 58 *European Coal and Steel Community (£m)*

		North	*Yorks Humbs.*	*East Mids.*	*East Anglia*	*South-East*	*South-West*	*West Mids.*	*North-West*	*Wales*	*Scot.*	*Nrth. Ire'd.*	*Multi.Reg. Projects*	*UK*
Loans	1974	14.4	13.4	2.2		0.2		1.4	0.2	6.5	3.6		18.0	60.0
	1975	26.1	24.2	4.0		0.4		2.5	0.4	11.8	6.5		32.6	180.5
	1976	71.4	66.3	11.1		1.2		6.8	1.1	32.2	17.9		89.2	297.1
	1977	43.6	40.5	6.8		0.7		4.2	0.7	19.7	10.9		54.4	181.4
Grants 1973–mid 1978														28.0

Table 59 *European Agricultural Fund–Guidance Section (£m)*

	North	*Yorks Humbs.*	*East Mids.*	*East Anglia*	*South-East*	*South-West*	*West Mids.*	*North-West*	*Wales*	*Scot.*	*Nrth. Ire'd.*	*Multi.Reg. Projects*	*UK*
1974													not available
1975	1.1	0.4	0.8	1.1	0.3	0.1	0.3	0.2	0.2	1.0	1.8		6.3
1976	0.5	1.5	0.4	0.5	..	0.6	0.0	2.0	0.4	5.9	2.8	0.7	13.0
1977	0.1	1.1	1.0	2.0	0.6	1.1	0.9	0.2	0.1	2.1	2.2		11.0

Table 60 *European Investment Bank (£m)*

	North	*Yorks Humbs.*	*East Mids.*	*East Anglia*	*South-East*	*South-West*	*West Mids.*	*North-West*	*Wales*	*Scot.*	*Nrth. Ire'd.*	*Multi.Reg. Projects*	*UK*
1974	15.6	12.0			7.0				8.0		2.5	20.4	79.9
1975	15.3	1.6							35.0	73.3		61.3	186.5
1976	34.4	19.7			17.3	12.6		9.0	46.2	20.8		99.0	259.0
1977	53.6	14.6				2.5		72.1	12.4	111.6	18.5	35.5	320.8

..: Negligible

Appendix 3 The financial sector

This appendix is concerned with the financial sector in the context of the regional money flows model. It is set out as follows. The first section outlines the sectors to which the financial sector relates. Then the different flows in the context of the regional model are examined and finally the data which have been generated is presented and the methodology used, is discussed.

The sectors

The financial accounts are classified by the Central Statistical Office as outlined in Financial Statistics. The sectors and their constituent components which relate to various flows are as follows:

Public sector: central government; local authorities and public corporations.

Banking sector: Bank of England, the National Giro, listed discount market institutions, listed banks and the larger finance houses.

Other financial institutions: These cover the remaining institutions: building societies; trustee savings banks (special investment departments); finance houses, National Savings Bank (Investment Account); insurance; superannuation funds; unit trusts; investment trusts, property unit trusts; special finance agencies and other miscellaneous institutions.

Industrial and commercial companies: All corporate bodies other than public corporations, banks, other financial institutions and agricultural companies.

Personal sector: Individual residents in the UK: unincorporated private businesses, sole traders and partnerships; private trusts and non-profit-making institutions serving persons.

In this study of financial sectors related to the regions of the UK, the sectoral divisions outlined above will be followed as far as possible. Complete adherence to these categorisations may not be possible due to the method and success in collecting statistics on a regional basis. Where it is feasible the constituent components of the sectors shall be treated in relation to the other sectors, and the rest of its own sector. For example, other financial institutions will be analysed by its component parts (as far as possible), and not consolidated as one grouping.

The various flows, as categorised in *Financial Statistics,* will be analysed for each of the above sectors (where applicable). Those will follow the order in *Financial Statistics* in the text with a commentary on methodology and source of data. The treatment of financial flows follows the CSO's *Explanatory Handbook (Financial Statistics)* and this is used for overall guidance.

Financial flows in the context of the regional money flows model

This section examines each category of financial flows in the context of the overall regional money flows model. Where greater regional data have been generated, reference is made to them in the next section. The figures for the flows for the country as a whole are presented at the end of this section.

Notes and coin

The issue of notes and coin is a source of finance for the central government. The figures for the public sector relate to the increase in the fiduciary note issue plus the increase in coin issued less the increase in holdings of notes and coin by the Bank of England Banking Department, (included in the item net government indebtedness to the Bank of England Banking Department).

The figures for the banking sector relate to changes in their holdings of note and coin less changes in Scottish and Northern Ireland notes issued. In terms of the regional matrix, this represents a flow between the government sector and the banking sector (supra-regional institutions).

Changes in holdings of notes and coin by other sectors are, for convenience, arbitrarily divided equally between industrial and commercial companies and the personal sector in the national flow of funds accounts. To get regional holdings, regional GDP is used as a proxy to apportion the national control totals. (The figures are given on p. 214.)

Market treasury bills

These comprise Treasury bills other than those held by the National Debt Commissioners, The Exchange Equalisation Account, central government departments and the Bank of England (all consolidated out as part of the public sector). Net sales by the public sector are equal to the increase in market Treasury bills outstanding less identified purchases by public corporations. Holdings are by the banking sector, by other financial institutions and by non-residents and these can be identified nationally. The residual between purchases and identified sales are attributed to industrial and commercial companies.

With respect to the regional money flows model these flows between the public sector and the other sectors is treated as flows between the government sector and other supra-regional entities. Holdings by industrial and commercial companies are not allocated to any specific region as these are likely to be held by the larger organisations.

British government securities

These comprise British government and government guaranteed marketable securities. Public sector sales are equal to total cash issues less redemptions less net purchases by the Bank of England Issue Department and the National Debt Commissioners (consolidated out as part of the public sector), and identified purchases by public corporations and local authorities (also consolidated out). Holdings are by the banking sector, other financial institutions, industrial and commercial companies and overseas. The residual difference between identified sales and purchases is attributed to the personal sector.

In terms of the regional money flows model all identified holdings are between the supra-regional entities and the public sector as with Treasury Bills. However in so far as local authorities hold any government securities, these could be attributed to the regions of the holding local authorities. The available data suggests that local authorities have not been holding these. Personal sector holdings have been allocated by regional

National savings

This comprises the following items:

1 *Deposits* (a) increases in outstanding deposits, including estimated accrued interest, with the ordinary department of the National Savings Bank and Trustee Savings Bank; (b) increases and deposits including estimated accrued interest with the Investment Account of the National Savings Bank and with the new Department of the Trustee Savings Bank.

2 *Certificates and bonds.* Net receipts from sale of premium savings bonds, defence bonds, national development bonds and national savings certificates plus the increase in accrued interest on national savings certificates plus the increase in accrued interest on national savings certificates.

National savings are treated as financial claims by the personal sector. Items 1 (a) and 2 represent financial claims on the public sector and items 1 (b) represents a claim on the other financial institutions sector.

With respect to the collection of data on national savings at the regional level the following apply:

1 It was not possible to separate which were financial claims on the public sector and which were on other financial institutions.
2 The Trustee Savings Banks' statistics related to the year ending 20 November, and these were used to apportion the financial years.
3 The figures for the Department of National Savings were used on a sample of savings by place of employment from the regional (voluntary) savings movement (now disbanded). Details of the sample and estimates for each form of saving at the regional level are given on p.178.

Tax instruments

This comprises the following items:

Certificates of tax deposits: these are available to tax payers generally and relate to payments of income tax (non PAYE and tax deducted from payments to sub-contractors), corporation tax, capital gains tax, capital transfer tax and petroleum revenue tax.

Tax deposit accounts: this was used to meet 'mainstream' corporation tax liabilities.

Personal sector flows have been allocated on the basis of regional gdp. All other flows have been allocated to the supra-regional sectors. (See p.214)

Net government indebtedness to Bank of England Banking Department

All transactions betseen the central government and the Bank of England Banking Department (part of the banking sector) are recorded under this heading. In terms of the regional money flows model, this represents flows between the central government and the supra-regional banking sector.

Local authority debt

Local authority borrowing is broken down for the country as a whole by various sectors. It is also classified according to type of borrowing. With respect to the latter, local authority debt is divided between:

1 *Temporary borrowing* which covers money repayable in less than 12 months, including borrowing on bills and bank overdrafts.
2 *Listed securities* which are securities listed on a UK stock exchange and all negotiable bonds (some of which are unlisted).
3 *Other long-term borrowing* which included loans by local authority superannuation funds to the parent authority.

With respect to the former, borrowing by local authority from within the public sector comprises borrowing from central government—mainly loans from the Public Works Loan Board—as recorded in the central government capital account, the take up of local authority debt by the Issue Department of the Bank of England and by the National Insurance Fund. As well there is borrowing from public corporations. Local authority debt acquired by the banking sector comprises advances and loans plus the sector's acquisition of local authority bills and of listed and unlisted securities. Lending by other financial institutions include loan by local authorities' superannuation funds.

For the country as a whole, the sources of these statistics vary. For the public sector, the central government capital account and the returns made by local authorities provide the data. The banking sector's and other financial institutions' own returns supply their data. For industrial and commercial companies local authorities returns are used. For the overseas sector, the statistics are taken from the balance of payments accounts. The residual between total net borrowing and identified borrowing from other sectors is allocated to the personal sector.

For borrowing by local authorities classified by region, the source of data is the regional information from *Local Government Financial Statistics Capital Income Account.* Although this does not give a sectoral breakdown, it does give figures on the inflow to each region in this category, and figures are presented in Appendix 2 on local authority incomes.

Deposits with banking sector

These are current and deposit accounts held with institutions classified to the banking sector by the other sectors. These include:

1 Deposits with the Bank of England Banking Department, other than bankers' deposits (intra-sector deposits) and the balance of the National Loan funds and Paymaster General.

2 Funds borrowed by the discount market outside the banking sector.
3 The banking sector's net liabilities to offices abroad and deposits and advances from banks abroad.

They exclude banks' own internal funds and all transactions between institutions classified to the banking sector. The regional apportionment of deposits with the banking sector is dealt with on p.208.

Deposits with building societies

These cover both shares and deposits with building societies. Increases in deposits are equal to receipts of principal plus interest credited and not paid out less withdrawals of principle. Nationally figures are allocated to persons, other financial institutions and industrial and commercial companies. For the regional apportionment, an approach to each building society was made to obtain end of year balances by region so that increases in deposits could be calculated. The regional figures are based on the response to this approach and are discussed in detail on p.194.

Deposits with finance houses

The main source of finance houses' funds are deposits, bills and bank advances. Finance houses provide hire purchase and other instalment credit to businesses for the purchase of plant and equipment, and to persons for the purchase of consumer durables. (The treatment of finance houses is treated separately on p.192).

Deposits with financial institutions, other

These are deposits received by financial institutions other than banks, building societies and finance houses. In the main these cover the special finance agencies and are treated separately on p.205.

Bank lending

All transactions between institutions classified to the banking sector are excluded. Included are:

1 *Advances and loans* including overdrafts.
2 *Commercial bills.* These are commercial bills drawn on UK and overseas residents and discounted by banks.
3 *Market loans.*

The sectors involved are the personal sector, local authorities, public corporations, other financial institutions, industrial and commercial companies and the overseas sector. (The regional apportionment of items in this sector is treated on p.208.)

Credit extended by retailers and identified trade credit

The figures relate for all years to debt outstanding on instalment credit to durable goods retailers. Identified trade credit consists of domestic trade debt (net) of public corporations and suppliers' trade credit and associated advance and progress payments on exports and imports. For the personal sector, regional sales of consumer goods has been used to distribute total to regions. For the company sector, regional GDP has been used as a proxy.

Loans for house purchases

This item consists of loans by:

1 *Local authorities.* Mortgages advances for house purchase and improvements, including loans for the purchase of council houses by tenants and loans to housing associations. These figures are obtained from the regional figure in *Local Government Financial Statistics* and *Local Financial Returns, Scotland.*
2 *Other public sector.* Loans made by the central government to private housing associations, loans made by the Housing Corporation to housing societies, and loans by new town corporations. These are obtained from the annual reports of the organisation, and are allocated to the regions concerned. In the case of the Housing Corporation, adjustments have to be made to their regions and these are discussed on p.110.
3 *Financial institutions.* Mortgage advances by building societies, loans by insurance companies and by banks. The advance by building societies have been calculated from the approach to the building societies and is discussed on p.194. For banks, figures are available for Scotland and Northern Ireland. For the remainder, including insurance companies, no information is available and new houses annually in each region has been used as a proxy.

Other loans by public sector to private sector

The figures relate to (a) transactions in commercial bills by the issue Department of the Bank of England (allocated nationally to industrial and commercial companies). For the regional model, this is treated as a flow between two supra-regional sectors; (b) to net lending to building societies (supra-regional flows); (c) and to industry and trade and

(d) other miscellaneous loans for education and other services. Items (c) and (d) have been allocated to regions as described in the public expenditure section (see p.84).

Also included is net lending by public corporations to the private sector, other than for house purchase.

Loans by superannuation funds to parent organisation

This includes loans made by their superannuation funds to public corporations and companies (this excludes local authorities which are included in local authority debt). These are treated in the regional money flows model as supra-regional flows (other financial institutions to multi-regional companies).

Other loans and mortgages by financial institutions (excluding banks)

These are made mainly by insurance companies and by special finance agencies. (The regional allocation of special finance agencies is treated in depth on p.205.) No data are available on insurance companies loans and population is used to allocate them to regions.

Unit trust sales

(This covers sales less repurchases of unit trusts. These are treated in greater detail on p.212.)

Company and overseas' securities

This item consists of:

1 *UK capital issues.* Nationally the estimates relate to new money raised by issues of ordinary, preference and loan capital by listed public companies and where they are identified, unlisted companies in the UK, and by overseas companies and overseas public authorities. Issues to shareholders are included only if the sole or principal share register is maintained in the UK.
2 *Capital issues overseas.* These include private issues of companies overseas.
3 *Other.* These are all other transactions in listed and unlisted securities which can be identified, including the acquisition of capital issues of stock.

Transactions by the public sector comprise cash expenditure on company securities, etc. (net) by public corporations less net cash receipts by central government sales. For the most part these will be in multi-regional companies, but some single regional companies may be included. These could be included in the region if identifiable.

Figures for the banking sector and other financial institutions are net transactions in both listed and unlisted securities. These have been allocated as flows between supra-regional sectors.

For the overseas sector figures in transactions in company and overseas securities are taken from the balance of payments statistics and allocated to the overseas sector in the regional flows model.

Information about transactions in company and overseas securities by industrial and commercial companies relates to their estimated cash expenditure on acquiring investments, their acquisitions of share and loan capital in overseas companies and to overseas direct investment in UK company securities and in the regional model, these are allocated to the supra-regional sector and the overseas sector.

The estimate of transactions in company and overseas securities by the personal sector are derived as a residual. With respect to the regional money flows model they have been allocated to regions in the basis of investment income.

Life assurance and superannuation schemes

This includes net receipts by the insurance companies and superannuation funds available for the acquisition of financial assets. The superannuation funds can be subdivided into local authorities, other public sector and private sector. (The allocation of these funds in the regional money flows model is treated on pp.184–191.)

Other identified home assets

This includes the following miscellaneous items:

For the public sector:

1 Repayments by nationalised steel undertakings of a loan from industrial and commercial companies. (Flow between supra-regional sectors.)
2 Redemption less issues of stock of Electricity Board for Northern Ireland. (Flow between Northern Ireland and supra-regional sectors.)
3 Borrowing by regional water authorities and trust ports other than from public and banking sectors. These can be identified from annual reports of organisations and can be allocated to region in which they lie. With the water authorities as their regional boundaries are not coterminous with the standard

planning regions, the nearest equivalent region has to be used.

For financial institutions

1 Increases in assets and liabilities which are not separately identified in the returns made by financial institutions. This includes borrowing from finance houses other than in form of deposits, and their deposits with the Bank of England. (Flows between supra-regional sectors.)
2 Property unit trust sales to charities and pension fund investment in property unit trusts and the Local Authorities' Mutual Investment Trust. (Flows between supra-regional sector.)

For industrial and commercial companies

Purchases of shares in retail co-operative societies. (These are likely to be between a supra-regional sector and separate regions, but no data are available; allocation is between supra-regional sector.)

Public sector transactions with the overseas sector

These include (a) allocation of special drawing rights; (b) official reserves; (c) inter-government loans; (d) transactions with IMF, etc., (e) refinanced export credits. These are all treated as flows between the government sector and overseas sector.

Intra-company investment overseas

This item represents private investment abroad, other than in securities less the corresponding overseas investment in the UK private sector. This is treated as flows between supra-regional sector and the overseas sector.

Other identified overseas assets

This is flows between the public and other financial institutions sectors and the overseas sector. The flow between the industrial and commercial companies is taken as a residual in the nations statistics, and it is considered a flow between the supra-regional sector and the overseas sector in the regional model.

Unidentified items

This represents the difference between the net acquisition in financial assets calculated from the difference on the capital and current accounts, and the sum of the identified transactions in financial assets.

Table 61

Public sector: transactions in financial assets (£m) (current prices)

	Notes and coins	Market treasury bills	British government securities	National Savings		Tax instruments	Net government indebtedness to Bank of England	Northern Ireland central government debt	Local authority debt	Deposits with financial inst.
				Deposits	Certificates					
1974–75	- 921	- 1,597	- 2,200	- 198	70	51	544	- 31	- 2,138	26
1975–76	- 619	- 2,166	- 4,157	- 209	- 291	4	- 292	28	- 1,044	391
1976–77	- 733	1,262	- 6,284	- 63	- 934	7	138	- 20	- 853	116
1977–78	- 1,282	572	- 6,684	- 341	- 740	- 436	- 800	2	- 488	60

	Bank lending to public	Identified credit extended by retailers	Transactions concerning certain public sector pension schemes	Loans for house purchases	Other loans to private sector	Loans by superannuation fund to parent organisation	Company secs;	Other identified home assets
1974–75	- 155	- 252	- 285	763	7	32	224	100
1975–76	84	38	- 307	454	- 288	12	473	57
1976–77	- 427	381	- 216	76	239	24	182	36
1977–78	137	120	- 216	67	140	28	-- 513	27

	Foreign currency borrowing by government	Official reserves	Inter government loans net	Transactions with IMF etc.	Re-financed exports and shipbuilding credits	Other identified overseas assets	Inidentified items
1974–75	- 1,067	280	152	76	454	- 602	- 68
1975–76	—	- 619	130	- 475	542	- 538	110
1976–77	- 584	2,166	24	- 932	576	- 1,232	- 780
1977–78	- 287	6,345	72	- 285	- 355	- 1,141	- 279

Acquisition of assets or reduction in liabilities is shown positive
Sale of assets or increase in liabilities is negative

Table 62

Banking sector: transactions in financial assets (£m) (current prices)

	Notes and coins	Market treasury bills	British government securities	Tax instruments	Net government indebtedness to Bank of England Banking Dept.	Northern Ireland government debt	Local authority bills	Local authority secs.	Deposits received: Public sector	Deposits received: Other financial inst.
1974–75	47	437	- 52	- 3	- 544	41	52	56	47	- 363
1975–76	156	1,875	375	—	292	- 10	- 14	- 233	- 279	- 32
1976–77	- 153	- 518	185	—	- 138	4	3	1	- 151	- 39
1977–78	117	– 512	976	61	800	- 3	- 45	- 11	- 128	- 1,863

	Deposits received: Industrial and commercial companies	Deposits received: Personal sector	Deposits received: Overseas	Advances and loans: Local authorities	Advances and loans: Public corporations	Advances and loans: Other finance inst.	Advances and loans: Industrial and commercial companies	Advances and loans: Personal sector	Advances and loans: Overseas sector
1974–75	- 203	- 2,091	- 6,332	225	114	- 52	3,015	- 122	4,934
1975–76	- 868	- 915	- 8,205	947	- 143	158	101	101	1,177
1976–77	- 1,286	- 1,310	- 11,435	- 27	425	255	3,193	628	2,605
1977–78	- 2,378	- 1,087	- 11,950	610	- 159	601	1,963	1,326	4,427

	Government dealing in foreign currencies	Commercial bills	Market loans	Intra-company government overseas	Company and overseas securities: Capital issues	Company and overseas securities: Other transactions
1974–75	820	656	- 103	—	- 66	82
1975–76	—	- 50	6,240	19	- 296	55
1976–77	534	120	7,685	- 21	- 236	131
1977–78	220	360	6,810	- 10	- 320	739

Acquisition of assets, reduction in liabilities is shown positive
Sale of assets, or increase in liabilities is shown negative

Table 63 *Other financial institutions: transactions in financial assets (£m) (current prices)*

	Market treasury bills	British government securities	Tax instruments	Northern Ireland Govt.Dept.	Local authority debt: Bills and temp.debt	Local authority debt: Other	Bank deposits	Deposits received: Savings banks	Deposits received: Building societies	Deposits received: Finance houses	Deposits received: Other financial inst.	Deposits received: Official loans
1974–75	34	1421	—	- 3	792	646	363	- 115	- 2,763	- 6	- 277	- 117
1975–76	302	3052	—	—	- 136	789	32	- 223	- 4,475	- 32	- 229	127
1976–77	- 80	3674	—	—	132	- 83	39	- 189	- 2,947	- 68	139	3
1977–78	317	4484	35	4	- 100	683	1863	- 792	- 6,495	7	68	5

	Bank lending: Advances and loans	Bank lending: Commercial bills	Market loans	Loans and mortgages: For house purchase	Loans and mortgages: By superannuation funds to parent organisation	Loans and mortgages: Other	Unit trust units	Company and overseas security: Capital issues	Company and overseas security: Other transactions	Life assurance and superannuation funds
1974–75	52	1	—	1,815	- 24	74	- 65	- 141	60	- 3,423
1975–76	- 158	- 5	- 128	3,096	12	90	- 99	- 303	2,221	- 5,049
1976–77	- 255	- 90	104	3,532	- 24	213	- 46	- 131	931	- 5,694
1977–78	- 601	- 28	- 92	4,248	28	492	- 71	- 116	2,071	- 6,493

	Other identified home assets	Intra-company investment	Other identified overseas assets
1974–75	67	73	- 53
1975–76	- 59	32	- 38
1976–77	- 85	142	125
1977–78	12	153	- 40

Acquisition of assets or reduction in liabilities is shown positive
Sale of assets or increase in liabilities is negative

Table 64 *Industrial and commercial companies: transactions in financial assets (£m) (current prices)*

	Notes and coins	Market treasury Bills	British government sectors	Tax instruments	Local authority debt: Temporary	Local authority debt: Other	Deposits: Banking sector	Deposits: Building societies	Deposits: Other financial inst.	Bank lending: Advances	Bank lending: Commercial bills	Bank lending: Market loans
1974–75	370	- 15	- 36	- 11	- 95	116	203	20	19	- 3,016	- 502	5
1975–76	117	506	130	6	19	- 28	868	41	25	- 101	89	53
1976–77	558	- 270	94	- 8	34	103	1,286	82	18	- 3,193	- 182	30
1977–78	662	13	52	234	- 197	- 79	2,378	154	10	1,963	- 518	- 128

	Credit extended by retailers	Identified trade credit	Public sector loans	Loans by superann. funds to parent organ.	Other loans and mortgages by financial inst. (excluding banks)	Company and overseas security: UK capital issues by listed companies	Company and overseas security: Capital issues overseas	Other transactions	Other identified home assets	Intra-company investment overseas
1974–75	20	141	45	8	- 60	- 814	- 10	142	- 69	241
1975–76	69	125	82	—	- 65	- 1,227	- 9	503	31	- 822
1976–77	142	- 76	- 305	- 1	- 107	- 1,399	28	840	- 27	246
1977–78	108	- 71	- 55	—	- 250	- 619	- 103	891	- 11	- 1,009

	Other identified overseas assets	Unidentified items
1974–75	126	- 194
1975–76	770	- 815
1976–77	318	- 218
1977–78	786	- 1,443

Acquisition of assets or reduction in liabilities is shown positive
Sale of assets or increase in liabilities is negative

Table 65 *Personal sector: transactions in financial assets (£m) (current prices)*

			National savings					Local authority debt		
	Notes and coins	British government secs.	Savings banks investment accounts	Other deposits	Certificates and bonds	Tax instruments	Northern Ireland government debt	Temporary	Other	Unidentified
1974–75	504	905	105	198	- 70	- 37	3	- 85	587	- 65
1975–76	346	659	221	209	221	- 10	- 35	- 34	- 45	- 372
1976–77	328	2,005	187	63	934	1	10	54	146	521
1977–78	503	356	785	348	740	106	- 3	- 58	- 19	- 286

	Deposits			Bank Lending					
	Banking sector	Building societies	Financial institutions	Advances	Market loans	Credit extended by retailers	Identified trade credit from public	Loans for house purchases	Other loans and mortgages
1974–75	2,091	2,743	13	172	45	–	66	- 2,628	- 21
1975–76	915	4,434	- 9	- 9	137	- 65	- 336	- 3,630	- 33
1976–77	1,310	2,865	39	- 571	- 89	- 159	- 402	- 3,658	- 114
1977–78	1,087	6,373	- 26	- 1,036	20	- 127	- 197	- 4,445	- 240

	Unit trust	Company and overseas sec.	Life assurance and superannuation funds	Other identified home assets	Unidentified assets
1974–75	65	- 1,029	3,708	- 113	- 1,154
1975–76	99	- 1,064	5,150	- 12	1,002
1976–77	46	- 1,468	5,910	68	209
1977–78	71	- 2,076	6,709	- 32	741

Acquisition of assets or reduction in liabilities is shown positive
Sale of assets or increases in liabilities negative

Table 66 *Overseas sector: transactions in financial assets (£m) (current prices)*

Sector	Market treasury bills	British government security	Local authority debt	Official reserves	Inter-government loans	Transactions with IMF	Re-financed export credits
1974–75	1111	- 38	- 91	- 280	- 152	- 76	849
1975–76	- 517	- 59	- 10	619	- 130	475	538
1976–77	- 394	326	- 31	- 2,148	- 24	932	1,282
1977–78	- 390	816	- 10	6,345	- 74	285	1,208

				Bank lending			Company and overseas sectors	
Sector	Deposits with banking sector	Deposits with other financial inst.	Bank advances and loans	Commercial bills	Market loans	Suppliers trade credit (net)	UK Capital issues	Other transactions
1974–75	6332	216	- 4934	- 114	53	25	43	810
1975–76	8205	133	- 1179	- 26	- 6263	169	46	- 227
1976–77	11435	- 93	- 2605	194	- 7793	114	64	312
1977–78	11950	9	- 4427	- 30	- 6532	167	42	4

	Inter-company			
Sector	By UK Overseas	By overseas To UK	Other private sector assets	Unidentified items
1974–75	- 1465	1151	- 168	426
1975–76	- 1060	1831	- 732	- 320
1976–77	- 2012	1645	- 443	1096
1977–78	- 1558	2382	- 746	2712

Acquisition of assets or reduction in liabilities is shown positive
Sale of assets or increase in liabilities is negative

The regional distribution of certain financial flows

In this section, the flows which are amenable to regional apportionment are discussed in detail. Figures for all the flows detailed in the last section as having been allocated to each region by proxy or otherwise are presented here.

National savings

National savings comprise the following:

1 *Deposits:* (a) increases in outstanding deposits, including estimated accrued interest with the ordinary department of the National Savings Bank and Trustee Savings Bank; (b) increases and deposits, including estimated accrued interest with the Investment Account of the National Savings Bank and with the New Department of the Trustee Savings Banks.

2 *Certificates and bonds:* net receipts from sales of premium savings bonds, defence bonds, national development bonds and national savings certificates plus the increase in accrued interest on national savings certificates.

National savings are treated as financial claims by the personal sector. Items 1 (a) and 2 represent claims on the public sector and items 1 (b) represent claims on the other financial institutions sector. However, as shown below, it was not practical to separate 1 (b) from the rest, so the figures that are shown here represent claims by the personal sector on the other two relevant sections. The description of the data collection is divided into the Trustee Savings Banks and the Department for National Savings.

The collective figures for Trustee Savings Banks and the Department of National Savings by region are presented in Table 67.

Trustee Savings Banks

The Trustee Savings Banks are basically regional entities, joined together in a confederation. After the 1976 Act which recommended that, provided the banks were prepared to amalgamate into larger units, they could develop along the lines of the clearing banks and carry out the business of banking, the seventy-two which then existed joined to form nineteen banks (now eighteen) whose common interests are now served by a Central Board.

The Central Board of the Trustee Savings Bank was approached regarding statistics on the operations in the regions. The response was favourable. The Central Board had themselves been engaged in collect-

Table 67 *National Savings by region (£m) (current prices)*

	North	Yorks Humbs.	East Mids.	East Anglia	South-East	South-West	West Mids.	North-West	Wales	Scot.	Nrth. Ire'd.
1974–75											
Trustee Savings Bank	16.3	18.2	15.3	17.9	40.0	10.4	31.3	36.7	4.8	43.9	10.7
Dept. for National Savings	1.0	1.8	2.2	1.0	- 7.8	3.5	0.3	9.8	0.1	5.0	2.2
Total	17.1	20.0	17.5	18.9	32.2	13.9	31.6	46.5	4.9	48.9	12.9
1975–76											
Trustee Savings Bank	25.2	19.1	36.2	2.9	34.9	12.8	15.2	46.3	24.1	70.5	16.6
Dept. for National Savings	23.8	35.7	26.7	13.9	170.0	34.3	44.0	44.2	17.9	31.8	3.7
Total	49.0	54.8	62.9	16.8	204.9	47.1	59.2	90.5	42.0	102.3	20.3
1976–77											
Trustee Savings Bank	7.6	19.2	26.7	12.9	44.7	19.3	18.7	52.5	8.6	67.6	12.0
Dept. for National Savings	65.6	89.9	66.0	38.2	381.8	81.6	126.0	110.0	14.2	42.1	5.0
Total	73.2	109.1	92.7	51.1	426.5	100.9	144.7	162.5	22.8	109.7	17.0
1977–78											
Trustee Savings Bank	24.8	35.3	40.6	18.9	64.2	20.5	42.8	69.5	13.1	73.2	14.2
Dept. for National Savings	112.2	186.7	103.1	66.5	677.6	155.9	194.5	219.1	49.9	79.0	18.9
Total	137.0	222.0	143.7	85.4	741.8	176.4	237.3	288.6	63.0	152.2	33.1

ing statistics for the nineteen new banks by aggregating those which had joined together to form a new entity. This formed the basis of the regional data for the money flows study.

The nineteen banks did not coincide with the eleven planning regions except for Northern Ireland. Some could be added together to form the region as in the case of Scotland. Others were wholly in one region, but some traversed regional boundaries. However, the Central Board provided details of these branches which had to be 'moved' from one region to another to obtain the banks' operations classified by standard planning region.

As the overall nature of the exercise is to ascertain whether it is feasible to produce a regional money flows model and collect data to fit the model, it was felt that the least burden put on the organisations which had agreed to provide the data, the greater the chance of success. Consequently although ideally data were sought for financial years, the accounting period used by the organisation itself would be acceptable. The accounting year for the Trustee Savings Bank ends on 20 November of each year. However, as the Banks produce monthly figures, figures on a financial year basis would be feasible, although would entail considerable more effort in their collation for the region.

The relevant statistics which are being collected, relate to the increase in deposits made by persons in each region which are available for investment by the banks. This figure is made up of various flows: payments less withdrawals in the accounting period plus accrued interest due to the person. (This assumes that any accrued interest which is withdrawn is included in with deposits; otherwise net accrued interest is the relevant consideration.) However, it is possible to obtain the sum total from the end of year balances for each region. By obtaining a time-series of end of year balances, the change in balances from one year to another represents the increase in funds available for investment. However, in some instances the figure could be negative, which show that overall withdrawals have been greater than deposits plus accrued interest.

The Central Board of the Trustee Savings Bank was initially approached in July of 1978. The data which were collected related to end of year balances from 1974 to 1977 inclusive. This gave net flows to the banks from persons for 1974–75, 1975–76 and 1976–77 (21 November to 20 November). The end of year figures for 1978 for the eighteen banks were used to estimate the 1977–78 figures. These are shown for each region in Table 69. Translating these statistics to a financial year basis by applying the regional distribution shown in Table 69 to the total net increase in funds (financial year) gives the figures as shown in Table 68.

Table 68

Trustee Savings Bank: estimated net increase in funds by regions (£m) (Current prices)

	1974–75[1]	1975–76[1]	1976–77[1]	1977–78[1]
North	16.3	25.2	7.6	24.8
Yorkshire and Humberside	18.2	19.1	19.2	35.3
East Midlands	15.3	36.2	26.7	40.6
East Anglia	17.9	2.9	12.9	18.9
South-East	40.0	34.9	44.7	64.2
South-West	10.4	12.8	19.3	20.5
West Midlands	31.3	15.2	18.7	42.8
North-West	36.7	46.3	52.5	69.5
Wales	4.8	24.1	8.6	13.1
Scotland	43.9	70.5	67.6	73.2
Northern Ireland	10.7	16.6	12.0	14.2
UK	245.5	303.8	289.8	416.9
Channel Islands	9.8	9.1	24.2	- 2.1
Total[2]	255.2	312.9	313.9	414.8

1 Year ending 31 March
2 Sum of regions may not equal total due to rounding

Table 69

Trustee Savings Bank: net increase in funds by regions (£m) (Current prices)

	1974–75[1]	1975–76[1]	1976–77[1]	1977–78[1]
North	21.6	23.9	5.9	29.3
Yorkshire and Humberside	24.1	18.1	14.9	41.6
East Midlands	20.3	34.3	20.7	47.9
East Anglia	23.7	2.7	10.0	22.3
South-East	53.0	33.1	34.7	75.8
South-West	13.8	12.1	15.0	24.2
West Midlands	41.5	14.4	14.5	50.5
North-West	48.7	43.9	40.8	82.0
Wales	6.4	22.8	6.7	15.4
Scotland	58.2	66.8	52.5	86.4
Northern Ireland	14.2	15.7	9.3	16.8
UK	325.5	287.8	225.0	491.9
Channel Islands	13.0	8.6	18.8	- 2.5
Total	338.5	296.4	243.8	489.4

1 Year ending 20 November

The Department for National Savings has evolved over more than a century and by the end of 1978 was comprised of: The National Savings Bank; National Savings Certificates; premium bonds; British savings bonds; save as you earn; and National Savings stamps and gift tokens.

The Department for National Savings were approached in August 1978 with a view to obtaining statistics on national savings in the context of the regional money flows research programme. The reply indicated that regional figures were not compiled and nothing beyond the national figures were available. It would also not be possible to provide raw data so that regional figures could be built up from individual returns.

Despite the failure of the approach to the National Savings Department, some data were found to be available. Figures on gross savings for Scotland and Wales are published in each country's *Digest of Statistics,* and net savings figures for Northern Ireland are produced in similar fashion. In addition, in the *Annual Report* of the Department for National Savings, the work of the National Savings Committees for England and Wales was reported. These committees were organised on a regional basis and statistics were given for gross saving in place of employment classified by region for all the categories of savings sponsored by the department.

The limited information published in these various forms have been used to provide some estimates of the regional distribution of the various forms of savings.

The regions which the National Savings Committee used were: Northern; Yorkshire and Humberside; East Midlands; Eastern; South-Eastern; Southern; London; South-Western; West Midlands; North-Western and Wales. The details for each region related to the gross savings by channel of investment and the numbers involved in the channel of investment. This allowed an estimate to be made of *per capita* holding in each form of saving by region.

Although some of the regions did not coincide exactly with the planning regions, the *per capita* figures of the savings committees' regions were used to represent the nearest planning region. Thus, the *per capita* figures for the Eastern region were used for East Anglia and the Southern, South-Eastern and London regions were aggregated to represent the South-East. The remaining regions appeared to have the same boundaries. The data related to the financial years 1974–75, 1975–76 and 1976–77. The committees were phased out in 1977–78 and no figures were produced in that year.

The regional figures for savings under the various headings were estimated by the following method:

1 The regional sample of gross payments from the National Savings Committee provided *per capita* figures for each region. These *per capita* figures were multiplied by the relevant standard planning region's population to obtain regional weights for each form of saving.
2 These regional weights were used to distribute the England total for the appropriate saving. The figures for Wales, Scotland and Northern Ireland were available from published sources. This gave the regional distribution of gross payments.
3 These gross payments were used to distribute net receipts for the regions of the UK. Northern Ireland was available separately.
4 The gross payments were used to distribute the net accrued interest (where relevant).
5 The average over the 1974–75 to 1976–77 period was used to distribute the 1977–78 national total.

The data which were used from the National Savings Committee provided a 'sample' based on location of employment and is shown in Table 70.

Table 70 *National Savings Committee regional coverage of total gross savings by channel of investment*

%

	1974–75	1975–76	1976–77
National Savings Bank	3.5	3.9	4.7
National Savings Certificates	3.3	1.8	1.4
Premium Bonds	4.3	4.1	4.5
British Savings Bonds	0.1	0.1	0.2
Save as You Earn			
(a) National Savings Bank	21.9	18.3	16.9
(b) Trustee Savings Bank	6.4	6.2	19.1

This section has looked at the availability of data on National Savings classified by standard region over the period 1974–75 to 1977–78. Figures have been produced using a variety of sources coupled with assumptions in the representativeness of the 'sample' and the relationship between gross savings and net receipts and accrued interest. However, the 'sample' data for the Department of National Savings is no longer available as the regional Savings Committees no longer exist. Obtaining data from the Trustee Savings Bank would not seem to pose the same problems as so long as goodwill is retained, the mechanics used to obtain the regional statistics in this book could be repeated. (This ignores the question whether the Trustee Savings Banks should be included with the financial sector as a whole in the future, or with National Savings.)

The Department for National Savings is increasingly moving to a mechanised system of handling their various accounts. The *Annual Report* for 1977–78 states that the following were processed by computer:

	000's
Dividends on the National Savings Stock Register	2465
National Saving Certificate repayments	1040
Save as you earn repayments	50
Save as you earn statements	606
Premium Savings Bonds Prize Warrants	1190
Premium Savings Bonds Repayments	514

In addition a total of 4.5 million holding of Premium Savings Bonds manual records have been converted to the computer system files, with a further 100,000 holding set up for new purchases.

It would seem that in the future, given goodwill between the Department for National Savings and the compiling of regional data, that it may be possible to collect the required data because of the storage of the raw data on a computer.

Life assurance, superannuation and pension funds

The financial assets of life assurance, superannuation and pension funds are regarded wholly as a claim by the personal sector upon the financial institutions in the main along with net receipts by the central government from those public sector schemes for which no special pension fund is maintained being regarded as transactions between the public sector and persons. The investment of the funds are treated as transactions of financial institutions.

With respect to the element which enters into the financial accounts, certain transactions have to be calculated. The element which is required is the net increase in the amount available for investment. This is obtained as follows:

Funded schemes (including life assurance)

Contributions of employers
Contribution of employees, individual premiums, etc.
Rent, dividend and interest receipts
Transfers from unfunded schemes
Less pensions and other benefits paid
Less administrative costs, etc.
Net increase in amount available for investment

Unfunded schemes

Contributions of employers
Contributions of employees
Other income
Less pensions and other benefits paid
Less transfers of liability to funded schemes
Surplus

However, the figures shown in Table 4.6 of the *National Income and Expenditure Blue Book:* Transactions leading to net acquisition of financial assets of life assurance and superannuation schemes by the personal sector (itemised above) is an amalgam of various genres of organisations. *Financial Statistics,* Table 8.13 gives statistics on investments by insurance funds, and Table 8.15 breaks down superannuation funds into investments by local authorities, other public sector funded schemes, and private sector schemes. However, in *Financial Statistics* life assurance and superannuation funds are considered together.

In attempting to collect figures of insurance and superannuation funds in the regional context the relevant organisations were approached. The initial advance was made to the Life Office's Association, the British Insurance Association and the National Association of Pension Funds as they were the main collators of data relating to national figures. As well the office of the Government Actuary was approached regarding their survey on occupational pension schemes.

None of the organisations named above were able to help directly. The Government Actuary had considered putting in a regional dimension in its latest survey but for the methodological reasons relating to financial organisations in the regional context did not pursue it in the survey itself. The Life Offices' Association offered advice about the activity of its members, but felt unable to take any active approach to individual organisations. This was in part due to staff time constraints and partly a reluctance to sanction any increase in data collection upon the membership. The British Insurance Association offered suggestions on indirect methods but were unable to help any further.

Consequently it was decided to approach the individual companies themselves and some 125 insurance companies were circulated with a letter requesting information on premium income, benefits and claims, and administrative costs for each of the economic planning regions in which they had conducted business since 1974.

The Life Offices' Association suggested that the only data many companies might have on a regional basis would be that relating to new business contracted since computerisation of their records. Consequently, mention was made of this in the letter, suggesting that such new business information would be appreciated.

In total some forty-three replies were received, but of these, only nine provided data that might feasibly be used, and several could only offer incomplete data.

The following table represents a crude classification of the reasons offered by the thirty-four respondents that could provide data.

	Number
Not readily available from records	
• non-EPR operational regions	6
• records kept not fully regionalised	10
• unspecified practical difficulties	13
Considered themselves too small	8
No UK business	1
	34

A particular problem raised by several companies was that a considerable portion of business came their way through intermediaries, in the form of brokers and pension schemes. Thus, whilst being able to identify the branch or location at which they themselves received the business, they could not identify the area of operation of the intermediaries, and therefore, the location of the customer.

As a result it was felt that this direct approach was not fruitful and that secondary sources of information had to be used.

Despite this there was one class of superannuation scheme which was available by region—the one relating to local authorities. From the Local Government Financial Statistics regional information, statistics are available for 1975–76, 1976–77 and 1977–78 relating to expenditure and income involved in superannuation schemes. (These are shown in Tables 72–74.)

For the remainder proxy methods would have to be used. The first major problem was obtaining control totals. Information on the components which make up the funds available for investment is on a calendar year basis while the remainder of the information relates to financial years; as well the control totals have to be net of local authority superannuation schemes. The relevant local authority statistics could be subtracted from each element of the components of funds available for investment (ignoring the different accounting period), and also from the funds of insurance and superannuation funds. A regional proxy based on the components figures would then be obtained and applied to the net funds figure to distribute to the regions.

The different elements ideally would be treated as follows (funded and unfunded schemes):

Contributions of employers. The CSO regional accounts estimates total employers' contributions as part of regional income from employment. They consist of payments made by employers to the National Insurance scheme, the National Health Service, the Redundancy Fund and to life assurance and approved public and private superannuation schemes. As there is no information on the contributions by industry or region to superannuation schemes these were allocated on assumptions relating to national accounts estimates by industry and regional wages and salaries bills. The proxies used here are built up for each region by subtracting from the CSO estimate of contribution of employers the estimates for National Insurance scheme, National Health Service and Redundancy Funds calculated for the taxation report. From these employers' contributions all local authority schemes are also subtracted. The remaining regional figures are used to allocate the control totals.

Contribution of employees. The Department of Employment's annual *Family Expenditure Survey* (FES) provides a series of regional estimates of various household expenditures. Part of this relates to direct premiums and contributions deducted from employees concerned with life assurance and pensions.

However, as the FES is a sample survey, a degree of sampling error is to be expected, especially in the individual regional figures where the sample size is necessarily less than for the nation as a whole. In an attempt to increase the sample size for the regions, the published FES regional estimates are an amalgam of the current and the previous year's surveys. Therefore, 1977 national data was apportioned to the regions using FES estimates for the two year period 1976 – 1977, and, similarly for 1974, 1975 and 1976.

Furthermore, certain regions are over represented, and others under represented in the FES sample, when compared with their shares of total population. For example, in 1976–77 FES estimates, the North region supplied 6.4 per cent of the households in the sample, and yet had only 5.6 per cent of the 1976 mid-year population of the UK. Conversely, the South-East region supplied 28.8 per cent of the sample, and yet had 30.1 per cent of the UK population. These discrepancies persisted even when considering the number of persons rather than households involved in the sample. To reduce the impact of this bias, the FES estimates are converted into average annual *per capita* expenditure and were weighted by the mid-year population estimates. From these the local authority employees' contributions are to be subtracted and the remainder are used to allocate the national totals (less authority schemes).

Rent, dividends and interest receipts. Rent, dividends and interest receipts by insurance and superannuation are received by the personal sector as income relating to their contributions. These are allocated by region in proportion to the contributions from which those funds are built up (employers' and employees' contributions). Investment income is available as a separate item for local authorities superannuation schemes and would be netted off both regional and control totals.

Pensions and other benefits paid. These cover the outgoings from the funds and are distributed along the lines of rent, dividends and interest receipts in the absence of any other data.

Administrative costs, etc. These are assumed to be in proportion to the amount of business in each region (employers' and employees' contributions).

Ideally the funds available for investment by life assurance and superannuation schemes would be assembled given the data situation as described. In practice for the 1974–75/1977–78 period, it was not possible to carry these procedures out due to local authority superannuation figures for the English regions not being available for 1974–75, and for Scotland (at the time of writing) for 1975–76 onwards. Figures for Northern Ireland were also unavailable. As a result, the procedure which was adopted did not adjust for local authority superannuation in the manner outlined above. Also for 1977–78 FES details and employers' contributions were not available and the 1974–75/1976–77 average for regions was used to distribute the UK total. The available data for local authority superannuation by region are also presented.

Corresponding to the receipts by these insurance and superannuation funds (their liabilities) is their use of these funds (their assets) for the funds as a whole nationally the figures are presented in Tables 75–76. In terms of the regional money flows model, the relevant assets are local authority bills and securities; loans from house purchase and on company policies; other loans to single region entities; new company securities of single region firms; and land, property and ground rents. Much of the assets are concerned with supra-regional entities such as British and overseas government securities, multi-regional company securities and unit trusts. No information is available on the incidence of the assets which can theoretically be assigned to a single region.

Table 71 *Estimates of funds of life assurance and superannuation schemes by regions (£m) (current prices)*

	North	*Yorks. Humbs.*	*East Mids.*	*East Anglia*	*South-East*	*South-West*	*West Mids.*	*North-West*	*Wales*	*Scot.*	*Nrth. Ire'd.* [1]
1974–75	163	237	155	86	1698	169	239	432	145	314	70
1975–76	256	398	305	99	2210	229	384	566	236	391	75
1976–77	276	443	327	107	2767	266	378	595	244	423	85
1977–78	316	490	358	133	3032	302	455	724	284	512	104

1 New life assurance premiums in Northern Ireland are published in *Digest of Northern Ireland* statistics

Table 72 *Local authority superannuation (£000s) – 1975–1976*

(Including police and firemen's pension schemes)	*North*	*Yorks. Humbs.*	*East Mids.*	*East Anglia*	*South-East*	*South-West*	*West Mids.*	*North-West*	*Wales*	*Scot.*	*Nrth. Ire'd.*
Contributions of employees	12652	17190	11154	4728	58501	12829	17254	25096	10133		
Contribution of employers	15294	25081	15642	8849	95754	18647	24097	37649	12953		
Rent, dividends and interest	8462	12409	7434	4568	53980	11453	11001	19834	1896		
Transfers (net)	- 184	607	788	163	- 7381	- 2265	- 2488	- 4387	- 555		
Other income	2323	3675	3717	1590	13021	2611	3669	8183	2204		
Less pensions and other benefits received	- 19285	- 27994	- 18849	- 8284	- 108304	- 24195	- 28226	- 50301	- 16767		
Net increase in amount available for investment	19262	30968	19886	11614	105571	19080	25307	36074	10974		

Table 73

Local authority superannuation (£000s) – 1976–1977

(Including police and firemen's pension schemes)	*North*	*Yorks Humbs.*	*East Mids.*	*East Anglia*	*South-East*	*South-West*	*West Mids.*	*North-West*	*Wales*	*Scot.*	*Nrth. Ire'd.*
Contribution of employees	14552	20378	13425	5519	68763	14615	19694	29221	11968		
Contribution of employers	19022	31188	18144	7883	109295	21633	28837	44980	16090		
Rent, dividends and interest	11642	17626	11235	5853	71513	14743	16107	26812	9382		
Transfers (net)	- 1148	1817	- 1200	369	- 1963	- 1103	- 1350	- 3563	181		
Other income	1743	4466	2614	1130	13923	2031	2059	5876	1623		
Less pensions and other benefits paid	- 29073	- 40701	- 27338	- 10981	- 137455	- 31646	- 38017	- 65832	- 24325		
Net increase in amounts available for investment	14955	34774	16880	9773	124076	20273	27330	37494	14919		

Table 74

Local authority superannuation (£000s) – 1977–1978

(Including police and firemen's pension schemes)	*North*	*Yorks. Humbs.*	*East Mids.*	*East Anglia*	*South-East*	*South-West*	*West Mids.*	*North-West*	*Wales*	*Scot.*	*Nrth. Ire'd.*
Contribution of employees	16105	22309	14314	5832	72897	15472	21255	31337	12572		
Contributions of employers	20236	32806	20180	8531	121042	23811	33461	47310	17559		
Rent, dividends and interest	14558	21172	13110	7615	90137	17922	22139	33711	11535		
Transfers (net)	7199	1669	- 594	- 160	- 1598	- 1501	- 667	- 1374	- 559		
Other income	3885	10124	4206	2552	26415	7581	2775	18896	5625		
Less Pensions and other benefits paid	- 33854	- 46665	- 30868	- 12745	- 166335	- 37756	- 47610	- 77278	- 28967		
Net increase in amounts available for investment	28129	41415	20348	11625	142558	26532	31253	52602	17765		

Table 75 *Superannuation funds*

Use of funds (£m) (current prices)

	1974–75	*1975–76*	*1976–77*	*1977–78*
Short term assets	151.0	- 255.3	136.5	111.3
Long term borrowing	298.5	- 51.0	- 9.1	- 26.6
British government securities	298.5	817.4	1422.6	834.5
UK local authority securities	2.5	33.2	72.1	25.7
Overseas securities	7.0	7.9	- 8.1	- 4.1
Company securities and unit trusts	319.7	1373.4	866.5	1569.5
Local authority	7.3	- 12.1	1.0	- 6.9
Property unit trusts	23.6	90.8	66.7	92.0
Loan and mortgages	136.6	- 47.3	- 13.2	- 98.0
Land market and ground rent	270.7	414.7	471.5	699.2
Other investments	7.5	11.0	31.4	75.3

Table 76 *Insurance companies*

Use of funds (£m) (current prices)

	1974–75	*1975–76*	*1976–77*	*1977–78*
Cash and balances	167.6	92.9	56.3	224.0
Short term assets in other FI	49.2	6.6	26.6	- 1.8
Treasury bills	23.8	65.5	76.9	- 16.4
Local authority bills and temp.money	165.7	- 104.6	22.3	- 91.0
Other	40.2	- 24.3	- 7.7	- 6.5
Loans and mortgages	158.3	45.5	- 69.4	- 8.6
Overseas loans	4.1	8.0	3.5	6.9
British government securities	525.9	1507.3	2130.6	2148.9
Local authority securities	20.0	71.9	57.1	158.9
Overseas securities	16.9	19.5	47.9	78.9
Company securities	42.1	561.1	153.9	711.5
Unit trusts	53.8	86.6	63.8	82.7
Land market and ground rent	3389.5	3944.0	465.4	445.8
Other	8.0	4.1	6.6	- 4.7

Finance houses and leasing companies

The main business of finance houses and leasing companies is the direct financing of instalment credit of motor vehicles, caravans and household goods mainly to persons, together with a substantial amount of farm, industrial and building plant and equipment to businesses.

The main sources of funds are deposits and borrowing and are shown in Table 77.

Table 77 *Finance Houses: source of funds*
(£m) (current prices)

	Deposits					
	Banking sector	Other financial inst.	Industrial and commercial companies	Other residents	Overseas	Instalment credit discounted by fin. ints.
1974–75	60	- 60	- 25	10	13	
1975–76	35	6	28	- 8	11	
1976–77	32	16	19	39	13	- 4
1977–78	132	35	11	- 26	8	- 1

	Borrowing				
	Commercial bills	Banking section	Other financial inst.	Other residents	Unearned credits charged to the residents
1974–75		12	4	—	
1975–76		53	—	12	
1976–77	28	44	18	- 6	28
1977–78	42	114	67	7	42

Note: Due to a different method of compiling these data, the statistics for 1974–75 and 1975–76 are organised on different basis than for later years.

From this it can be seen that the majority of funds come from the supra-regional sections either in the form of borrowing or deposits and in terms of the money flows model deposits and borrowing with other residents (personal sector) may be credited to regions.

Figures for loans and advances of the finance houses are included in flow of funds accounts under 'Other loans and mortgages by financial institutions' (excluding banks) (see p.168), and the finance house element is shown in Table 78.

Table 78 *Loans and advances to UK residents*
(£m) (current prices)

	Financial institutions	Retailers[1]	Industrial and[2] commercial companies	Individuals	Cash and deposits in banks	Other current assets incl. treas. bills.
1974–75	6		- 233			3
1975–76	35		51			25
1976–77	36	2104	347	110	3	4
1977–78	10	2399	791	241	4	- 8

1 Retailers table 8.4 and 8.5 *(Financial Statistics)*

2 Industrial and commercial companies 8.4; finance houses 8.5 *(Financial Statistics)*

The importance of flows with respect to the regional model are those loans and advances to UK residents (retailers, industrial and commercial companies, and individuals).

The Finance House Association and The Equipment Leasing Association were both approached with a view to obtaining data on their members' activities in the regional context. Following discussions with the Associations a formal request for such statistics was put to the Taxation and Accountancy Committee of the Finance Houses Association and the Statistics Sub-Committee of the Equipment Leasing Association. The latter request coincided with a similar one from the Department of Trade.

The response to the requests was not favourable. The Finance Houses Association held the view 'that they could not recommend members of their Association to undertake such a mammoth task as an analysis by merchandise by standard regions. The information is not available at present and members see little or no commercial value in it.' The reply from the Leasing Association was that 'meaningful results could not be obtained without a disproportionate effort, and they could not recommend members to participate in such an exercise'. However, they agreed to undertake a more limited survey based on five categories: England, Scotland, Wales, Northern Ireland and other (mainly offshore). 'In the light of this country analysis the committee may reconsider the regional analysis. However, given the limited commercial value it would be unlikely.'

The reaction to the request for regional data was considered, not unnaturally, on the commercial value of such an exercise; as a result it would seem unlikely that any direct data on the operations of finance houses or leasing companies will be available, and that proxies would have to be used to allocate national totals to regions. However, with respect to leasing companies the analysis of assets purchased during 1978 shows the following:

	%
England	72.7
Northern Ireland	0.7
Scotland	10.7
Wales	4.7
Other*	11.2

* mainly ships

This unfortunately is not of great use in allocating the figures shown above as they do not cover the whole operation. Suggested proxies are expenditure on consumer durables for individuals and gross domestic fixed capital formation by region and these have been used to allocate the national figures for 1976–77 and 1977–78. The figures for 1974–75 and 1975–76 have not been allocated as the statistics are not on such a disaggregated basis and the selection of a suitable proxy less easy.

Table 79 *Finance Houses and leasing companies (Estimated advances by regions) (£m) (current prices)*

	Advances to retailers and individuals		Advances to industrial and commercial companies	
	1976–77	1977–78	1976–77	1977–78
North	133	135	23	53
Yorkshire and Humberside	181	216	26	59
East Midlands	149	177	20	45
East Anglia	74	88	10	22
South-East	746	890	91	208
South-West	187	223	20	45
West Midlands	200	239	25	57
North-West	225	268	30	68
Wales	106	127	29	43
Scotland	177	211	37	85
Northern Ireland	55	65	10	22

Building societies

Building societies are playing an increasingly important role in the institutional control of money within the national economy. Operating as they do, through a network of local offices, branches and agents, and yet often with national coverage, the building societies clearly have the potential to transfer considerable quantities of money into and out of the several regions of the country. Also, the smaller societies act as local institutions through which money enters and leaves the region.

In attempting to build up a detailed picture of the regional operations of the societies, the first step was to contact the Building Societies Association (BSA), both for comment on the feasibility of the exercise, and if possible to gain their active co-operation; thereby hopefully improving the chances of success. Currently, the BSA, with the Department of the Environment, conducts a rolling 5 per cent sample survey of new mortgages agreed by building societies. The results are published in *Housing and Construction Statistics,* and much other information in official publications on the private sector housing market draws on these results.

Based as it is on the details of the gross value of newly completed mortgages, the BSA-DOE survey, concentrates on the changing number and size of mortgages, albeit with a regional disaggregation and comparison. However, the present study is not concerned with the scale of building society activities in the housing market, per se, rather, it seeks to identify how these operations channel funds between the regions.

The Survey. The BSA was most helpful in providing information on their membership, and in offering advice on the difficulties involved in any survey of the individual building societies. Unfortunately, they were unable to take part directly in any such special exercise. However, they did offer to act as a clearing house through which information might be channelled and aggregated whenever individual societies felt concerned about confidentiality.

A flow of funds from one region to another can be measured by examining sources and uses of funds. Funds available for lending are derived from net new receipts from depositors, interest credited to accounts, and any mortgage principal repaid to the society. These funds are used to finance lending but also to build up the liquid assets of the society. Consequently, the sum of sources of funds is not directly comparable with net advance, unless the assumption is made that any region's share of the increase in liquidity from year to year is in proportion to its share of receipts.

Nevertheless, it was decided to proceed with a complete survey of the building societies, through the medium of a letter to each. In this letter, a request was made for details of that society's receipts (net of any repayments to depositors) and lending on property (net of any repayments of principal), for each and every region in which they conducted business. Altogether, some 230 building societies were circulated with this request.

An article in the April 1978 issue of the BSA journal, *Facts and Figures*, had suggested that this type of analysis was feasible. The article was concerned with the operation of the Scottish housing market, and as part of this analysed the activities of BSA members within Scotland. It gave detailed breakdowns of monies received, and monies lent by building societies operating in Scotland during 1976–77. This had been achieved according to the business transacted by the Scottish located branches and agencies of some thirty-four societies. Whilst clearly capable of conceptual refinements in terms of inter-regional flow measurement, the article confirmed that, for Scotland at least, our requests could be met, and if for Scotland, then probably for the other regions. Furthermore, the BSA have provided a copy of an internal study conducted by them in 1978 on the activity of British based building societies in Northern Ireland for the period 1971 to 1977. Reference to the *Facts and Figures* article was made in the letter of request to the building societies, and its table of results held up as an ideal format.

The response to the requests for information were mixed. Many societies did not answer, despite a subsequent communication, and of those that replied, not all were able or willing to provide the figures as asked.

In some cases, building societies did not seem to be directly concerned about the geographical distribution of their activities, and whilst sympathetic to the request, found themselves unable to help. Clearly this problem is greater when the society operates over much of the UK from a single office. Occasionally, the society was able to offer an appropriate percentage distribution of their activities between several regions.

Other societies, more aware of the spatial dimension, were also unable to help as well as they might, due to differences between their operational regions and the planning regions. At least one society used the commercial TV regions.

Certain societies organise their information according to the regions and were able to meet our requests in full. Information was also provided by some societies according to the activity of their branches, though often with the caveat that customers retain contact with a particular branch when no longer residing in its local area.

Finally, many of the smaller societies that responded to the survey considered their business effectively exclusive to the region in which they were located. On several occasions they provided copies of their annual reports from which the necessary data could be gleaned. In other cases, the annual reports published in the BSA *Yearbook* were used to supplement information provided directly.

On balance, the middle sized societies found the greatest practical problems in meeting our requests—their records being imperfectly suited to meeting our needs, and yet the society not restricted in activity to a single region. More than one small society considered its activities insignificant in the national total, many more did not answer and, for various reasons, several of the largest societies felt unable to furnish data. In a few cases, building societies were reluctant to co-operate due to seasonal peaks in administrative workload, resulting from the end of their financial year. Of the members of the BSA, some 70 per cent have a year-end at 31 December. Therefore, the positive response rate might conceivably be raised by careful timing of the request to societies.

The question of relative size is quite significant when considering building societies. If the value of assets is used as an indicator of rank, then according to the BSA *Yearbook,* nearly 80 per cent of all assets were under the control of the eighteen largest societies in 1977, two of which merged with each other in the course of that year.

The range of variation in size of building societies suggested that each individual respondent cannot be of equal significance. Consequently, when discussing the result of the survey, the size of total assets (as of 1977) is used as an indicator of the relative importance of the societies. Due to the specific interest in inter-regional transfer of funds, the larger societies gain even more importance. It seems reasonable to assume that the scope for such transfers from within the societies' funds is greater with the larger societies, and consequently, the top seventeen or eighteen societies, might conceivably be responsible for more than 80 per cent of such transfers. Conversely, concentrating solely on these larger societies might introduce a geographical bias to the survey, particularly if that response rate is not 100 per cent. Most societies have local origins, and their relative significance varies between the regions. Furthermore, despite the smaller societies being less involved in internal transfers of funds they can act as local intermediaries, channelling funds into or out of the region. Therefore, whilst a survey of the activities of building societies must try to gain the co-operation of the larger societies if it is to gauge the scale of activities, this will not necessarily ensure a fully representative picture of their regional distribution.

The results. During the period 1974 to 1977, there existed at one time or another, a total of 315 building societies, with membership of the BSA. By the time of the survey (late 1978), this number had fallen to 230, due to numerous amalgamations and several changes of name. For those societies in the top seventeen, (controlling 80 per cent of the movement's assets in 1977) that had not replied by 1979, a further approach was made. Ultimately, 88 societies answered, of which 43 were able to provide the data directly, or give sufficient information to enable the data to be obtained from their annual reports, whether supplied directly or as published in the BSA *Yearbook,* for the years 1974 to 1978 inclusive. These 43 societies, whilst only 19 per cent of those contacted, were responsible for 34 per cent of the movement's assets in 1977, and the 88 soceities who replied, represent 73 per cent of these assets. A synopsis of the coverage achieved in the survey is given below.

	Number (%)	Assets £m (%)
Societies contacted	230 (100)	28,199 (100)
Replies received	88 (38)	20,166 (73)
• without data	45 (20)	11,111 (39)
• with data or information	43 (19)	9,504 (34)

Those societies supplying information, were able to do so in different ways. Many of the smaller societies stated that their business was effectively local in nature, certainly for advances on property, if not for the receipt of funds. Consequently, all their receipts and advances were attributed to the region specified. The data were sometimes provided by the society on the model of the article in *Facts and Figures,* sometimes obtained from the *Annual Reports* sent by the society, and sometimes gleaned from the figures in the BSA *Yearbook.* A smaller number of societies who replied operated in more than one region, but being unable to identify directly the location of their business, offered percentage distributions that could be applied to their total business.

Other truly multi-regional societies were able to provide directly data of their receipts and advances for each region in which they had conducted business, often following the lines of the article in *Facts and Figures.* Overall, these different methods applied to the following breakdown of assets.

	Assets—£m
Local societies	752
Percentage distribution	193
Multi-regional data	8,559
	9,504

Some societies were unable to give information for all four years requested, sometimes as a result of a merger during that period. In these cases, no attempt was made to extrapolate available figures for the missing years. Other societies found it easier to identify details of their receipts than advances, or vice versa. Again, no attempt was made to fill the resulting gaps. Whilst 31 December is the end of year date for the majority of building societies, a significant number operate on a variety of other financial years. A purely pragmatic approach was adopted in the analysis of returns received with non-standard year-ends. All financial years that came to an end up to 30 June were considered as ending on 31 December the previous year, and those ending on or after 1 July were considered as ending on 31 December of the same year.

Following these practices, all available data was grouped together to give estimates of total surveyed receipts and total surveyed advances for each region for 1974, 1975, 1976 and 1977. (These are presented on pp.199–200).

Because of the gaps and approximations, these figures must not be used directly to make time series analyses, nor should comparisons be made of net regional inflow and outflow of funds. However, for any one year, and for receipts or advances alone, the figures are comparable, and so can be used to weight an allocation of the total UK building society receipts and advances as found in the CSO *Annual Abstract of Statistics.*

Table 80 *Building societies—survey results: net receipts (£) (current prices)*

	1974	*1975*	*1976*	*1977*
North	34,728,628	83,121,621	75,322,806	104,816,503
Yorkshire and Humberside	42,945,997	127,041,489	93,245,582	153,404,688
East Midlands	24,978,982	85,518,818	66,065,963	106,501,494
East Anglia	10,927,391	34,324,657	29,859,098	47,807,497
South-East	147,559,442	378,356,842	304,145,747	549,588,676
South-West	34,775,878	135,420,412	109,102,035	177,924,477
West Midlands	38,557,789	121,793,840	96,300,231	161,897,978
North-West	266,103,073	390,193,701	396,355,697	503,831,432
Wales	27,186,846	76,356,135	75,593,135	108,695,584
Scotland	27,198,397	87,911,955	64,840,790	119,896,497
Northern Ireland	7,519,000	18,545,988	14,350,307	22,417,099
Total	662,481,423	1,538,585,458	1,325,181,391	2,056,781,925

NB: Some individual building societies included in these figures could only furnish regionalised information for certain years, or only for net receipts or net advances. Therefore, these figures must not be used directly to make time series analyses nor to compare net receipts with net advances, for any one region.

Table 81

Building societies—survey results: net advances (£) (Current prices)

	1974	*1975*	*1976*	*1977*
North	7,105,842	54,792,120	71,819,606	74,320,323
Yorkshire and Humberside	14,523,950	89,577,149	120,705,123	144,407,779
East Midlands	17,015,317	75,580,533	106,276,711	113,053,231
East Anglia	2,896,997	23,715,053	34,929,313	38,945,651
South-East	91,505,500	368,256,467	513,100,606	545,017,239
South-West	25,691,240	92,969,856	119,708,896	130,826,704
West-Midlands	27,940,290	88,892,564	114,330,374	127,960,283
North-West	100,844,891	206,375,338	283,449,590	307,858,069
Wales	10,059,343	45,664,708	61,169,708	68,069,604
Scotland	15,124,802	80,498,467	105,318,011	101,059,956
Northern Ireland	1,499,000	15,465,845	21,707,446	24,942,100
Total	314,207,172	1,141,788,100	1,552,515,384	1,676,460,939

NB: Some individual building societies included in these figures could only furnish regionalised information for certain years, or only for net receipts or net advances. Therefore, these figures must not be used directly to make time series analyses, nor to compare net advances with net receipts, for any one region.

The previous section examined the survey which was undertaken to obtain figures relating to lending and deposits in the building societies' movement. This section relates the figures already presented to the complete operations of the societies.

The breakdown of building societies assets and liabilities is shown in Table 82.

Table 82 *Building societies: liabilities and assets (£m) (current prices)*

Liabilities

	Net shares and deposits			*Official loans*	*Reserves*
	Persons	*Companies*	*Others*		
1974–75	2743	20	4	- 281	90
1975–76	4416	41	23	- 125	194
1976–77	2865	82	1	- 3	168
1977–78	6373	122	7	1	234

Assets

	Mortgages	*Cash and balances at bank*	*Sterling certs. of deposits*	*Treasury bills*
1974–75	1706		448	
1975–76	3036	43	94	19
1976–77	3512	- 141	- 108	- 16
1977–78	4326	484	- 4	24

	Tax inst.	*Overseas*	*Local auth. debt.*	*Govt. securities*	*Others*
1974–75			568	293	46
1975–76	–	–	1459	677	97
1976–77	–	- 2	- 72	- 75	106
1977–78	54	–	542	833	319

In relation to the regional money flows model, the relevant items which have a direct regional incidence are net shares and deposits, mortgages and local authority debt. As already described, the emphasis on data collection related to shares and deposits and mortgages. No information was obtained on the regional holding of local authority debt. (This topic is tackled from the local authorities' liability rather than the assets of holders of debt in the relevant section.) Consequently, the usefulness of the survey relates to deposits and advances. With respect to deposits, all deposits irrespective of sector have been aggregated. The percentage distribution between regions of the figures shown in Tables 80 and 81 has been applied to the relevant totals to obtain estimates of regional net advances and deposits. These are shown in Tables 83 and 84.

Table 83 *Estimated net receipts received by building societies by region (£m) (current prices)*

	1974–75	*1975–76*	*1976–77*	*1977–78*
North	145	242	168	331
Yorkshire and Humberside	179	370	207	485
East Midlands	104	250	147	337
East Anglia	46	100	66	151
South-East	616	1101	676	1737
South-West	145	394	243	562
West Midlands	161	355	214	512
North West	1111	1136	881	1593
Wales	114	222	168	344
Scotland	114	256	144	379
Northern Ireland	31	54	32	71

Table 84 *Estimated net advances by building societies by region (£m) (current prices)*

	1974–75	*1975–76*	*1976–77*	*1977–78*
North	39	146	162	192
Yorkshire and Humberside	79	238	273	373
East Midlands	92	201	240	292
East Anglia	16	63	79	100
South-East	497	979	1161	1406
South-West	139	247	271	338
West Midlands	152	236	259	330
North-West	547	549	641	794
Wales	55	121	138	176
Scotland	82	214	238	261
Northern Ireland	8	41	49	64

The figures shown in Table 83 and 84 are the best estimates of deposits and advances by building societies. Reference has been made to the BSA's figures for Scotland and Northern Ireland, and although the estimates for these countries shown here are not the same as the BSA figures, they are in the same order of magnitude. (The two sets of figures are not directly equivalent as they represent slightly different accounting periods.) The question of reliability is important and at first sight the estimates suggest that either the South-East is under-estimated, or the North-West is over estimated with respect to the deposits. However, it is flows, not stock that is being considered and flows can reflect more than the size of the region as other categories of the financial sector show.

Table 85

Estimated loans for house purchase: the banking sector: (£m) (current prices)

	North	Yorks Humbs.	East Mids.	East Anglia	South-East	South-West	West Mids.	North-West	Wales	Scot.	Nrth. Ire'd.
1974–75	2.6	4.3	4.7	2.6	14.5	5.4	4.2	4.9	2.9	12.8	1.0
1975–76	1.9	3.5	3.2	2.0	9.9	3.8	3.2	3.4	1.8	11.3	1.0
1976–77	1.9	3.2	3.0	2.1	10.9	4.0	3.0	3.5	1.8	13.4	7.0
1977–78	6.8	11.7	10.9	7.5	39.8	14.6	10.8	12.7	6.7	11.2	3.0

Table 86

Loans for house purchase: new towns: £000s (current prices)

	North	Yorks Humbs.	East Mids.	East Anglia	South-East	South-West	West Mids.	North-West	Wales	Scot.	Nrth. Ire'd.
1974–75											
Loans	346		86	53	6173		76	497	87	10823	
Repayments	34		23		674		8	52	7	1159	
1975–76											
Loans	331		104	43	5833		60	595	78	11355	
Repayments	26		46		592		8	68	6	1245	
1976–77											
Loans	292		108	33	5221		46	108	76	11807	
Repayments	29		57		500		66	81	5	1261	
1977–78											
Loans	311		191	21	4755		41	191	62	11956	
Repayments	29		57		457		5	98		1250	

Table 87 *Loans for houses: local authorities: (£m) (current prices)*

	North	*Yorks Humbs.*	*East Mids.*	*East Anglia*	*South-East*	*South-West*	*West Mids.*	*North-West*	*Wales*	*Scot.*	*Nrth. Ire'd.*
1974–75											
Loans										22.4	
Repayments										6.1	
1975–76											
Loans	30.8	30.3	45.3	28.3	286.4	11.5	31.1	63.0	19.6		
Repayments	9.4	9.1	7.7	3.6	118.7	10.8	10.2	15.2	9.5		
1976–77											
Loans	26.5	23.3	16.7	12.2	217.0	23.5	26.8	43.6	14.9		
Repayments	15.4	13.0	9.8	5.5	196.9	21.0	12.7	17.6	12.0		
1977–78											
Loans											
Repayments	16.4	16.5	12.2	7.8	229.2	20.4	23.2	30.2	13.3		

Special finance agencies

Special finance agencies are institutions set up, generally with official backing to provide finance in the main, to borrowers who are unable to raise money through more usual channels. Some of them provide temporary and longer term finance for industrial businesses to supplement other sources of finance where developments are in the national interest. Currently they comprise: Agriculture Mortgage Corporation, Commonwealth Development Finance Co. Ltd., Equity Capital for Industry, Exporters Refinance Corporation, Finance for Industry Ltd. and Scottish Agriculture and Securities Corporation Ltd. Finance for Industry Ltd. is the holding company for Finance Corporation who in turn has Technical Development Capital Ltd. and Estate Duties Investment Trust Ltd. as subsidiaries.

Each of the special finance agencies was approached for information on the liabilities and assets in the context of the regional money flows model. The response was favourable and much useful data were generated.

Source of funds. Most of the funds of the special finance agencies are received through debenture or borrowing from other financial institutions and as a result do not enter the financial accounts because they are consolidated out. There are occasionally some deposits but these are from large companies, merchant banks, pension funds, investment trust, etc. All items can be assigned to the supra-regional sector.

Use of funds. These are included under other loans and mortgages by financial institutions (excluding banks) in financial statistics and investment in company securities. It was possible to analyse these uses of funds in the context of the regional money flows model. Some of the special finance agencies do not operate in this country. For example, the Commonwealth Development Finance Company Ltd., privides finance for companies incorporated and operating outside the UK. The Exporters Refinance Corporation can also be classified to the overseas section. The remaining agencies are those which help industry or agriculture to expand by providing finance of one form or another.

The Agriculture Mortgage Corporation Ltd. and the Scottish Agriculture Securities Corporation Ltd. lend money to farmers and farming companies in England and Wales for the former and in Scotland, the latter. Finance for Industry Ltd. has a variety of roles. Industrial and Commercial Finance Corporation Ltd., (ICFC) assists small and medium sized business. Due to the size of the business these can safely be assumed single region entities; so that ICFC lending could be assigned to the region in which it is made. Technical Development Capital Ltd.'s function is to help entrepreneurs create new, or expand existing, businesses based on worthwhile technicological invitation. Those, like ICFC firms are small businesses and can be regionalised. Finance Corporations for Industry's prime function is to assist the larger firm needing medium to long term finance. Here the firm is likely to be of the multi-regional kind. Equity Capital for Industry provides equity finance for firms who have outgrown their existing financial resources; these firms are likely to be a mixture of sizes.

Pressure of space prevents the presentation of the full details of each of the different special finance agencies and the figures presented in Table 88 show their aggregate activities in each region and in the multi-regional sector. However greater detail is given in Short (1980) where each agency is discussed. For instance, the lending by ICFC is presented in terms of regions and industry.

Finance for Industry has activities in leasing and plant hire; in shipping, and in property markets. While it was not possible to obtain a breakdown of these due to the organisational set up in dealing with these activities because of the centralisation of the management structure and the activities of middlemen between them and the final user (or region), some figures for broad regional categories were produced (North, Midland, South and Scotland) for the leasing activities, but these are not reproduced here.

The figures given in Table 88 relate to gross investments in loans and shares, and while these figures are a better indication of the scale of activity in relation to import, net investment (gross less payments) is important in considering money flows. While gross figures are better indications of the scale of activity in relation to impact, net investment (gross less repayments) is important in considering money flows. Although net payments could be analysed in the same manner as gross payments, it is possible to obtain a picture of the payments, it is possible to obtain a picture of the payments pattern.

For 1974–75 and 1975–76 the split of ICFC/TDC's investments between loans and shares was as follows:

	1974–75	1975–76
Loans	70	84
Shares	30	16

Based on a reasonable sample of loans advanced in 1974–75 the repayments schedule over time is:

	1974–75	*1975–76*	*1976–77*	*1977–78*	*1978–79*	*1979–80*	*Thereafter*	*Total*
%	Nil	5.2	8.7	10.7	11.7	10.2	53.5	100.0

Table 88 *Special Finance Agencies: shares and lending by region (£m) (current prices)*

	North	*Yorks Humbs.*	*East Mids.*	*East Anglia*	*South-East*	*South-West*	*West Mids.*	*North-West*	*Wales*	*Scot.*	*Nrth. Ire'd.*	*Multi-Region*
1974–75	4.5	4.6	6.0	3.4	13.2	10.8	7.1	4.1	3.1	15.5	0.2	12.1
1975–76	2.3	2.7	4.0	2.2	14.6	7.6	4.3	3.1	2.7	15.7	–	117.1
1976–77	3.7	5.2	5.9	3.4	17.9	11.1	8.5	4.6	4.0	17.4	0.3	66.2
1977–78	4.4	9.1	8.3	5.9	30.3	12.3	10.1	9.9	5.0	18.8	–	44.3

Conclusion. The special finance agencies provide a good illustration of the problems of assigning money flows to particular regions. They deal with the multi-regional company, the single region company and the flows between supra-regional sectors. As such, they show that the model adopted can provide a comprehensive account of all flows, but cannot assign them to single regions. This is not a weakness of the model but a problem of data classification.

The banking sector

The banking sector is one of the most important channels for financial flows in the economy. The coverage of the banking sector includes the Banking Department of the Bank of England, the National Giro, listed discount market institutions and listed banks which include the London clearing banks, the Scottish clearing banks, Accepting Houses, other British banks, overseas banks and consortium banks.

In order to ascertain whether statistics were available on a regional basis, the various banking associations were approached via The Committee of London Clearing Banks; The Committee of Scottish Clearing Banks, the Foreign Banks and Affiliates Association; The American Banks Association of London, The British Overseas and Commonwealth Banks Association; The Accepting Houses Committee and the National Giro as a separate institution.

From the ensuing correspondence it emerged that the role of most of these associations was to represent the views of their members in discussions with the authorities on matters of banking procedure and policy. Any data queries such as the ones which were of concern to the regional money flows study would have to be referred to the individual banks. However, most of the business of the foreign banks is involved in transactions in the finance of trade between countries and they did not have a great regional role, if any, as outlined in the model. The relevant organisations which had a role to play were the domestic based banks covered by the London and Scottish Clearing Bankers Commit tees, the Northern Ireland Banks and the other non-affiliated banks such as Yorkshire Bank, Co-operative Bank and Girobank.

In the approach to the Clearing Banker Committees, the regional money flows model and the availability of data were discussed. From the outset it became clear that the banks did not provide any data on a standard region basis, although some of the banks had their own regional structures, and had data relevant to these. However, these regions did not coincide with the planning regions. Moreover, the organisations did not think an analysis of banks corporate lending (or deposits) would be meaningful due to the fact that many companies operated one account irrespective of the location of their activities.

This problem was overcome in theory by creating the supra-regional methodology. The personal sector could be analysed in principal.

The question of a special exercise that could be mounted to collect banking figures for the regions was raised. For such a request to be successful, it was felt that the official channels of communication should be utilised. The Bank of England should be approached first and the request would be considered alongside all the others, and judged in the light of their relative importance. At present, due to the heavy demands on the banks in this direction, it was felt that such a request would merit fairly low priority even though the request was reasonable and sensible.

Given that no direct data are available, the possibility of obtaining proxies for the standard planning regions through the banks' own regions was raised. However due to the differences in the regional boundaries and the differences in the regional boundaries and the difficulties in obtaining suitable benchmark populations for the banks' own regions, such proxies were thought impossible.

The flows between the banking and other sectors are presented below:

Table 89 *Banking sector: current and deposit accounts (£m) (current prices)*

	Public sector	*Other financial institutions*	*Industrial and commercial co.*	*Personal sector*	*Overseas*
1974–75	47	- 363	- 203	- 2091	- 6332
1975–76	- 279	- 32	- 868	- 915	- 8205
1976–77	- 151	- 39	- 1286	- 1310	- 11435
1977–78	- 128	- 1863	- 2373	- 1087	- 11950

Table 90 *Banking sector: Market loans and commercial bills (£m) (current prices)*

	Public sector	*Other financial institutions*	*Industrial and commercial co.*	*Personal sector*	*Overseas*
1974–75	155	- 53	3512	217	4995
1975–76	- 84	291	- 41	128	7466
1976–77	427	225	3345	660	10204
1977–78	- 137	721	2609	1016	10989

The sectors which have a regional relevance are primarily the personal sector in toto and the single region industrial and commercial companies. The remainder can be assigned to flows between the banking data and supra-regional institutions.

Regional allocation of banking sector deposits and advances

The personal sector. Although no direct data exists on the personal sector's deposits and lending, there have been studies related to a regional dimension. Jack Revell and Cyril Tomkins in *Personal Wealth and Finance in Wales* produce figures for 1969 and 1970 for personal sector deposits and advances based on analysis arranged by the Committee of London Clearing Banks of Members' branches in Wales. These figures were not the same as figures for the bank deposits and advances of Welsh residents because many bank accounts are maintained at branches other than place of residence. However, it was felt that although this difference would be great in relation to companies, it would be marginal for persons. As a percentage of UK deposits and advances the Welsh figures for persons were:

Wales as a percentage of UK

	1969	*1970*
Deposits	4.97	4.92
Advances	6.16	6.12

For Scotland, data on total personal deposits of the Scottish banks are available at December 1978 and at June 1979 (but not earlier). These cover total sight and time deposits in sterling and other currency of 'persons, households and individual trusts', corresponding to the personal sector. As with the Welsh figures it is reasonable to assume that these will form a good proxy for Scottish residents even though not all persons resident in Scotland will bank with a Scottish Clearing Bank, and not all those who bank with a Scottish Clearer will live in Scotland. The Scottish figures as a percentage of total UK personal deposits was 5.72 per cent in December 1978.

For lending to persons by the Scottish Clearing Banks a comprehensive time series is available covering lending for house purchase and other (lending for house purchase is treated under a separate heading in *Financial Statistics).* Again the assumption that the advances to the personal sector by the Scottish Clearers equals lending by the banking sector to persons in Scotland is made.

Although the Northern Ireland Bankers' Association include two banks with head offices in the Republic of Ireland, figures relate to the liabilities and assets of their banking offices situation in Northern Ireland are published in *Financial Statistics.* However, only advances are categorised by sector.

As far as the regions of England are concerned no direct data are available. *Personal Savings and Wealth in Britain,* an EAG Business Research Study suggests from their evidence that there is a strong association between having bank accounts and income. The survey found that for current accounts there are considerable regional differences with Scotland (18.3 per cent) having the fewest accounts relative to its population and the South-East (45.6 per cent) most. For deposit accounts Wales had the highest proportion in relation to population (24.2 per cent) followed by Scotland (22 per cent) with London having the lowest (16.1 per cent). However this survey says nothing regarding the average holdings by region. (Also their regional classification used for the sample differs from the planning regions).

As a result personal bank deposits for England and Northern Ireland was allocated to the regions by personal disposable income by region and bank advances to persons was allocated to regions of England using the same proxy. The figures for Wales and Scotland deposits were obtained by applying the average percentages reported above to the UK figures. Advances to Scotland and Northern Ireland were taken from *Financial Statistics,* and those for Wales were obtained by applying the 1969–70 ratio.

Table 91

Banking sector: estimated current and deposit accounts of personal sector by region (£m) (current prices)

	1974–75	1975–76	1976–77	1977–78
Northern	116	51	71	59
Yorkshire and Humberside	183	80	113	94
East Midlands	141	62	86	71
East Anglia	63	28	42	34
South-East	716	314	448	372
South-West	157	69	100	83
West Midlands	193	85	124	103
North-West	250	109	155	129
Wales	103	45	65	54
Scotland	120	52	75	62
Northern Ireland	47	21	31	26

Table 92

Banking sector: estimated advances to personal sector by region (excluding for home purchase) (£m) (current prices)

	1974–75	1975–76	1976–77	1977–78
Northern	11	7	36	57
Yorkshire and Humberside	19	10	58	89
East Midlands	14	8	44	68
East Anglia	7	4	21	33
South-East	76	42	230	355
South-West	17	9	51	79
West Midlands	21	12	63	98
North-West	26	15	79	123
Wales	13	8	41	62
Scotland	-6	11	25	38
Northern Ireland	20	2	11	14

The industrial and commercial sectors. The flow between the banking sector and industrial and commercial companies is considerable; however as discussed above there are considerable difficulties involved in obtaining a breakdown of these flows by region.

The Bank of England analysises advances to industry broken down by broad industrial sectors; such an analysis does not provide any clues to the regional incidence as it cannot be ascertained whether industries are comprised of single region or multi-regional companies. As a result, the whole of the deposits and loans are allocated to the supra-regional sector for companies.

Flows between the banking sector and other sectors are between the supra-regional organisations.

Unit trusts

Unit trusts invest mainly in ordinary shares. They are set up under trust deeds, the trustee usually being a banker or an insurance company but they are administered by independent management companies. Units representing a share in the trust's assets can be bought by the public or resold at any time. In the financial accounts all transactions in unit trusts, other than those identified on the returns of other OFI's are assumed to be with the personal sector. In the financial accounts sales with OFI's are consolidated out. The breakdown of their assets and liabilities is shown in Table 93.

Table 93 *Unit trusts: (£m) (current prices)*

	Net sales		*Short term*	*British*	*UK LA*	*Overseas*	*UK Co.*	*Overseas*
	Pensions	*OFI*	*assets*	*govt. sec.*	*secs.*	*govt. secs.*	*secs.*	*company secs.*
1974–75	65	53	-96.4	26.8	5.6	-1.0	119.1	6.9
1975–76	99	90	24.5	-16.3	-0.2	0.7	175.2	67.0
1976–77	46	84	32.9	89.0	0.3		88.4	-26.5
1977–78	71	92	23.6	-4.3	-1.2		62.9	44.8

Many assurance companies run schemes which are linked with unit trusts. Some of the respondents in the assurance survey were able to provide details of their sales by regions regarding these schemes but the response was not enough to justify any further usage. Holdings by persons have been allocated by region according to regional disposable income and are shown in Table 96.

Investment trusts

Investment trusts are holding companies with their own equity and loan capital which manage a portfolio of UK and overseas securities. On the whole they raise finance from borrowing or by issuing shares on the stock market. An analysis of their assets is given in Table 94.

Table 94 — *Investment trusts (£m) (current prices)*

	Short term assets	Brit.govt. securities	UK L.auth. securities	Overseas govt.secs.	UK co. secs.	Overseas co.secs.	Other UK	Overseas
1974–75	31.1	55.6	- 16.4	12.6	- 80.6	- 235.6	14.3	5.8
1975–76	- 208.4	45.6	- 6.3	- 12.3	150.2	50.6	1.0	- 1.1
1976–77	70.4	33.3	- 3.1	0.6	26.9	- 145.8	- 1.1	4.6
1977–78	- 31.9	116.9	- 0.5	- 2.6	- 9.9	- 71.8	7.4	1.5

Given the nature of investment trust operations both in source of funds and then use, the majority of their transactions are allocated to the supra-regional sectors.

Property unit trusts

Property unit trusts invest in commercial property and their assets are held in the name of a trustee and managed by a separate company. Their holdings are restricted to pension funds and charities. The pension fund holdings are consolidated out in *Financial Statistics* while the charities holdings are included in *Other identified home assets.*

Their net assets and liabilities are as shown in Table 95.

Table 95 — *Property unit trusts (£m) (current prices)*

	Net sales		Net transactions				
	Pension funds	Charities	Cash and bals.	Other current assets	Current liabilities	Property	Other assets
1974–75	14.3	- 1.2	- 3.8	2.4	2.5	8.5	7.5
1975–76	92.7	2.4	49.6	0.4	- 0.7	42.5	1.9
1976–77	72.3	—	- 1.9	- 2.7	- 3.0	74.5	4.8
1977–78	149.0	1.5	57.9	9.7	0.2	77.1	13.9

The net sales can be allocated to the supra-regional sector, while no information is available on their assets by region.

Tables 97 to 100 show the regional incidence of these financial flows where the methodology for regional apportionment was indicated in the section 'Financial flows in the context of the regional money flows model', viz. *Notes and Coin* (p.162), *British Government Securities* (p.163), and *Credit Extended by Retailers and Identified Trade Credit* (p.167).

Table 96 *Unit trusts: estimated sales to persons by region (£m) (current prices)*

	1974–75	*1975–76*	*1976–77*	*1977–78*
North	3	5	2	4
Yorkshire and Humberside	5	8	4	6
East Midlands	4	6	3	4
East Anglia	2	3	1	2
South-East	22	33	15	23
South-West	5	7	3	5
West Midlands	6	9	4	6
North-West	7	11	5	8
Wales	3	5	2	3
Scotland	6	9	4	6
Northern Ireland	1	2	1	2

Table 97 *Notes and coin (holding by region by persons and companies (£m) (current prices)*

	1974–75		*1975–76*		*1976–77*		*1977–78*	
	Persons	Co.	Persons	Co.	Persons	Co.	Persons	Co.
North	26	19	18	8	15	32	29	33
Yorkshire and Humberside	42	31	28	13	24	50	45	51
East Midlands	32	24	22	10	18	38	35	39
East Anglia	15	11	10	5	9	18	16	18
South-East	174	128	118	53	97	204	187	210
South-West	35	26	24	11	20	42	38	43
West Midlands	47	34	32	14	26	54	50	56
North-West	57	42	39	18	32	68	62	70
Wales	22	16	15	7	13	27	25	28
Scotland	44	33	31	14	26	54	50	56
Northern Ireland	10	8	7	3	6	13	12	13
Banking Sector	47		156		153		117	

Table 98 *Tax instruments (£m) (current prices)*

	1974–75	*1975–76*	*1976–77*	*1977–78*
Banking sec	- 3	–	–	61
Other financial institutions	–	–	–	35
Industrial and commercial co.	- 11	6	- 8	234
Personal sector	- 37	- 10	1	106
North	- 2	- 1		6
Yorkshire and Humberside	- 3	- 1		9
East Midlands	- 2	- 1		7
East Anglia	- 1	..		3
South-East	- 13	- 3		36
South-West	- 3	- 1		7
West Midlands	- 3	- 1		10
North-West	- 4	- 1		12
Wales	- 2	..		5
Scotland	- 3	- 1		10
Northern Ireland	- 1	..		2
Public sector	51	4	7	- 436

..: Negligible

Table 99 *British government securities: sectoral holdings and estimated regional personal holdings (£m) (current prices)*

	1974–75	*1975–76*	*1976–77*	*1977–78*
Banking sector	- 52	375	185	976
Other financial institutions	1421	3052	3674	4484
Industrial and commercial co.	- 36	130	94	52
Overseas sector	- 38	- 59	326	816
Personal sector	905	659	2005	356
North	46	35	106	19
Yorkshire and Humberside	75	54	166	29
East Midlands	57	43	128	23
East Anglia	26	20	60	11
South-East	313	226	683	121
South-West	63	45	139	25
West Midlands	84	61	182	32
North-West	102	74	227	40
Wales	39	29	90	16
Scotland	80	59	182	32
Northern Ireland	19	14	43	8
Total	- 2200	- 4157	- 6284	- 6684

Table 100 *Credit extended by retailers and identified trade credit by sector and estimated regional credit by persons and companies (£m) (current prices)*

	1974–75 (persons)	*1974–75* (companies)	*1975–76* (persons)	*1975–76* (companies)	*1976-77* (persons)	*1976-77* (companies)	*1977–78* (persons)	*1977–78* (companies)
Overseas sector	25		169		114		167	
Personal sector	66		- 401		- 561		- 326	
Industrial and commercial companies		161		194		66		37
North	3	8	- 20	10	- 29	3	- 17	2
Yorkshire and Humberside	5	13	- 33	16	- 46	5	- 27	3
East Midlands	4	10	- 28	13	- 38	4	- 22	2
East Anglia	2	5	- 14	6	- 19	2	- 11	1
South-East	23	56	- 136	66	- 189	22	- 110	13
South-West	5	11	- 33	13	- 47	5	- 28	3
West Midlands	6	15	- 38	18	- 51	6	- 30	3
North-West	7	18	- 42	22	- 57	7	- 33	4
Wales	3	7	- 18	9	- 27	3	- 16	2
Scotland	5	14	- 31	17	- 45	6	- 26	3
Northern Ireland	2	3	- 10	4	- 14	1	- 8	1
Public sector	- 252		38		381		120	

Bibliography

Beckerman, W., *An Introduction to National Income Analysis,* Weiderfeld and Nicolson, London, 1976.

Begg *et al, Expenditure in Scotland 1961–1971,* Scottish Academic Press, 1975.

Catsambas, T., *Regional Impacts of Federal Fiscal Policy,* Lexington Books, 1978.

Commission on the Constitution, *Written Evidence 10,* The Revenue Department, London, HMSO, 1973a.

Commission on the Constitution, Research Paper 10, D. M. King, *Financial and Economic Aspects of Regionalism and Separatism,* HMSO, London, 1973b.

Central Statistical Office, 'Estimates of Gross Domestic Product: England, Wales, Scotland and Northern Ireland, *Economic Trends,* June 1976a.

Central Statistical Office, 'UK Regional Accounts', *Economic Trends,* November, 1976b.

Central Statistical Office, 'Studies in Official Statistics', *Regional Accounts,* No.31, HMSO, 1978.

Hochwald, W., (ed.), *Design of Regional Accounts,* Committee on Regional Accounts, The John Hopkins Press, Baltimore, 1961, includes Ruggles, R.N., *Regional Breakdowns of National Economic Accounts.* Levin, C., *Regional Income and Product Accounts: Construction and Applications.*

Izard, W. and Cumberland, J., (eds.), *Regional Economic Planning,* OECD, Paris, 1960, including Stone, R., *Social Accounts at the Regional Level: A Survey.*

Local Government Finance (Layfield Committee), Cmnd. 6453, May 1976.

McCrone, G., *Scotland's Economic Progress 1951–60. A Study in Regional Accounting,* Allen and Unwin, London, 1965.

Maurice, R., (ed.), *National Accounts Statistics—Sources and Methods,* HMSO, London, 1968.

National Bureau of Economic Research, *Regional Income Studies in Income and Wealth,* Vol.21, Princeton University Press, 1954; including Hochwald, W., *Conceptual Issues of Regional Income Estimation;* Perloff, H., *Problems of Assessing Regional Economic Progress.*

Northern Region Strategy Team, *Strategic Plan for the Northern Region,* Vol.5, Public Expenditure Priorities, HMSO, London, 1977.

Northern Region Strategy Team, Technical Paper 12, *Public Expenditure in the Northern Region and Other British Regions 1969/70–1973/74,* 1976.

Short, 'The Regional Distribution of Public Expenditure in Great Britain, 1969/70–1973/74', *Regional Studies,* Vol.12, 1978.

Short, J., *Public Expenditure and Taxation in the UK Regions,* Gower, Farnborough, 1981.

Short, J., Defence Spending in the Regions of the UK, *Regional Studies,* Vol.15, 1981b.

Short, J. and Nicholas D. J., *Money Flows in the Regions of the UK, 1974–75 to 1977–78.* Department of Economics Research Paper University of Durham, 1980.

Statistical Office of the European Communities (Eurostat), *Regional Accounts Economic Aggregates, 1970,* Luxembourg, 1976.

Strategic Plan for the North West, Technical Paper No.2, *Needs and Resources,* North West Joint Planning Team, 1973.

Strategic Plan for the South East, *Review Report of the Resources Group,* DOE, 1976.

West Central Scotland Plan, Supplementary Report 3, *Public Expenditure,* West Central Scotland Plan, 1974.

Woodward, V., *Regional Social Accounts for the United Kingdom,* Cambridge University Press, 1970.